Borderlands

Volunteering among Europe's Displaced

By

Jesse O'Reilly-Conlin

Borderlands: Volunteering among Europe's Displaced

By Jesse O'Reilly-Conlin

This book first published 2025

Ethics International Press Ltd, UK

British Library Cataloguing in Publication Data

A catalogue record for this book is available from the British Library

Copyright © 2025 by Jesse O'Reilly-Conlin

All rights for this book reserved. No part of this book may be reproduced, stored in a retrieval system, or transmitted, in any form or by any means, electronic, mechanical photocopying, recording or otherwise, without the prior permission of the copyright owner.

Print Book ISBN: 978-1-83711-178-7

eBook ISBN: 978-1-83711-179-4

Contents

Introduction xv

1: Belgrade 1

2: Calais 47

3: Sarajevo 93

4: Samos 127

5: Nicosia 186

6: Subotica 220

Afterword: Ukraine 261

References and Further Reading 271

The following pages about my experiences volunteering with NGOs assisting displaced people represent only a moment in time. A lot has changed since 2021 and 2022. The NGOs I volunteered with have closed some projects and opened new ones. They must constantly juggle the competing demands of respecting budgetary constraints and meeting the needs of asylum seekers. They must adapt and do the best with what they have.

As for the displaced people themselves, the situation has only gotten worse. Pushbacks continue in the Aegean, more people have drowned in the English Channel, and the violence inflicted in the borderlands goes unpunished. Opinions towards displaced people in Cyprus have become more hostile. Europe has struck more externalization deals with countries, such as Tunisia and Mauritania, to stop people from trying to reach European territory. These arrangements have resulted in human rights abuses and great suffering. Until the underlying causes of displacement are addressed and curtailed, people will continue to seek safety elsewhere, and their right to do must be respected. No amount of deterrence will stop them.

I have changed the names of the people with whom I interacted, both volunteers and the displaced, to protect their anonymity. I have not included the names of the NGOs I volunteered with so as not to conflate my position and perspective with theirs. The opinions expressed herein are mine alone.

Introduction

This book is about the ongoing refugee crisis occurring at Europe's borders. It is not a crisis of numbers but of policy and parochialism. It is a crisis of inaction and xenophobia—of callousness. European leaders refuse to understand the most brutal containment practices in the world will not prevent a man, woman, or child from fleeing a burning house. And that stubbornness breeds the violence, both physical and psychological, inflicted on people fleeing burning houses at Europe's outposts.

From the summer of 2021 to the end of 2022, I volunteered with several NGOs working at different refugee hotspots across the continent: Serbia, France, Bosnia and Herzegovina, Greece, and Cyprus. We provided humanitarian aid to displaced persons trying to make the increasingly perilous journey from their home countries to Western Europe. I saw firsthand how Brussels has made it policy to make finding sanctuary in Europe increasingly difficult, dangerous, and sometimes even deadly. I heard stories from people who had experienced violence at the hands of border patrol officers and who had lost friends and loved ones on their journey to Europe. And I understood how Europe's increasing shift to the right and its steadfast determination to prevent any irregular migration across its borders have made a mockery of the human rights legislation European leaders claim to hold sacrosanct. In this book, I share these stories and reflections.

My aims here are modest: I only bear witness to what I saw. I do not present any solutions to displacement because we already know how to prevent it: End war, poverty, and persecution. Stop climate change. Protect human rights. If these propositions seem overly idealistic, I wonder how we in the West have become so comfortable with watching the suffering of others, as if we somehow play no part in the war and poverty engulfing other parts of the world. We do play a part. We are accountable, and we have a responsibility to confront and challenge these injustices.

This book is a consciousness-raising activity. My audience is a Western one. I want them to know that human rights have ceased to exist in the borderlands—on Europe's edge. My goal with these words is to spur action among those in the West who have grown indifferent to the suffering of others. Empathy is not enough. We must rethink what it means to belong to a community in a globalized world. We must fight our fear of difference. We must learn to accept the other within our midst not only because it is the ethical and moral thing to do but also because it might be us, one day, knocking on another's door and asking for shelter.

In the long history of humanity, movement has been the norm, not the exception. Among the settled and comfortable of the West, the anti-migrant cheerleaders, exists a curious myopia about the past and future. Is their privileged position making them forget their forbearers moved or were forced to move? Do they not realize their children or maybe their children's children or maybe even their generations further down the road will have to move, too? Do they think their present will exist into infinity? Do they believe their future family will not have to seek the hospitality and protection of other, foreign communities? And how would they like them to be treated? Nothing lasts; all empires eventually crumble. Everything is only ice.

I am not a refugee. War, poverty, persecution, or environmental destruction have never displaced me. I have never sought safety and security from another country. I have never knocked on another's door asking for help.

I am not a refugee. I am its opposite.

I have lived most of my adult life comfortably in Canada, a peaceful and prosperous nation, and for those years I did not, my Canadian passport allowed me easy access to other countries to study, work, or simply visit. Through my twenties and into my thirties, I danced and fluttered from country to country. Travel was easy and painless. I collected passport stamps as one would baseball cards or comic books. For border guards, my Canadian passport humanized me more than my words, thoughts, or actions. I had to prove nothing to them other than my birthplace. My passport spoke for me. It gave me access to the world and the privilege to move. The more I travelled, however, the more I saw how border guards were not always so welcoming to others with more suspicious documentation. Border guards had more questions for them. I became more aware of how the world of movement was a profoundly unequal one. I was called "courageous" or "adventurous" for embarking on a months-long trip, yet people travelling overland through Central America, Mexico, and into the United States (US) for the chance of a more dignified life were called "rapists" or "criminals" and those travelling across the Aegean or Mediterranean and into Europe to escape war and persecution were called "terrorists."

The inability of nation-states to effectively respond to refugees lies not, entirely, in their selfishness but in their inability to perceive, and thus protect, human life outside their legal systems. If human rights are innate and exist beyond the borders of any state, then refugees by their very nature should trigger a comprehensive and unassailable protective system. But because human rights have become tied to citizenship through the nation-state, mass displacement reveals the fiction of any notion of universal human rights. In the modern conception of sovereignty, in which states are responsible for their citizens on a particular territory, human beings do not exist outside their citizenship. To strip a person of their citizenship—that is, to cast them as a refugee—is to render them rightsless. Instead of an aberration, or people simply out of place, the reality of mass displacement severs the linkage between human beings and citizens. Most frightening for nation-states is displacement allows us to imagine future political communities that do not take the nation-state as their foundation.

Unsurprisingly then, hysteria typically accompanies discussions about asylum seekers, refugees, and what to do with them among Western countries. Every day, politicians bemoan the increasing fragility of borders and devise increasingly punitive measures to deter their coming. Every day, citizens speak about asylum seekers and refugees in terms of "floods" or "tsunamis," an uncontrollable and destructive force, and advocate for further restrictions on their movement. Every day, psychological and physical violence is committed against the displaced in the name of protecting nation-states and their borders. Every day, legal avenues for asylum seekers to reach the West evaporate.

Judging by this alarmist rhetoric, and the draconian policies it has spawned, one might assume that the world's 90 million displaced people were together knocking on the door of the West and demanding entry. Yet a glance at UNHCR statistics shows that 74 per cent of these 90 million are hosted by low-income countries and that 69 per cent are hosted by a country neighbouring their country of origin. Instead of opening more legal pathways to asylum or providing more opportunities for resettlement, Western countries have instead expended much money and resources containing the displaced in their area of origin, trapping them in a state of limbo in which they are kept alive but also kept from living. Western governments make deals with authoritarian regimes to keep the displaced locked away and out of sight. Humanitarian responses to displacement, which were once temporary, have extended into perpetuity. The emergency has become the norm. Some refugee camps have transformed into cities in which generations of families now live and die. Many refugee situations have become protracted and have lasted decades. NGOs offer short-term relief but no permanent solutions. In their host countries, refugees themselves are often denied the legal right to work or attend school; to survive, they must navigate the informal sector, where chances of exploitation are rife. Opportunities for personal development are scarce; talent and creativity are wasted. In exile, dreams often go unfilled. People are forced to wait and then wait more for a solution that may never come. But waiting is exhausting. Through their containment policies, Western countries have criminalized any decision other than to wait. If refugees refuse to sacrifice decades of their lives waiting in camps, their movement is criminalized, and whatever violence befalls them during their journey is said to be their fault.

But most refugees stay in their home region, eke out an existence, and hope they can either return home or be resettled in another country. This book is not about them. This book is about a small minority with the means and connections to journey to Europe to restart their life in a place of relative security. This book is about what happens when they arrive at Europe's borders.

1
Belgrade

September and October 2021

War has shaped Serbia. In the 1990s, violence and conflict whittled Yugoslavia down to a mere sliver of its former size and power. Borders were created, and others were redrawn. In February 1999, representatives from Kosovo and Serbia, as well as from the US, the European Union (EU), and Russia, met at the Chateau de Rambouillet near Paris in an attempt to end the Kosovo War. The Rambouillet Agreement maintained the territorial integrity of Yugoslavia while granting Kosovo significant autonomy. Milošević rejected the deal, refusing to accept the presence of international forces in Yugoslavia or to stop his military campaign in Kosovo. The bombing then soon commenced.

Beginning on March 24, 1999, NATO bombed Belgrade and other Serb-controlled areas for seventy-eight days. Unsanctioned by the United Nations (UN), NATO's campaign damaged twenty-five thousand houses and apartment buildings and destroyed hundreds of kilometres of roads and railways. In terms of civilian casualties, estimates range between five hundred and twenty-five hundred. On June 10, Milošević agreed to the withdrawal of all Serbian forces from Kosovo and to the arrival of thirty-six thousand peacekeepers. Serbs today still hold deep antipathy towards NATO and the West for the destruction they wrought and for which they enjoy impunity.

From 1991 to 1998, when war engulfed the former Yugoslavia, the violence displaced 3.2 million people. Within the three months of the NATO bombing campaign specifically, fifty thousand Serbs fled their country, with most seeking refuge in neighbouring Hungary. Although a sizeable percentage of the displaced were mothers and their children fleeing the bombs falling on Belgrade, fifteen to twenty thousand were also men fleeing the draft and the long arm of the Serbian military.

Those who fled Milošević's Serbia comprised the dictator's most pointed critics, including professors, journalists, photographers, opposition leaders, and protestors—those very people whose voices Milošević's architecture of fear and intimidation tried to silence. Together they lived in exile in Hungary, unable to go back and unable to move forward, and wait for a time they may restart their lives free from oppression.

Belgrade now knows peace, but the displaced still roam its parks and streets. In the summer of 2015 and into 2016, hundreds of thousands of people fleeing war, poverty, and persecution passed through Belgrade on their way to Western Europe. The city did not have the resources to cope with the influx, resulting in a humanitarian crisis. The EU has since tried to close the Balkan route and make travel more difficult and dangerous through the region for displaced people. With the aid of smugglers and vast communication networks, however, the displaced still ply this route with the hope of reaching Germany, France, Italy, or the United Kingdom (UK). Although the number of displaced people passing through the Balkan route no longer reaches the numbers seen in the summer of 2015, thousands still pass through Belgrade. However, the city has few resources to support them.

One issue is hygiene. People on the move rarely enjoy the pleasures of a shower. They can go days, even weeks, without one. Even though showers can seem peripheral to survival, or even an indulgent luxury to those who take them for granted, dignity, not to mention health, is correlated to the ability to clean oneself. Noting this connection, one NGO transformed an old bakery in the centre of Belgrade into a wash centre, offering showers and laundry services to people on the move and Serbs experiencing homelessness or poverty. I volunteered at the centre for six weeks and met many people passing through Belgrade. Here are some of their stories.

The Showers

When the showers get busy, and people are waiting downstairs for their turn, I am sometimes not as detailed in my cleaning of the showers as I would like. I sometimes must sacrifice thoroughness for expedience. People are waiting. They are on the move, maybe leaving this afternoon or evening. They want to shower. No, they need to shower. And I am holding them back.

During calmer moments, when I do not hear any commotion coming from downstairs, this is what happens. A beneficiary exits the shower, and I direct him to the hamper he can throw his dirty towel. As he looks at himself in the mirror, passing a comb through it or applying almond oil at his leisure, I take my bottle of detergent and enter the shower. I spray the three shower walls and floor and wash it all away with the shower head, watching the bubbly remnants of soap and shampoo travel towards the drain. Periodically, I peek my head out to see if the beneficiary needs anything else or whether he would like to exchange his socks for a new pair. If he requires nothing further, I then watch to see if anything is obstructing the water's passage, and, if so, I put on my green latex glove and go digging for the culprit, which usually takes the form of a clump of matted hair. I then spray the shower again. If I am lucky, the water will pass easily, leaving behind a clean floor of immaculate white. If I am unlucky, however, the water will leave behind strands of hair or other small pieces of dirt or debris, requiring further work to remove the pieces. While I am squatting and wiping away whatever remains, I remind myself how I would like to find the shower if the shoe were on the other foot. Would it matter that I was a refugee? Would my status and situation warrant I be treated with less respect or given a shower a citizen would find unacceptable? Would I be expected just to shut up and be grateful? These thoughts propel me to wipe away any remaining dirt or pick up any hairs that stubbornly refuse to go down the drain. When I am satisfied with the stall's state, I call downstairs to say I have one shower available. I then grab a clean towel and wait for the next beneficiary to arrive.

When things get a little more chaotic, though, when beneficiaries begin to ascend and descend three at a time, when there is a queue forming downstairs, I do not have the time to be so exhaustive. I still disinfect the walls and floor and ensure that nothing plugs the drain, but the second passing sometimes gets overlooked, and sometimes once the water drains, hair and other things get left behind. I justify this oversight in the name of expediency. We try to serve as many people on the move as possible in a dignified way, so when time does not allow such a deep clean, I comfort myself with the thought that at least we are getting people through the door. And, I admit, I comfort myself with the thought that a person on the move, someone sleeping rough and fighting for their survival, would not begrudge me an errant hair or piece of debris. They must be satisfied with the shower, soap, shampoo and with the feeling of warm water hitting their skin and washing away all the dirt, mud, grime, and even blood that had accumulated there over the past days, weeks, months; indeed, who can say the last time they showered, so they must be grateful just for the shower, just for the chance to be clean again.

These thoughts swirl as I maddeningly spray the shower walls with disinfectant and water and watch it all slowly sink into the drain. Nothing seems to plug its passage. The water flows as it should. I yell downstairs to the shift leader to send the next person and then soon hear the footsteps ascending. I do one last quick spray, grab a clean towel, and direct the beneficiary to his shower. I glance at my watch to see how much time the other two showering beneficiaries have left, since we try to limit each shower to five minutes, especially when it's busy. But when I turn to go inform them they have only about one minute left, I am met by the beneficiary, now shirtless, whom I had just met. He is pointing towards the shower stall with an unamused expression on his face. Although his English is almost nonexistent, he knows the words to convey his displeasure. He is direct: "Dirty," he says. I follow his finger to the shower, and sure enough, a dozen or so hair strands have coated themselves to the white floor. They look like emaciated worms desperately trying to reach the drain to again find sanctuary and safety within the darkness of the pipes. I am angry with myself. If I had waited another minute or two for the water to drain instead of calling this beneficiary up, I would have noticed these obstinate hairs and their refusal to disappear. I would have removed each either by hand or water. I would have made them go away. I would have. I swear I would have. In that moment, those remaining hairs represent my privilege as a citizen of the world. Someone with papers, someone with money, someone with security. I would never accept a dirty shower stall, but it's good enough for them. That's what the hairs scream. They should be grateful. Yes, grateful. The Serbian police round them up like dogs. The Serbian people treat them with disdain and derision. They sleep rough in parks or under bridges and are exposed to daily threats of violence. They have nothing but the clothes on their back, maybe a rucksack, maybe a cellphone. We are here to help. We are doing our best with the limited resources at our disposal. We need to serve as people as possible. I want to say this to the beneficiary. Sometimes, corners are cut. Sometimes, shortcuts are taken. But it's better than nothing, right? An imperfect shower is better than no shower at all, right? Why can't you just be grateful?

No. I do not say this. These thoughts thankfully do not stay long.

Dignity does not exist in a hierarchy.

I grab my green gloves, pull them on, and get to work. I kneel over the floor, showerhead in hand, and attack each strand of hair, each stubborn little worm. Some I send hurtling down the drain; others, the more obstinate, I grab with my thumb and forefinger and fling into the garbage. In a few minutes, the floor is as white as it should be; all traces of the former showerers have disappeared. I spray the walls one last night and watch the water flow down the drain. The beneficiary enters, and I hear no further comment or complaint, only the water coming to life.

Rahim

We have a mirror in the shower area. It's a dignity thing. People on the move can examine themselves once they exit the showers; they can use the combs and oil we provide to brush and style their hair if they so choose. And most do. Appearance remains important regardless of immigration status. The thing about the mirror, though, is it rests against a wall because it appears too tough and solid to allow the passage of a nail or screw to hang the glass. So it sits on a crate and leans against the wall, which means that some of the taller people must crouch slightly to see their reflection. Because the mirror stands close to one of the boilers, not quite underneath it, a taller person can, if he is not careful, bump his head on said boiler after checking his appearance and standing tall once again. Some beneficiaries also check themselves for wounds.

One afternoon, two beneficiaries make their way up the stairs. Their movement is laboured, unconfident. They seem to have trouble keeping their balance. They are distant, seemingly occupying a different plain of reality. In essence, they appear stoned, which worries me slightly, since our centre has a zero-drug policy. We do not tolerate drug use on our premises, and we do not serve people under the influence.

One plops down on a chair and starts removing clothing from his backpack. The other heads towards the mirror, kneels, and inspects an ugly gash he has on his neck. He removes a pair of scissors from his jeans, the dull kind children use while doing arts and crafts, and takes one point and presses it against the red spot on his neck. He grimaces and says something to his companion in Arabic. He is in obvious discomfort, and I can feel my anxiety rise. We are not a medical centre; we have a First Aid kit. That's it. We can provide some Band-Aids and bandages. We can inform people on the move when Médecins Sans Frontières (MSF) will next visit the city, which is once a week at the best of times. We have neither the skills nor the resources to offer any medical assistance beyond that. He pokes his wound and then grimaces. Again and again. And I wonder just how dull that blade is, whether it can pierce skin, an artery. The neck is notoriously vulnerable, and here he is poking it with a scissors' point. Should I intercede? What if he cuts himself? What if he further hurts himself? What if? What if? Just as I am about to direct him away from the mirror and towards the shower, he stands from his kneeling position and bangs his head on the boiler. Rage envelops him. I see it. It's the culmination of a million indignities, small and large, suffered on his journey from there to here. No more suffering. No more humiliation. This is the final straw. I am a human being, and I will no longer tolerate this degradation. And as if to prove to me beyond a shadow of a doubt he is a man who possesses agency and can affect, nay disrupt, the happenings around him, he violently grabs the mirror and lifts it a centimetre or two from the ground. I think he will smash it. The mirror is already cracked. It wouldn't take much. There would then be shards everywhere, each a threat, a chance, an unknown variable. In those seconds, he grasps the mirror; I do not begrudge him his decision. I do not judge him. Fuck the boiler. Fuck the mirror. If it were me. Fuck the endless hell of my life. Fuck the gratitude I must display, the incessant grovelling, just for some crumbs, a pair of socks, a hot shower. Fuck these volunteers who hand me towels and tell me I have five minutes for a shower. Fuck the way they try to humanize an inhuman situation. Fuck their benevolence and good intentions. Fuck their empathy. Fuck how good they must feel for handing me a towel when all that separates me from them is pure chance.

At the last moment, though, he stops himself. He exhales and relaxes his muscles. He has walked himself back from the edge, the precipice. I take the mirror from him and lean it against the wall. "No problem," I say, directing him towards the shower. "No problem." He follows my hand and disappears behind the shower curtain. His friend, meanwhile, still sits on the chair, rifling through his backpack for this or that, removing and repacking items, never completely sure what he is looking for. Now and then, he shouts something to his showering friend, who sometimes replies and sometimes does not. He strikes me as unpredictable and combustible. His demeanour can change at a moment's notice. His build is athletic and strong. He can handle himself; he has handled himself. The scars shock me. When he removes his shirt, I see long, thin cuts covering his torso. It was as if a group had held him down and someone had dragged a rake or a spading fork across his chest. They are pronounced; they are difficult to avoid. I cast my gaze downwards out of respect and disgust. I have never seen such wounds before—those caused by the intentional violence of another. What souvenirs people get on their journey to Europe. What memories they must daily suffer through, their horrible echoes and shrieks only rendered mute by narcotics. The world's callousness has tattooed itself across his body, forever marking it.

Once he shuts the shower curtain, I rush downstairs to tell the two other volunteers what happened, about their demeanour and scars. The shift leader tells me to watch their behaviour and see if either wishes to divulge how they received their injuries or about what happened to them. The NGO is partnered with an organization that takes testimonies from people on the move who have experienced violence from the police and then uses them for advocacy purposes. There are signs taped to the wall explaining about the network in Pashto, Farsi, Arabic, Urdu, and English, and the shift leader says to point out the sign to them to see if they wish to share. If their violence is police related, their disclosure will not lead to any tangible benefit for them, except the knowledge maybe that someone has heard their story, someone has believed it, and someone has tried to use it to prevent from such violence from visiting other people in the future.

I ascend the stairs, wondering how I will broach the topic, how I will ask the men whether they want to share something intimate and horrible with a stranger. Beside the shower, I stand, hands behind my back, on the ready, waiting for the men to emerge. Yet something suddenly does not sound right, something does not feel right. It then hits me: I can hear only one shower running. I glance towards the middle stall, which should be showering the man with scars across his chest, but see no movement. No curtains are rustling, and no water is running from the shower head. No signs of a person. I ask if anyone is there while peaking behind the curtain. Empty. Just the stool, the wooden mat, and two containers full of shampoo and soap. In an instant, I know what has happened and where the man has vanished to. There is no secret. But I don't want to believe it.

We have a washroom on the second floor, a metre away from the showers. Volunteers use it to relieve themselves and other mundane yet essential tasks like filling the water jug or the disinfectant bottle. People on the move cannot use it, for incidents have occurred, or so I was told. One man, allegedly, barricaded himself inside to do drugs, much to the chagrin of the volunteer who was pleading for him to exit, to get the hell out. Since then, people on the move are forbidden to enter, which creates some discomfort when some see the mysterious door and ask whether there is a toilet inside, and I must lie and say no or that the washroom is only for staff. We tell them they may find public toilets at Republic Square, a fifteen-minute walk away, but we know many of them will not venture that far into the city, preferring instead to hang around the bus station, where exit, or escape, is more feasible. As someone with an unpredictable bladder and who has been left in perilous situations on many long bus journeys, I sympathize with the desire to use a toilet whenever one presents itself.

I knock on the bathroom door, and someone knocks back. I knock again, and he knocks back. "You have to get out now," I say, but I am only met by silence. What is he doing in there? I picture a syringe and a vein. I picture a knife. I picture wounds and blood. I picture an ordeal. "Please, you have to get out now," I beg. "The bathroom is for staff only." I hear a sputtering of Arabic and a little bit of movement. But the door remains shut. Anger has replaced anxiety. My body stiffens and tightens. "Get out now," I scream and bang on the door. My anger, though, does not resemble that of the beneficiary who bumped his head on the boiler. He was frustrated at the injustice of his situation. At the barricades people mounted between himself and hope, between himself and a future.

At the little and large humiliations he has suffered to get a chance, only a chance, to show himself worthy of safety, somewhere where carnage and mayhem do not fall from the sky. In contrast, I am angry at the disorder this man in the toilet has caused. He has flouted the rules and displayed an utter lack of respect for how we do things in the wash centre. We do not ask for much, just politeness and decorum, a little reverence for the rules. We do not wish to be thanked. We have no interest in being hailed as heroes or saviours. All we want is to get as many people through the door as possible. All we want is to perform our roles with as little hindrance as possible.

"Get out now," I shout. I try to pull it open but again am met by resistance, but in the slight crack, I see him for a second in the middle of getting changed. Was that all he wanted? More room to change? A little more privacy? A taste of dignity? Am I depriving him of the very thing we seek to provide?

"Jesse!" The shift leader is calling from downstairs. "We have a problem." I wonder how she knows about the man in the toilet, but when I look over the rail and see her standing at the bottom of the stairs, I realize she is talking about a very different problem. Water is falling from a pipe from the bathroom across the first-floor ceiling and is quickly pooling on the stairs. I grab a container in which we ask people on the move to leave their shoes, and we situate it under the waterfall.

"A man has locked himself in the bathroom," I tell the shift leader, somewhat sheepishly, since I am still chastising myself for my dereliction of duty.

A native German speaker, she pauses to see if she correctly heard me.

"He won't come out," I say.

"He must," she says.

I race back up the stairs, leaving her to inspect the pipe from which the water is falling. For the sake of decorum and sensitivity, women volunteers are prohibited from going upstairs when men are showering. When I arrive at the showers, the beneficiary with the wound on his neck, who did take a shower, has emerged fully washed and clothed. I ask him to please tell his friend he must leave the toilet immediately. The beneficiary bangs on the bathroom door and yells some instructions in Arabic. Muffled words can be heard in return. "He is coming. He is coming. One minute. One minute." I shake my head. "No. Please tell him he must come out now."

"Jesse." I turn to see the shift leader at the bottom of the stairs. "Can I come up?" The second man has dressed, so I indicate she may. She knocks herself, once and then twice. "You need to come out now. This toilet is for staff only." A pause. "Okay. Okay," the voice says. "I am coming." She turns to his friend. "Tell him he must come out now." The friend says, "Sister. Sister. This is not my fault." He points to me. "You see, I took my shower. No problem." We reassure him we don't blame him, but his friend must come out. So he again bangs on the door, and he shouts some words in Arabic, and again we hear some muffled words in return. "Soon. Soon," the friend says and returns to organizing his clothing. "Jesse, once these two guys leave, we will close the showers for a few minutes to see where the leak is coming from." I nod, and she descends. A moment or two later, the toilet door swings open, the athletic man appears, half-dressed and with a bag in hand, his scars as present as ever, but instead of finishing getting dressed next to his friend, he darts into the shower and closes the curtain behind him. "No, the showers are closed," I scream. "You can't shower. We have a leak." I tell his friend to tell him he cannot shower, and a shouting match soon erupts between them in Arabic. From the stall, I hear the athletic man say, "Just two minutes. Please, just two minutes." I lean over the rail and shout downstairs: "He has gone into the shower." She appears in a flash, just in front of the falling water, which has not decreased in volume, and tells me in no uncertain terms he cannot. A maelstrom of English and Arabic passes through the room as his friend and I beg him to please stop. I use the simplest expressions, the most basic of body language, wagging my finger, making an X with my arms, but it's no use. The man understands what I want. There is no ambiguity. Nothing is lost in translation. He has chosen to ignore me: The man has decided to shower. He has undressed and has turned on the shower. "Jesse," the shift leader is calling me. "Has he come out?" I lean over the rail. "No. He is showering. There is nothing I can do."

A calm settles over the shower room. Gone are the noise and drama. A quiet descends. It's as if nothing had happened. The friend combs his hair, gathers his things, and soon skips down the stairs. The water has stopped leaking for now. I stand with my hands behind my back, replaying the previous minutes in my mind. If I had only not gone downstairs, he would not have gone into the toilet, and none of this would have occurred. Why did I go downstairs? Was the information that pressing? Couldn't it have waited ten or fifteen minutes? Of course, it could have. The steam rises from the shower stall and floats underneath the light. I hear the man cough once or twice. He spits. I wanted to feel as a valued member of the team. I wanted to have something to share, pressing information to which only I was privy. I wanted them to hang on my every word and realize that, yes, I belonged and had something valuable to contribute. Insecurity breeds overcompensation. Wanting to impress is its own kind of imprisonment. Yes. This situation could have gone quite differently if I had only been a little more secure in my skin, a touch more resolute in attending to what matters: the dignity of the people we encounter. He only craved a little more room to change. He casts an imposing figure, and the space between the two shower curtains, where we have put a stool and a wooden floorboard, is simply too constrained to accommodate him. Will he be banned from using our services? Perhaps. Will he be expelled for expecting something we take for granted daily: space and privacy?

The water has stopped, and there is movement behind the curtains. He exits bare-chested, with jeans on. He passes me without apology or regret and stands in front of the mirror. He takes a t-shirt from his backpack, situates it over his head, and then rolls it down over his chest, concealing once more his scars, the irrefutable evidence something is not quite right. He applies cologne and fixes his hair in the mirror. You'd be forgiven for thinking he was grooming for a night out and not preparing to face another uncertain afternoon and evening on the streets of Belgrade. He sits his cigarettes, lighter, and bills on the chair and ponders which pocket each should go. He is in no hurry. Nothing rushes him. Although his movements still strike me as unconfident and wobbly, he is calmer than he was fifteen minutes ago, less unpredictable, less prone to antics. He finally grabs his backpack and throws it over his shoulder, and without looking at me, he says, "Thank you, friend," and walks down the stairs and leaves the centre. The shift leader asks me if everything is okay. I nod.

"What is his name?" I ask.

"Rahim," she says.

Rahim continues to visit the wash centre—still demanding and unpredictable. He and his friends possess a chaotic energy. They demand a shower or to have their clothes washed. Lines and time slots do not seem to matter. They are unstable and shaky. Trouble follows. Knife wounds often grace their bodies; one man has a large, vertical cut from the ear lobe down his neck and another one just past his eye. They take drugs; they may even deal drugs. I don't know. One once told me they had been in Serbia for eight years; "a shit country," he said. There is a local man who hangs around the centre, collecting bottles and scavenging the local trash bins, who once he told me, pointing to Rahim and his group, those Arabs are all dangerous drug dealers and we shouldn't wash their clothes or give them showers. I ignored the racist caricature and went on with my day. We judge behaviour done in the centre, not outside. Although Rahim and his crew have come to the centre intoxicated and high one or two times and are a little difficult, they have done nothing to warrant being banned. We think they are from Algeria, and I find it ironic Europeans would castigate people from the Maghreb seeking better futures in Europe when just one hundred years before, Europeans were settling in North Africa searching for the same thing.

It's raining when the group arrives. They come in with umbrellas and demand a shower because they will catch a bus in a few hours. I look around but cannot see Rahim, who is not hard to spot, towering as he does over the rest of his mates. Tim, the shift leader, kindly tells them to put on a mask, because of our COVID-19 regulation, which they reluctantly do, and then informs them that all the showers are occupied and will have to wait thirty minutes. They protest and cannot seem to fathom how another person could be showering when they want to shower. Their demeanour is not threatening, just playfully obnoxious. They are almost charming in their demands. One, Farhad, the ostensible leader without Rahim, gets close to Tim so they are less than a metre apart. He has something he wants to tell, a secret he wishes to divulge, a burden to cast away. "Rahim is dead," he says and runs his finger across his throat. He says a few more unintelligible words, maybe something about a train station, maybe something about the police, maybe something about a knife. Tim looks suspiciously at Farhad, cognizant of how this group likes to exaggerate and even lie. And as if sensing Tim's disbelief, Farhad repeats himself: "Rahim, he is dead." But then he laughs at Tim and me. "Are you joking?" Tim asks. Farhad laughs some more. "No, no. Rahim is dead. He is dead," he says, again running his finger across his neck. "Are you serious?" Tim asks again, but Farhad has returned to his friends, and they continue to demand a shower as soon as possible. "You will have to wait," Tim says. "Twenty minutes. Wait twenty minutes." The crew go outside for a cigarette. "Is Rahim dead?" I ask Tim. "I don't know" is all he says.

The Translator

Most days on outreach, we communicate with people on the move through a smattering of English, body language, and our translation pages. We aim to find people on the move, tell them about our services, and book appointments for them. We note their name, gender, language spoken, and appointment time. All the people on the move I have so far encountered have been male and young. We do not ask for their country of origin, only their first language to know better about the communities we serve and ensure we have the necessary translations of all the languages we encounter. Most people we meet speak Pashto, one of the national languages of Afghanistan, followed by Farsi.

We need people to visit our wash centre and use our services. They must come to us; we cannot go to them. We must inform people about our wash centre. We must go to the parks and find people to inform. So, what do you do? You enter a park and see dozens of people. Do you ask every person whether they would like a shower or to have their laundry done? Such an approach would be the most equal and the least problematic. We are operating on the assumption that everyone—regardless of race, gender, religion, sexual orientation, and immigration status—could potentially benefit from our services. Yet not everyone needs our services, and we are not, practically speaking, in a position to offer showers and laundry to everyone. We are here to provide services to people on the move, people who have fallen through the cracks, people who do not have access to the many things we take for granted, and people who are sleeping rough and who might not have had a shower or had their laundry done for weeks on end. So, we target people on the move.

We profile. We look for clues and markers. We search for an unkempt appearance, old and beaten shoes, or a backpack. We hunt the parks for groups of young men sitting together on benches, scrolling through their phones. Most of all, we seek those with nonwhite faces, who stand out from the crowd and appear as though they do not belong. It's dangerous to reduce a person to a stereotype—to have an image in your head and then look for people to confirm it. We are often right, but there are other times when we examine a body from a distance, note his shoes and clothes, and cannot say whether he is passing through.

We use the same method as the police when they go hunting for migrants. They know what to look for. The hints. The tells. They know what a Serbian looks like, who belongs and who does not, who deserves to be left alone and who deserves to be stopped, questioned, and detained. Police cars and vans buzz around the parks like ravens over carrion. They are here to convince the locals they have control, which they do not. They are here to show the locals that even though the Serbian economy is weak and the educated and young cannot leave the country fast enough, what matters is keeping migrants out of city parks, off benches, out of sight. These roundups keep no one safe, but they are not meant to. They are symbolic actions. They are about borders, control, and order.

When we approach a group of people on the move, we say our usual prattle: "Hello, good morning. How are you? We are an organization that provides showers and laundry to people on the move for no cost." We then wait to see if they have captured the meaning of our words. Today, though, a young man in jeans and a hoodie does not hesitate: "You are from an organization." We nod. "You provide free showers and laundry to refugees." We nod again. He repeats our message in Pashto to the group of ten guys surrounding him. They seem interested, and we ready ourselves to make appointments. "It's not enough," the man suddenly says. "Showers and laundry are not enough." He looks at us hard, and I feel my body temperature rise. The look is not one of hostility but of frustration. Absolute frustration. His leg twitches; there is irritation in his voice, as if he cannot believe he needs to explain his point. "Tell me, what do we do after the shower? We come back here and sit in the park? And then what? Where should we go? What are we supposed to do?" A voice rings in my head: Just listen. All you can do is listen. "Last night, it rained. It was cold. Winter is coming. We do not have the clothing for winter." He points to his clothing and then to the guys surrounding him. They are inadequate. Sweaters. Jumpers. Hoodies. Trainers. They will not suffice. Out on the road or deep in the forest, they will not suffice.

At the wash centre, I sometimes check the shoes of the showering people. They are often extraordinarily ruined, held together by only the thinnest of threads. Their structure has lost all integrity; their shape has become warped and flimsy. There is no support. The elements have ripped the tongue from its place; the sole is cracked. Laces are missing. Grime, dirt, mud, and grass all cake the outer material. The smell is pungent, remarkably so. When a person on the move does come in with a new pair of trainers, they seldom fit properly, and when they struggle to put them on, when they have to jam their foot into the too-small opening, I know blisters and rashes and an assortment of other foot ailments will soon follow. I see their feet when they are changing. I see the swelling, the discolouration, the wounds. I see them grimace when they apply bandages or Band-aids to their sores. I see their pained expression when they walk. I see the disappointment on their face when we tell them MSF only comes to the park once a week, on Thursdays, to treat people on the move, and today is only Friday or Saturday. We tell them they can see a doctor in the camps, but most would rather suffer through the pain than go to a camp. I hope they do not see me when I see them. I hope they do not see my disjointed, alarmed face when I see them at their most vulnerable, when I see their open sores, and when I watch them dry their wet, worn feet. As a runner, I know the value of a good pair of shoes and healthy feet. And it shocks me these young men are travelling halfway around the world, roughing through mountains and forests, wearing shoes I would not walk a kilometre in.

"I was a translator," the man is saying. "I worked with the British and American forces in Afghanistan." He pauses. "And they left, and the Taliban came." The group of men has formed a semi-circle around him. Someone says something in Pashto, and the man translates for us, Westerners, as he always has. "For twenty years, we fought for the idea of democracy. We worked with the Western powers. Now we are not safe." A man says something in Pashto. "Each of us is in danger. We all have family members in danger. And how does Europe help us? They close the borders." Another man says something. "This man," the translator says, "tried to enter Romania, and the police took his food, money, and phone and then pushed him back into Serbia. Why would they do that? Why would they rob a refugee?" More and more voices rise in the background. "They all have stories about the police, about being pushed back from the border. Bosnia. Croatia. Hungary. They all have stories." He catches his breath. "And if they take our fingerprints in Romania, Croatia, or Hungary, we are sent back there if we are caught in any other European country."

A realization comes to me, standing there amid these young men and boys. This is all we can do for them. We become a recorder, nothing more. We take their stories in our hands—their hurt and anger—and put them someplace safe. "We are human beings," he says. "Just like you." We absorb each horrible detail, each scar and wound, each humiliation and degradation. "If they don't want us here, they should build a wall around their borders, but now that we are here, what should we do? What should we do?" We say together: "I'm sorry. I can't imagine what that must have been like." A few minutes later, we say it again. And a few minutes later, again. "I'm sorry. I can't imagine. We wish we could do more. It's not fair. It's unjust. It's awful." We don't engage further. We don't ask for more than they are willing to disclose. We make no promises we cannot keep. We listen and offer showers and laundry. But it's not enough. "Please bring media to these parks," the translator says. "We need more attention to our situation. We need you to take our voices to the European Union. They must know what is happening." We tell him about the network we have partnered with and how they take the stories of those who experienced violent pushbacks and present them to the EU or the UN to advocate for more humane treatment. We ask him whether anyone in the group would like to share their story. But he has become increasingly agitated, unwilling to let this opportunity to speak with a receptive audience go to waste. "Europe wants our drugs. They want Afghanistan's drugs. Look at Amsterdam. Where do the drugs come from? Why are the drugs allowed to arrive? Why should they take drugs but not people? How can drugs pass so easily across borders but not people?" We nod and then nod again. "Yes, it's awful," we say. "But would anyone here like to share their stories of border violence?" "Of course, we want to share our stories," the translator says. "We all have stories. That's why we need you to bring the media here. We need people to know our stories." He reiterates his countrymen's stories about being robbed at the border and the violent pushbacks. "All we want is a chance. We are young men. We want to work. We can help Europe. We can do the work Europeans do not want to do. Europe benefits, too. Don't forget: Europe benefits, too."

We have been listening for about fifteen minutes now. I don't know how much more I can take. I am uncomfortable. I am anxious. I feel exposed. I have arrived at a fire without an extinguisher. How do you exit gracefully from such an encounter? "We wish you all the luck in the world" in the world sounds disingenuous. Luck has nothing to do with it. Specific and calculated actions have produced their situation. People's choices have led them here to Belgrade, existing in a park, surviving on the meagre benevolence of strangers or whatever resources and connections they may have, unable to go anywhere but in circles or to camps or, worse, back to from where they came. Our governments, the Western world, played a not-insignificant part in creating the context that pushed these young men from Afghanistan and into an outside world wanting nothing to with them. "Good luck"? No. Not after they believed us. Not after they swallowed what we fed them for twenty years about the virtues of democracy, the wonders of an open and free society. Not after they fought for us for twenty years only to be abandoned, only to wind up in the same position they started—with the Taliban. "Have a nice day" does not suffice either, for what does "nice" mean for a person on the move in Europe? Their day will be full of uncertainties and threats. They must dodge the police here in Belgrade and at the border of whichever country they try next. They must avoid those who would take advantage of their precarious situation. They must find shelter from the rain and the cold. They must find somewhere to sleep. They must get money if they can. They must buy food, new shoes, and a jacket if they can. They must get data for their phones if they can. They must do all that, and chances are only a few will.

The translator thanks us for listening, apologizes for taking so much of our time, and reminds us to use their voices to effect change. We ask him one last time if he would like a shower, the most concrete thing we can offer him, and he reiterates his position with a little more annoyance: "I don't need a shower. I need something more."

Zoran

Zoran is a local Serbian man who occasionally uses our services. He is older, fifty-something, and has mobility issues. Diabetes has decimated his left foot, rendering his movement precarious. He needs time and space to undress and then undress again. And space is something we have in short supply. At the wash centre, the three showers are located on the second floor, requiring the visitor to climb a rather steep flight of stairs, which is not a problem for younger people, who comprise most of our visitors, but for the older ones, these stairs can prove treacherous. Of equal concern is the lack of space upstairs. Between the chairs, boilers, clothing bins, towel hampers, and showers, little room exists for people to move about, organize their things, take off their shoes, and put on the shower sandals, especially when there are four people up there: me and the three showerers. We ask people to change within the shower stall. Each stall has two curtains, one for the shower and one for changing. In between each is a sliver of space, equipped with a blue plastic stool and wooden shower mat, where people can undress in relative privacy. The young and small have the nimbleness required to manoeuvre in such a small space, and it is not an issue; they are in and out. The task is more challenging for larger people or those with mobility issues. They cannot get undressed in such a small space, so they disrobe out in the open, in plain view of everyone else. On quieter days, this is not a problem; they may take their time and use the space afforded to undress and sort through their clothing. On busier days, however, when the showers are a revolving door of people coming and going, their presence can be problematic, not only because they take longer, depriving others of showers but because their near nakedness may make others feel uncomfortable. I look away. My eyes search the ground or wall for some interesting design or secret I had failed to notice. I don't want them to see me staring at their body. Their sores. Their discolouration. The stains of disease or of simply living rough for so long. But they change without shame or embarrassment. They seem experienced in having no privacy, of stripping in the company of other men, strangers.

Zoran has his left foot wrapped in a bandage, and because he does not wish to ruin it with water, he covers his foot with a plastic bag. He often tells me about his various ailments, how he is in and out of the hospital, and how dreadful diabetes is. "Sugar is no good," he says. But as he discloses the intimate details of his life to me and removes piece of clothing after piece of clothing, all I think about is what happens if a group of people on the move suddenly arrive wanting a shower. Would I tell him he needs to hurry up? Would

I tell this man of fifty or sixty, whose body has been ravished by diabetes, that he must hurry up because a group of twenty-year-old Pashto speakers has arrived, our key demographic, and wants to shower?

Zoran is not alone today. He has just finished his shower and is now delicately drying his feet, sitting on a chair at the top of the stairs. Across from him sits another man with serious foot problems, but he is a person on the move. He, too, is drying his feet with the towel, but each time he touches his swollen and cracked feet, a look of intense discomfort reveals itself on his face. He can barely put any weight on them. I hand him the bandages he has asked for. We have a rudimentary first aid kit with only the most basic supplies.

Zoran stares at the man's feet with obvious concern. "You need to see a doctor," Zoran says, quietly. When the man does not understand his words, Zoran looks at me and repeats his assessment: He needs to see a doctor. I only nod in agreement, but inside, I am frustrated: What doctor, Zoran? He is undocumented. He cannot access any medical services. Hospitals will not admit him. Ambulances will not come. Previous shift leaders have tried to call for medical help, but when they hear English, they hang up. No public help exists for him because, for them, this man does not exist. He is not here right now. He is a ghost, appearing and disappearing. A phantom. A spirit. Tomorrow, he will be somewhere else. Someone else's problem. No public money should be allotted to treat ghosts; it's unfair to the hard-working taxpayer, those citizens of flesh and blood.

I explain to the man it would be more comfortable to apply his bandages downstairs. He gingerly rises, grimaces, and then begins his painful journey. I yell for the shift leader to watch his movements if he needs support on the stairs. He steps slowly, planting each foot with as little pressure as possible. He grabs the handrail hard to remove any unnecessary weight from his feet. His pain is obvious, beyond a doubt, punishing. All I can do is watch. We do a lot of watching while volunteering. We do a lot of feeling helpless. A person on the move arrives at our centre feeling relieved they have finally found a friendly face, someone who will not cast them aside or inflict violence on them. We then watch the hope drain from his face when we tell him we do not offer shelter, we do not offer new shoes or jackets, we do not offer medical help, and we do not offer legal advice. We stand there, hopeless, and pray they will be satisfied with our silent promise not to forget.

The man sits on a chair, applying new bandages to his feet. The shift leader explains to him through Google Translate that MSF visits every Thursday, but since it is Saturday, he may consider visiting the Obrenovac camp to see a doctor. He is adamant in his refusal to go to the camp, preferring to take his chances outside in the rough, with his crumbling feet. Zoran watches the man apply his bandages as if hypnotized. "No," he whispers to himself, shaking his head. "Not like that." He kneels before the man, forgoing the discomfort movement undoubtedly gives him, and proceeds to unwrap the bandage the man had just finished wrapping. The man does not appreciate Zoran's interference, even if it does come from a good place, since Zoran has intimate and expansive knowledge about bandaging feet. "Zoran, please stop," the shift leader says. "I will show him how," Zoran replies. "I will show him how to do it correctly." The man reaches down and tries to pull the bandage from Zoran's hand, indicating his displeasure with Zoran's unravelling of his work. "Zoran, thank you, but he doesn't want your help," the shift leader says. Zoran ignores our pleas and continues to work as if we do not understand the genius of his work or what he is trying to accomplish. "Zoran, please look at him. He doesn't want your help," the shift leader says, tapping Zoran's shoulder. He raises his eyes to the man's and sees the exasperated, desperate look and his arms forming an X across his chest. "Okay. Okay," Zoran says, rising to his feet. "I was just trying to help," Zoran says. "We know, Zoran." "He needs to see a doctor." "We know, Zoran."

The Teenager

I have seen this young man before. Once or twice. It's hard to keep track of all the faces passing through the showers. But him, yes. I know him. I have handed him a towel, cleaned the shower after he finished, watched him run almond oil through his hair and then style it with a comb, and offered him a clean pair of socks. Our interactions have been rudimentary and mechanical, as they should be. He has not asked me where I am from, and I have not asked him where he is going. These conversations are inappropriate, regardless of how human they may feel. I am a body filling a need, only part of the larger wheel. Here, in the showers, I am not allowed to ask questions; I am only allowed to hand out towels, clean showers, and offer socks. And this is good. This is important. Respecting boundaries is sacrosanct, as is revering my limitations. I am not a saviour. I repeat this line ten or twenty times a day. Especially when I feel good. Especially when a person says, "Thank you, sir." I am not a saviour. I do not want thanks. I loathe cookies. All I want is to get as many people through the showers as possible. All I want is to add a little more dignity to this situation.

The young man has put his shoes on and is tying his laces. They seem relatively new—black trainers with orange stripes. I have seen other young men wearing similar shoes, and I wonder if they got them from the same donation drive. He stands and moves towards the mirror. He straightens his jacket and fixes his hair. You'd be forgiven if you thought he was getting ready for a date or a job interview—something important. I even detect a smile. "Today," he says, "I am going to Germany." He is young, somewhere between a child and twenty. He has his life in front of him. And maybe he can finally see it now in the mirror. That future he has long dreamed about, that hope, which kept him going through the bleakest of moments. The light. Maybe he sees in the mirror in twenty years sitting at a café in Berlin, Munich, or Frankfurt, sipping a coffee or tea, chatting with his friends about the promotion he just got or the child his partner just gave birth to. Maybe he has already told them about his long journey from Afghanistan to Germany, or maybe some things you just want to bury and forget.

The young man smiles at me, and I smile behind my mask, which we must wear to prevent the transmission of COVID-19. I hope he can tell from my eyes I am smiling and that I wish him the best. There are many things I want to say to him, but none are appropriate, except for "My friend, don't forget to put on your mask," which he does. His eyes are radiant, little balls of light, and as I watch him bound down the stairs, I try to rebury a thought arriving from my more cynical side: He will be back here in less than a week.

Muhammad

A young man from Afghanistan wants to know why I am doing this. He is sitting and drying his feet with the towel. His name is Muhammad, and he can speak English. The shower has refreshed him, and he appears genuinely pleased to have had the opportunity to apply soap and shampoo to his person. He is talkative, almost loquacious. He wants to know where I am from, wants to know about Canada. I give basic, rudimentary responses, never providing too many details. Yes/No answers. A lot of nodding. Body language. But he keeps probing, dancing around my defense mechanisms. What am I doing here—a Canadian volunteering at a wash centre in Serbia? I stutter and panic. What is an appropriate response? I am tired of simply reading about asylum seekers in books, articles, and policy papers. It was time to put action to my beliefs. I was tired of sitting in my armchair, barking criticisms to anyone who would listen. I wanted to contribute, however small, to a vision of a world uncarved by borders. But I say none of this to Muhammad, none of this nuance and complexity, the undergirding of any human decision. I default to something comfortable and banal: "I am here to help." I say, "I am here to help." For the sake of convenience and expediency, I betray all that I had learned, all that I had held to be sacrosanct.

The verb "help" implies hierarchy and stark power imbalances. I am above, and he is below, and with a little help, he may reach my level, may stand where I stand. "Help" says I have something he lacks and wants, some quality or thing, and it's in my power to give. I could give it, but only if he politely asks. "Sir, may I have some socks?" "Sir, may I have a razor or toothbrush?" He is lost at sea, and I am the lighthouse. He is a wound, and I am a bandage.

He is in trouble, and I am the rescue. He must look around the wash centre at all the white faces, the men and women from Canada, the US, Germany, Spain, Belgium, who are so financially secure they can go weeks, even months, without working, and think they are the answer. I want to be like them, he might say, and with a little help, I just might be. One day, I will. One day, in some country in the West, I will look at myself in the mirror and see them.

Nothing separates us in reality. We both have the attributes of human beings. We think feel, act, etc. There is no natural or obvious explanation for why I am distributing towels, and Muhammad is taking one. No laws stipulate or mandate this arrangement, about why I am here and he is there—only history. Muhammad has ended up in this wash centre through no fault of his own. His present predicament resulted from powerful people pushing buttons and pulling triggers.

Help naturalizes the kind of brutality Muhammad experiences and makes it seem as if brown and Black people fleeing to Western countries were as natural as rain falling from the sky. Help obscures this history of violence and hides it under a blanket of benevolence and promises of charity and donations. And we, the volunteers, do not get to divorce ourselves from this reality. We are part of this world. We have benefited and have thrived. This is why we are in the wash centre, and they are just passing through.

Muhammad graciously takes my statement. "You are helping," he says. "Thank you, my brother." I try to swallow the glow enveloping me—the goodness I suddenly feel because of his thanks. It feels warm, like wrapping a blanket around yourself on a cold night. I push the euphoria back down inside, but still it pushes back, hard, until it overflows and comes crashing out of me. Does he sense it? Does he feel the glow radiating from me? I dislike it and want to put it away, hide it in my closet or under my bed, like something shameful or forbidden. Yet it still comes and comes and comes. I never say, "You are welcome," though, because that implies his "thanks" is necessary, required, and that I am providing some service, which necessitates his thanking me. I say, "No problem."

"My brother," he says, "May I have a new pair of socks." "Of course, of course," I say, opening a drawer. I hand him a new pair, not a rewashed one, which people on the move sometimes look at rather sheepishly. "Thank you. Thank you," he says, and the feeling comes again stronger and more forceful.

"My brother," he says again, "May I use the oil," and I nod and casually and nonchalantly direct his attention to its whereabouts as if he needn't have bothered asking. It's yours to use, my body language says. He squeezes some onto his hands and runs it through his hair. I remember on my first day in the showers, a young man climbed the stairs who did not have any hands. I had to help him apply oil to his forearms after he finished showering. He could manage everything else, getting undressed and holding the shower head between his arms. He just could not remove the cap from the oil bottle, so I did and squeezed the contents onto his awaiting arms. No pride and elation emanated from me then, just a profound shock, which I hope the young man did not see.

"My brother," Muhammad says as he secures his backpack and takes a final look at himself in the mirror, "Thank you for everything." I wave and provide my standard "No problem," and he is gone. I have noticed the Arabic speakers I have encountered often refer to me as "my brother," which I found curious at first but have come to like, despite my intellectual criticisms. I don't have a brother. And maybe that explains my affinity to the declaration "my brother." But, no, it's more than that. "My brother" transcends the biological, relationships based solely on blood and genes and speaks to something loftier and nobler. My brother. Muhammad and I are not brothers; we are separated by culture, language, and the cruelties of history. Yet "my brother" attempts not to override those differences and somehow render us the same, which we are not, but instead points to a chance of solidarity. My brother. There is an affinity in those words, some secret that may help us see through and beyond what has been presented as natural.

Igor

Igor is a friendly giant—tall, big, and gregarious. He is one of those people who seem at ease whenever meeting someone new. He has no nerves, no anxiety, and as a result, neither do you. You meet Igor, and within five minutes, you feel as if you two have been friends for years. He has a deep, baritone voice—a voice one could imagine God possessing—yet his playful, lighthearted demeanour gives the impression he would be a benevolent if mischievous God.

Igor meets me outside his apartment complex in the centre of Belgrade and takes my hand. I will stay at his apartment for the six weeks I stay in the city. "Welcome," he says and leads me inside. We pass through a heavy, steel door and into a dimly lit corridor.

"Throughout the day, that door is open," he says, motioning to the black door behind me, "but it is closed at night." He smiles. He has a scruffy beard and oozes safety and security. He could be a bouncer. Or a bear. "People feel safer with it closed," he says. At the intercom, outside a second door, he punches in a code, and the door buzzes open. An ancient, tiny elevator meets us, and Igor flips open the two side doors as if he were opening a box, and the two of us, my large backpack included, squeeze inside. "We are at the top," he says, pressing for the fourth floor, and the elevator struggles to life, producing all the stereotypical sounds one would associate with an old, run-down elevator, and then lifts us gently to the top. We emerge, unscathed, and turn to meet another flight of stairs. "Only a few more steps," he says, never explaining why the elevator does not go straight to the top. He opens two more doors and finally shows me into my apartment.

It is a generous space for a single person. Wooden beams run across the white ceiling, giving it a rustic feel. The bed sits on a loft overlooking the apartment. The kitchen is small but adequate, as is the washroom. There is a television, a couch, a table, and a plant. But the apartment's highlight is the view. Through the windows, I can see Belgrade fall before me. I can see the Sava River and all the development transforming that once sleepy side of the river into one of the city's most affluent neighbourhoods. I see the construction teams finishing buildings, putting in the missing parts, here and there, as if adding the last pieces to a puzzle. The cranes are busy moving heavy parts around, trucks busy themselves moving about, to and fro, back and forth. I can see the rooftops of all the buildings leading down to the river, and they show their age.

"A wonderful view, isn't it?" Igor asks. And before I can answer, he draws my attention to an old movie screen standing below, sandwiched between two old buildings, and before the theatre sit dozens of plastic chairs, neatly organized into rows. "On Friday and Saturday night, they show films here. Entrance is cheap. Like a euro," Igor says. I like the theatre and how the community has taken a derelict and disused space and transformed it into something unique and purposeful. Despite the seeming incongruence with its surroundings, the theatre is oddly at home outside and among the concrete and brick of Belgrade.

Igor is leading me into the washroom and pointing at the washer. "The guy before you was a bit of a problem. Messy, loud. I don't know what he did to the washer, but it no longer works. A new one is coming this week. Please don't do laundry before the new one comes." He shows me the air conditioner. "It's been a hot summer," he says and laughs. "Last week, my girlfriend and I went to Kotor on the coast, just so I could get my ass into the sea, and of course, when we get there, the temperature never got above twenty." "Isn't that always the case," I say, mechanically, hoping he might turn on the air conditioner. He shows me the television, the modem, stove, fridge, and heater. His explanations are pithy and succinct, with a joke sprinkled here and there. He is good at welcoming people and making them feel as if they were the only people in the world who mattered.

He hands me the keys, and I have already forgotten which one does what. "The big, black door downstairs, did you say I will have to open and close it whenever I leave and come back?" Igor's generous smile immediately melts any anxiety I had about the silliness of my question. He disarms my defense mechanisms and makes me feel at ease. "No, no. Don't worry about that door. It stays open during the day, but at night, we close it, so if you ever leave or return late at night, you will need this key to open it." He points to a long silver one in my hand. "We never used to lock the door, but the residents sleep better knowing it's locked," Igor says. "It's a peace of mind thing." I nod and do not expect him to provide any further details. His explanation is sufficient and logical, and I have no concerns or criticisms, yet I can tell he wants to provide something more, another detail or two, to justify the decision to lock the big, black door at night. "A few years ago, we had a big problem with migrants. They used to sleep in the hallway downstairs and bother the residents, so we started locking the door." I need him to stop talking. I don't want to know anything else about him or his beliefs. I want to keep a simple image of Igor in my mind. He is my host. The man I go to if I have a problem with the apartment or a question about the city. That's all. I want to see him as nice and friendly—a cute, cuddly bear. Nothing more. But the unnerving smile that creeps upon his face says he has much more to say on the subject, and I wonder what about me has made him believe that I would find such anecdotes relevant or entertaining. "Two years ago, two migrants broke into my apartment, which is just down the hall from yours. Luckily, I was at home. Luckily, I heard them." Something sinister then falls across his face as he clasps his hands together and looks to the ceiling. "When I heard them, I just said, 'Oh thank you. Oh thank you.' 'Yes.' 'Yes.'" I understand he is thankful for the justification to do something with these migrants he had no legal reason to do before. He could only watch them on the streets and in the parks with derision and antipathy. But inside his home, with a legal pretext to protect himself from any intruder, he would be legally protected from any punishment that might befall him for putting his hands on their bodies. He has carte blanche. He may take out his frustrations freely and comprehensively. Igor's smile disturbs me. And although he never tells me what exactly transpired in his apartment, I see he is satisfied with himself and happy with the opportunity, in his mind, to right a few wrongs.

"I never asked you what you are doing in Belgrade." I do not hesitate: "I am a freelance copyeditor. I just need my laptop and an internet connection to work. So, I jump around from country to country, city to city." "And how is the pay?" Igor asks. "It pays well enough. I can do what I want." This excites him. "Exactly. If you only chase money, money ends up chasing you. Before the pandemic, I used to manage a dozen properties; now, I just manage one. I am an IT engineer by training, but I work when I want. I am happier for it." I think he sees the exhaustion in my eyes. "Well, I will let you unpack and settle in. But text me later, and we can grab a coffee or beer and chat." Two minutes ago, I would have said yes. Two minutes ago, I would have grabbed a coffee or beer with him and told him I was volunteering with an organization providing services to people travelling through Belgrade. I would have told him I just wanted to contribute in a small way to adding a little humanity and dignity to their otherwise degrading and dehumanizing journey from danger. But in the last seconds, I have decided against this path. I will not tell him my true reason for being in Belgrade, and I will avoid him to the best of my ability. I will be busy. I will be quiet. I will give him no reason to inquire about me or my stay. I will take that part of myself and bury it. I will act as if I did not exist. Is this cowardly? Maybe. Perhaps Igor told me his story for my benefit. Perhaps he thought that as a guest in his apartment, I would want to know he would do everything in his power to keep my stay safe and drama-free. Perhaps he exaggerated his story because he thought I would appreciate such embellished details. Or, perhaps, he is tired of the never-ending stream of destitution passing through his city, with the larger European community unwilling to do anything to address it. Perhaps he once did feel compassion for these migrants, but after so many years and so little change, perhaps, he is just tired of it all. Perhaps he wonders why Serbia—only a middle-income country itself—should be expected to support people on the move when his country cannot support its citizens and when the educated and wealthy are exiting to the West en masse. Perhaps there is more grey to Igor than I have given him credit, more nuance and complexity than a nationalist caricature, a portrait I would discover if only I had a coffee or beer with him. Or perhaps he is just a racist.

Dragan

Dragan is drunk. I hear Mike mention this to Brenda, today's shift leader, when I go downstairs to get some clean towels. "We probably shouldn't let him shower today," Mike says. Dragan is a local who often visits the centre with his mother, Lara. He is in his forties, has short black hair, and wears a black and red coat. His beard exudes a roughness, a shield that has protected him from the many hard nights he has had. He and his mother were polite when they dropped off their clothes to me the other day; they were kind and courteous. If Dragan had been drunk then, I did not see it, but then again, I wasn't looking, concerned as I was with correctly recording their order and identifying each article of clothing they left. So, I think nothing of Mike's proclamation when I return to the second floor and continue organizing shower times, cleaning stalls, and distributing towels. Twenty minutes later, at 1:00 p.m.,

I descend as I assume Lara will be showering during the designated women's time slot and Brenda must supervise her shower. "Everything okay?" I ask when I see Brenda and Mike standing at their stations with concerned looks on their faces. "Drama," Brenda replies. "Big drama." I look at both for elaboration. "Dragan pulled out a knife outside against a person on the move," Mike says. I learn Karl and Marie, the two volunteers on outreach, had been doing their postshift debrief outside when they saw Dragan remove a knife from his pocket and gesture towards a person on the move. Nothing had provoked him. Nothing had been said. Perhaps the person on the move got a little too close for Dragan's liking, representing some perceived threat he thought warranted the appearance of a blade. Whatever the reason, in the matter of a second, Dragan went from a man using our services to a man holding a knife and threatening a person on the move. The situation did not escalate, but now we must decide how to respond—what to do with Dragan?

At the wash, there is a three-strike system for handling people causing problems: yellow for the first offence, orange for the second, and red for the third, or first warning, second warning, and banning. The offences usually comprise insulting and offensive language directed against the staff or people on the move. Local Serbians often make derogatory and racist comments against people on the move, and people on the move sometimes make sexist comments against female volunteers. We have a code of conduct written in half-a-dozen languages taped to the desk explaining these rules, but incidences happen sometimes. Dragan had no colour attached to his name; this was his first offence. But it was a big one. In seconds, he had turned the centre into an unsafe space. We like to envision the centre as a safe space where visitors can escape the stress and danger of their lives for twenty or thirty minutes. They can shower, sit, and have tea or a piece of fruit. Of course, the violence of outside can still enter our premises, especially in the guise of police officers who frequently hunt for people on the move nearby. But we do everything conceivable to try and limit those threats inside.

"In my opinion," I say, "we must ban him." I have reservations about the bluntness of my position. I dislike taking from people who already have so little. I dislike removing services from people who already have access to so few. And although we can refer him to ADRA, an organization dealing only with Serbians experiencing poverty and homelessness, I still wish another solution existed. But one doesn't. Dragan threatened the life of another with a deadly weapon. We cannot tolerate such behaviour and agree he must go. Brenda, Mike, and I decide when Dragan returns tomorrow to retrieve his laundry, we will tell him and explain to him as clearly as possible why we have banned him. Brenda is again shift lead tomorrow and asks Marie and I, who will be on outreach, come and assist her in barring him. "Just message us," I say, "and we will come."

The next day, Marie and I are about to make shower appointments for a large group of people on the move when Brenda's message arrives: "Dragan is here. Please come." We tell the group we will return in a few minutes and then rush back to the centre. I confirm to Brenda we are on our way, and Marie types out the English explanation of why we have banned him in Google Translate in case we must explain in Serbian. We soon see Dragan and Lara standing outside the centre. Brenda waits for us inside, and we decide what to say.

"Dragan, can we talk to you for a moment?" Brenda asks. He nods and stands in front of us near the wash entrance. "There was a problem yesterday, no?" Brenda begins. Dragan looks confused, disoriented. His eyes glitter. He may be drunk again. "You came to the centre drunk…" Dragan throws his arms in the air and lightly laughs, seemingly relieved the issue is nothing serious. "Oh that's no problem," he says. "Everyone drinks in this country." Brenda tries to regain control of the narrative. "Yes, it was a problem because you——" Dragan raises his voice: "Okay. Okay. I won't come when I am drinking. Okay. No problem. There's no problem." Marie cuts to the point: "I saw the knife, Dragan. I saw you pull out your knife and threaten a person on the move." There is a glint of recognition in his eyes. He remembers. "Oh, that was nothing," he says. "Nothing." I can feel the situation escalating. "It was not nothing," Marie says. "This is a safe space for people on the move, and we cannot tolerate any kind of violence or threat of violence here." Dragan has become agitated and angry. The hate comes. "These people," he says, motioning to the young men sitting inside the centre, "are dangerous criminals. They are drug dealers." Marie tries to counter but is met by Dragan. "Why do you think the police are always around here? Because they are dangerous. I have a right to protect myself." Brenda and Marie counter his claims and reiterate the centre is a safe space, yet this far into the conversation, we still have not arrived at the crux of the matter; we have not yet told him he is banned. I feel the conversation is spinning out of control, going around and around in wild, unhinged circles. Our task here is not to assist Dragan in unlearning the racism he has cultivated in his forty-plus years of living. We cannot debunk every racist stereotype he believes. We have one goal here: to ban him.

"Dragan, you can no longer come here," I say. "You are banned." I surprise myself with the directness and rigidity of my words. There is no ambiguity, no chance of misunderstandings. Dragan understands because I see the anger percolating just below his skin. He understands yet cannot believe what he is hearing. He understands because he launches into a deranged diatribe about the injustice of our position. He says he is Serbian, born and raised in Belgrade—"I have lived here my entire life"—and is entitled to certain rights and privileges because of his citizenship. "What are you going to do?" he asks, looking between us. "Call the cops? Go ahead and call the cops. But you won't call the cops, will you?" He turns to his mother and explains the situation in Serbian. The news does not seem to shock her; her face remains expressionless, mysterious. She goes back to sorting through her laundry. I recognize the word "immigrant" in Dragan's rant, and I can only imagine the Serbian words he has sprinkled before and after it. Brenda returns inside to tend to the shower appointments, while Marie and I listen in silence as Dragan switches between Serbian and English to voice his displeasure about migrants and his own expulsion. We do not engage. We absorb each of his blows. I look past him and focus my gaze at the market across the street. He is only sound and fury at the moment, just another example of a man blaming migrants for the failures of his government, just another piece of evidence highlighting the lies and inherent violence of nationalisms. I dislike reducing people to caricature, but Dragan has devolved into simply a xenophobic mouthpiece, completely devoid of any original thought or nuance. I want to say if he only looked closely and put aside his prejudices, he may see that he and people on the move may have more in common than he thinks, both being examples, albeit to different levels, of a severed relationship between a human being and their government. I want to say if his government put as much effort into funding social programs for people like Dragan and Lara as they do in paying cops to round up people on the move, displaying the latest military aircrafts they have purchased, and extolling the virtues of Serb unity across borders and stoking fears of another war, then Dragan and Lara may no longer have to use our services to wash their clothes and bodies—nor, perhaps, would people on the move.

Dragan eventually exhausts himself. He is deflated, defeated. Lara has gathered her laundry, and the two prepare to leave. Before departing, though, Dragan spits a few more insults in Serbian in our direction. I don't know what they mean, but I can guess their flavour. They walk slowly, side by side, up the road, past the market, and towards an unfinished or abandoned apartment block. Lara carries her laundry bag, and Dragan only carries himself. "We did the right thing," Marie says. "But I feel we have only worsened his opinion towards migrants." Dragan and Lara ascend the hill and then disappear. "Maybe," I say. "But we did the right thing."

The Police

When cops emerge, people on the move run. A cop can clear out a park in seconds. Those that do not move fast enough are cornered and questioned, and if their paperwork does not satisfy the cops examining it, the men, and some boys, are whisked away in the back of a van and deposited at a police station, a camp, and sometimes even the Northern Macedonian border, hours to the south.

The cops know who we are, too. They know what we do and what we offer. They know where to find the wash centre. Vans pull up sometimes in front and take away six, seven, or eight people in the blink of an eye. Team members communicate with one another over WhatsApp. We let each other know whether police are present in the parks or near the centre. We try to keep people away when the cops are lurking. We are not always successful. It's a horrible feeling when one of the people we send to the wash gets apprehended by the police. There's a sense of betrayal, of complicity. A feeling we served them up on a big plate to law enforcement. A feeling we took their trust in our hands and broke it into a thousand pieces. A feeling for all our good intentions, we are leading them to disaster.

Marie and I have finished our outreach shift and stand outside the centre discussing the morning's happenings. We do a debrief after each shift, share difficulties we encountered, and brainstorm about potential improvements. A young man leaves the centre as we talk; he has just showered and waves to us as he passes. Two men and a woman appear from around the corner and approach and crowd him. But the young man wants nothing to do with them, so he tries to walk around them and get by. But no matter how hard he tries, the three block his passage, and their body language grows increasingly belligerent—fingers pointing, arms waving, voices raising. The young man tries to brush them off, but the largest of the group grabs his arm and tries to pull him in a direction he does not want to go. The three have enclosed him, ensnared him in a trap, and the young man in his desperation looks back at me, pleadingly, as if asking, no begging, for me to do something.

I have watched the unfolding drama with concern, taking a step closer as the group inches a step away. What is going on? Is he being robbed in broad daylight in Belgrade? Are these nationalists taking the law into their own hands? The young man with strangers' arms around his body keeps looking back over his shoulder at me, and his face has the unmistakable look of betrayal. I trusted you, he says. You asked me to come, so I did. There is an urgency to my step. I move closer. And then closer still. I do not know my course of action, yet I am pulled to the commotion just a few dozen metres away. The three have noticed me approach, since the young man keeps pointing at me and shouting. Their eyes are on me. I am in this now. I keep walking, and one of the three breaks away and comes towards me. He is big and burly and walks with authority, but I match his step, and soon we face each other. "What's the problem," I ask, my voice failing to hide my disgust at what is unfolding in front of me. The man has prepared himself for my question, though, and he reaches into his coat pocket and pulls out a badge, which stops me in my tracks, in the same way a gun might. My bravado has vanished. I am deflated. A popped balloon. I am on the defensive, trying to minimize the damage as much as possible. I am surprised by the effect the badge has on me. It deserves my unquestioned deference. This I have been taught. It deserves my utmost respect even though the man who wields it does not. No. He and his colleagues do not deserve my respect. Yet his badge, its mere appearance, has robbed me of my righteousness, my confidence to do the right thing. It is gone.

"Do you know him?" the police officer asks, pointing to the young man, still in the clutches of the other two. "He used our shower," I say, keeping my sentences short and as unhelpful as possible. "Are there any more showering?" the police officer asks. "I have no idea," I say and regret my answer. Marie, who without my knowledge has followed me, says, "No. There's not." The police officer returns to his colleagues, and we return to ours. A second later, the officers and young man are gone. The street continues to bustle with activity. People and cars go about. There is nothing out of the ordinary. You could never haved guessed something grotesque happened just a few seconds earlier. There are no traces. No evidence. The young man has been taken. I keep picturing the man's hands on the young migrant's body and his struggle to free himself. I see the shock and fear in his eyes, his helplessness and mine.

2
Calais

October to December 2021

In front of Town Hall sits one of Calais's most famous sites: Rodin's the Burghers of Calais. The bronze monument is of six men dressed in robes. They all are barefoot, and some have ropes around their necks. Emaciated and haggard, they all exude a pronounced sense of despair. There is something fatalistic about their body language. The men have succumbed to whatever awaits them, whatever comes in the next few minutes. Such a depressing scene seems out of place in front of the Town Hall, the symbolic heart of Calais, especially in this festive season, when around the gaunt and faded men stand Santa Clauses and reindeer and teddy bears and children mesmerized by the fun of it all.

During the Hundred Years' War, Calais passed between British and French hands like the proverbial hot potato. The scene Rodin depicts comes from the war's early days, in 1347, after King Edward III of England had laid siege to the coastal city for almost a year. Edward prized the coastal city because controlling it meant keeping the channel open for English soldiers to pass. Yet since Calais rested on a marsh, which made a full attack difficult, the king decided to construct a small garrison outside the city's walls and starve the city to death. For eleven months, the burghers of Calais waited for King Philip VI of France to rescue them, but he never came, and with starvation close at hand, the inhabitants surrendered. Sir Jean de Vienne, a military commander of Calais, met Walter Manny, representing King Edward, who told the soldier Edward was angry at the inhabitants' intransigence and had decided to execute them. After talking with his advisors, Edward eventually decided to spare the burghers, except for six, whom he ordered to appear in public with nooses around their necks and with whom he ordered beheaded. The men appeared before the king gaunt, barefoot, and dishevelled and prepared themselves for their sacrifice. At the last moment, Edward's wife, Queen Philippa, threw herself at her husband's feet and begged her husband for mercy. The king relented, and the men were spared.

Interpretations of the sculpture have emphasized the bravery and sacrifice of the burghers. Yet what Rodin's sculptor does not show is the act of six burghers sacrificially presenting themselves in front of Edward was neither spontaneous nor particularly unique for the times. What the men were performing was a ritual of surrender, a kind of theatre of capitulation and rather commonplace in Medieval Europe. It was pageantry, a performance. The king and the inhabitants drafted the rules of surrender well in advance, and to solidify the submission of the people of Calais, a ritual was required. The burghers did leave the city walls wearing nooses, but the town's men-at-arms also accompanied them for protection. The execution was purely symbolic, a ceremony to restore the glory and majesty of the English crown, which the burghers had sullied and threatened. Far from being patriots or representing an incipient French nationalism, the six burghers were merely following tradition and doing what the vanquished had always done.

And around Rodin's statue, children do not ask questions but stare wide-eyed at the night sky, as fireworks crackle and burst. It's Christmastime in Calais, the season of magic. But like the statue, the merrymaking hides more than it reveals.

Even though people on the move have journeyed to Calais in northern France to cross the English Channel and irregularly enter the UK for decades, the city and its migrant population captured the world's attention with the creation of the Jungle, a sprawling informal refugee camp housing thousands of displaced people, and its subsequent destruction on October 24, 2016. Such an act of force was meant to dissuade other migrants from coming to the French seaside and pitching their tents. Yet six years after the Jungle's destruction, people have not stopped arriving at Calais; some two thousand still live on the city's outskirts, in wooden areas or in and around abandoned buildings, waiting for their chance to cross the channel by dinghy or truck.

The French police operate what Human Rights Watch calls "a strategy of enforced misery." Every forty-eight hours, French police conduct eviction operations that force migrants to leave the land they occupy. Authorities say evictions prevent mass encampments like the Jungle from generating; others say the efforts are used to make migrants' lives as miserable as possible to encourage them to leave Calais. During these mass evictions, police often seize the tents, sleeping bags, tarps, blankets, and whatever other meagre possessions the displaced might have. The migrants are then forced to go the centre d'accueil et d'evaluation des situations administratives (CAES), migrant reception centres. Only those people who wish to make an asylum claim in France can stay in the centres for longer. For most people on the move, however, no such claims are possible, for under EU law, they should have applied for asylum in the first EU country they arrived. Most do not even want to stay in France. Their hopes lie thirty-three kilometres to the northwest in the UK. Between October and December 2021, I volunteered at an organization in Calais assisting people on the move. Here are some of their stories.

BMX

Distribution days begin with a debrief. The team leader lays out the day's plan: We are distributing NFI (non-food items) at the BMX site, an informal camp of about sixty to seventy Eritreans. We will distribute forty-five tickets, determined by an algorithm based on factors like the number of people and time of year. With a ticket, a person may choose items from our catalogue. The order taker notes the choices, and the volunteer in the van retrieves the items. Our catalogue is taped onto our distribution table. Among the first column items, a person can have one of each, such as t-shirts, jumpers, hygiene packs, and SIM cards. The other two columns contain higher-value items, such as jackets, shoes, and belts, from which the person can only have one item from each column. Today, we are a team of five. Stephen and Franz will take orders; Kate and Tony, the two more experienced volunteers, will monitor the line and handle exchange requests; and I will collect the requested items in the van.

After loading the van, we drive to the old BMX stadium. Calais hides its scars well. Driving or walking through the city centre, a visitor would never guess thousands of people are sleeping rough in forests and fields on the city's outskirts or under bridges. The streets are romantic, especially in the fall, with the leaves falling and the nights getting colder. The bakeries, bars, and butchers are all open. The city centre possesses the quaintness one would expect from a European city: low-rise townhouses and boutique shops. There are no evident signs of distress. But moments occur when the façade drops, and the unfolding humanitarian crisis unveils itself. The flashes quickly happen. Young men of colour huddled together outside a Catholic church or congregated around the train station and parks. Tents erected under bridges. Police vans patrolling the streets.

We park the van next to the abandoned BMX stadium and prepare the distribution. We set up the table and hang a cardboard chart of the available items. The people, predominately men, have already begun to form two lines behind the table. They know our system and know the closer they are to the front, the better chance they have of getting the better, more valuable items, such as jackets, belts, and scarves. What makes BMX one of the more relaxed distribution points is the homogeneity of the people. They are Eritrean. One community. They live together and support one another. As a result, tensions do not rise between communities, as they can at other sites.

The wind is strong this afternoon, and ominous clouds hang overhead. It could rain at any moment. We will need to be quick. I hand out half of the tickets to the men standing in one line, and the sight of these grown men, some of whom probably had successful professions in Eritrea, queuing politely in line does bother me. Each takes a ticket and thanks me. Forcing them to line up for necessities infantilizes these men. They become children eager to please the teacher, desperate for a good grade. Once the tickets are gone, I climb into the van and look at each crate. I visualize flowing from each one with ease and little effort. I need to be fluid. Tony says we can begin, and Stephen and Franz start taking orders from the two lines. I gather the items as quickly as possible, double-checking I am grabbing from the right crate and repeating the item out loud to confirm with the order taker. We repeat this pattern. The line moves well.

Within a few minutes, a little girl climbs into the back of the truck with me and demands to help. During the morning's briefing, the team leader said this would likely happen. Stephen appears and asks for a medium jacket, which I grab and then hand to the girl, who then passes it to Stephen. With the UK now on their horizon, the need for English has become more pressing, which perhaps explains the girl's repetition of each word—or maybe it's just fun, a brief respite from the never-ending monotony, and terror, of living rough in a field.

The girl takes a break from distributing the goods and sits on the bench we have set up in the van. I sense her staring up at me while I collect the items and focusing on my ponytail, which now hangs over my left shoulder. I see her fixated on my hair, trying to understand it, trying to match me, what I look like, with it, the long hair. She is working it out, making internal calculations, as if I were a math problem. I smile because I know her question, that question, will inevitably come, as it has for most of my life. She points to my hair and asks without any hesitation, "Are you a boy?" "I am a boy," I reply, grabbing a hygiene pack and handing it to Franz. "But you have long hair," she says, and I nod, "I like long hair." She seems satisfied with my response and points to her hair, which has been tightly braided in long rows, and asks what I think. "Very nice," I say, and she then asks whether I want my hair braided. I only reiterate how much I like her hair. Again, she seems satisfied.

Two more children jump into the van, and my work area becomes a playground. The little ones rifle through the crates, examining the items and asking their names. A boy grabs a hygiene pack and notices the brown bar of soap inside, which he mistakes for chocolate. Excitement takes him. "Chocolate, chocolate, chocolate," he says, showing the soap bar to the other children. I tell them the bar is not chocolate but soap, used for washing the body, a process I mime for them, but they look at me blankly, suspiciously, shocked I could tell them something so cruel. The boy and the others lose interest in the soap-chocolate and rummage through other crates, asking what each is, what it does, and whether they can have it. After a few more minutes of playful chaos, parents come to claim their respective ruffian, and calm returns to the van.

Items disappear from the shelves. I tell the order takers we no longer have jackets, jumpers, and boxers. The lines become smaller until we have taken our last order. We pack up the table. A police van stops on the parking lot's edge, and three officers get out. Since there was an eviction this morning, they will likely only watch. And what do they watch? People chatting around the generator and waiting for their phones to charge. Young men kicking a football around. Children chasing one another around the parking lot. Satisfied with what they have seen, they drive off, leaving Steven and me to ponder over their visit and what purpose it served other than to intimidate. Some Eritreans return to their tents with their belongings while others kick a football around. Now, they will wait until the time is right to cross the channel.

Old Lidl

It's November in Calais. The days are shorter, and the weather has turned cold. The city has a biting wind that can pierce through even the thickest of jackets. It rains a lot. And then it rains some more. The coordinators have decided to distribute around seven hundred tents to people camping around Calais, many going to the Old Lidl site.

The site has a reputation for unruliness. It's a mixed community, home to people from various countries, which makes distributing there challenging. The Sudanese community outnumbers the other groups, dominating the distro lines and making it difficult for other nationalities to access our services. Another problem is the sheer number of people. A few weeks earlier, the distro team had to evacuate because the lines had disintegrated and become too chaotic.

Before going to Old Lidl, we strategize. Bethany, the team leader, has sketched the site, indicating where the van will park and where each volunteer will stand. I am to cover the small space between the van door and the railway fence, ensuring no one tries to access the van from that side or cut to the front of the line. We can only give one tent to two people. I see myself on the paper, a little X with my name written on it, and try to visualize myself blocking access to potentially life-saving goods.

We leave in four cars and drive past shops, buildings, homes. Calais again feels ordinary and banal. But as we drive along Rue Beau Marais and pass under the A216 overpass, I see a long line of people walking towards the Old Lidl site. We park on the side of the ride, next to a row of quaint little bungalows. As dinner time approaches, I wonder if the family inside is preparing their supper, readying to sit down for a meal. Their proximity to Old Lidl is striking, a site home to four or five hundred people on the move at any given time. How tragedy has come entwined into the fabric of this city again astonishes me. A row of houses disintegrates into a space of encampment.

The beneficiaries have already formed a long line. The van transporting the tents has backed into a space next to the train tracks, blocked by a large green fence. The volunteers assemble and go to their designated space. One volunteer jumps into the van to distribute the tents and tarps; another stands at the van's front to hand the goods to the people waiting. One table separates the van from the beneficiaries. A few more volunteers circulate the line to ensure everyone is queuing in pairs. An Arabic-French translator also stands at the table to clarify any confusion. The rest of the volunteers survey the line and try to keep its structure intact by blocking anyone who tries to enter it from the side.

Problems develop immediately. Although everyone has queued in pairs, it soon becomes obvious they do not know each other well and have no desire to sleep in the same tent together. Some pretend to share, and the same faces asking for tents appear again. When a volunteer asks a single person where their friend is, they always motion to the side, by a few boulders, where people have huddled. "My friend is there," they say. They call out a name, and a friend does appear. Before long, however, the friend they have called rejoins the line after their friend has called them. The line slows to a crawl. We interrogate those we have seen before and explain they will have to share with the man with whom they already claimed a tent. We navigate these various scenarios as best we can. We tell them they cannot call friends over; they must be in line together. The volunteers go down the queue and determine who will share a tent. "You and you," they shout. "You and you." We put people together. We want them standing in pairs. We want them to follow our rules.

I try to envision myself in that situation, being forced to share a tent with a stranger, but I do not linger long there. I cannot. I must focus on preventing this man from accessing the line between the fence and the van, even though he points and shouts he is only trying to get to his friend. I tell him to go around the van and join the others at the back of the line. He shouts at me some more, and I absorb each of his protests and reply, "I am sorry my friend, but you must go around." Distributing is 80 per cent apologizing for the things we do not have or the things we cannot give to everyone.

It is now dark and cold. The line crawls along. A high-speed train flies past us. I wonder for those commuters, for whom a journey past Old Lidl is daily occurrence, whether the sight of men living in squalor and surviving from the charity of others still gives them pause, or has the sight become so common they may only register the men in broken shoes and flipflops before returning to their phones?

We have completed our task yet do not feel like celebrating. As we pack up, I watch the men with their tents scatter in different directions. Some walk along the train tracks, and others vanish between nearby buildings. Some even walk along the main road and past those quaint little bungalows. Inside, parents ready their children for bed, tucking them in tightly and maybe even reading a bedtime story. Outside, the men with tents walk by their windows, never daring to peek inside or draw attention to themselves. They only hope to enjoy a night's shelter before the police come.

Macron

Hundreds of people are awaiting our arrival. We have returned to Old Lidl for our weekly distribution of NFI. Two volunteers have already driven ahead to hand out the one hundred tickets we are distributing. Each group of twenty tickets is represented by a different colour: 1–20 yellow; 21–40 blue; 41–60 red; 61–80 green; and 81–100 orange. With this system, only the people with the colour and numbers being called should be waiting around the distribution table, yet people still hang about, seeing what we have in our catalogue and trying to catch a glimpse into the van to see if our stock is dwindling.

Erick, the volunteer surveying the line, notices some tickets circulating among the people who do not have today's date on them, which we include to distinguish valid tickets from fraudulent ones. He asks one guy where he got the ticket, and the man just brushes him off and returns to trying to access the table. We explain to him that without today's date, the ticket is not valid; he replies in Arabic, sprinkled with a few English words, and despite the language barrier, we can understand his frustration. We find a guy with a proper ticket and show the aggrieved man the date, highlighting the difference between a real and a fake ticket. We ask him where he got his ticket, but he storms off and disappears into the crowd. Minutes later, a man with a bowl of soup asks if he can have a ticket. "Sorry," I say, "but we have distributed all our tickets." I spot the annoyance in his eyes and sense he will not take my words so generously. "When can I get a ticket?" he asks. "We come here every Tuesday at twelve," I say, "but you should line-up for tickets at 11:40 or 11:30 to ensure you get one." He looks at me hard and holds an anger he desperately tries to contain. "So you are not back for another week?" he asks, and I prepare the most frequently used phrase on distribution: I'm sorry. "Sorry," he repeats. He knows this word. He has heard it many times. He shakes his head but keeps his eyes locked on me. He will not let me go sharing his feelings, and he will certainly not let me leave him thinking I have done something good here, something I should feel proud about. "Everywhere I go," he says, pointing to our van and then to another nearby van distributing soup, "I hear sorry. Sorry, sorry, sorry, sorry, sorry." He stares at me, daring me to say it again.

I spot the man with the fraudulent ticket; he has returned to the crowd assembled around the table. I ask to see his ticket. It is a different one, but there is still no date. "You cannot use this ticket," I tell him. "It needs to have today's date." His expression hovers between incredulity and hostility. He cannot believe what he is hearing, but instead of arguing with me further, he shows me, unambiguously, he has had enough: He takes the little ticket in his hands, holds it in front of me, and rips it into a dozen pieces. As the tiny pieces drift towards the ground, the man leaves, shouting his feelings in Arabic, truly expressing himself, much to the amusement of those who can understand him.

I drift through the crowd and do not anticipate him. This man comes seemingly out of nowhere. His movements are volatile and unhinged. He is in my face, and I can smell the alcohol on him. His speech is slurred; his words are a mixture of French, English, and Arabic. He is angry. I assume he wants a ticket, but I am incorrect. He wants nothing from me except my ear. My presence. He speaks to me in French and then in English. "I can speak both," he says. "Which do you prefer?" He wants me to know he can express himself in European tongues and I cannot hide behind a shield of miscommunication. He understands me, and I will understand him. He is boastful and confident. The alcohol has released him from any penchant for gravel in front of the white aidgivers. No. He will tell me how he feels. "Fuck France," he says, and asks whether I agree. His words are a melange of languages, and I have trouble following his rant. I wonder if he wants a reaction from me, for me to take offence to his words. "Fuck France," he says again. "Fuck Macron." The saliva flies from his mouth, and I see the wild frenzy in his eyes. I do not engage and do not ask any further questions. I nod and agree. I become a sponge to soak up his anger.

He is pointing to somewhere in the distance. He is talking about borders, something about borders. Something about movement. My silence seems to anger him more. He wants a reaction. He comes closer. "Fuck Macron," he says again. "And fuck Elizabeth." "Do you agree?" he asks. "Do you agree?" Again and again. I nod. People around us are watching, wondering how this encounter will end. "Fuck Macron and fuck Elizabeth." I cannot detach myself from this barrage. "Fuck Macron and fuck Elizabeth." There is no exit. "Fuck Macron and fuck Elizabeth." Each time I think he has exhausted himself and will vanish among the others, he regains his strength and launches into another enraged soliloquy. He is relentless and uncompromising. How long has it been? Five minutes? Ten? It feels like hours. He exhausts me. His words weigh on me, a fucking boulder on my shoulders. I am his punching bag. He need not censor himself. He has no fear of reprisal. These words have long festered within him, growing, multiplying, metastasizing until they had nowhere to go but out. How long must I endure them?

Something has distracted him. A police van lurches through the field, and the men part for the police. The disgruntled man, too, vanishes. From the vehicle, two officers survey our distribution, perhaps debating whether it is worth their time to ensure we have the proper paperwork to give away essential items to displaced persons. Locals are unhappy with people camping in their vicinity. Not happy with their presence or with the things they leave behind. They are displeased with us. We sometimes hear their irate opinions when they see us pulling up, but as they share their grievances from the comfort of their doorstep, I always wonder what they are upset about. They complain to the police and local government, who do not need much incentive to make life even more difficult for the displaced calling this dirt patch home. These authorities have the blessing of Macron and Elizabeth, too.

Candles

Park Richlieu sits in the city centre. A small park, its most interesting feature is a sculpture of the map of France, which becomes illuminated in red, white, and blue at night. From the park's entrance, on the main street, I watch people pass through the map and pass through the country, as it were the easiest thing to do. We have gathered here tonight, the couple hundred of us, to hold a vigil for those displaced people who have died trying to find safety and security. Two people drowned trying to cross the English Channel, and another was hit and killed by a train while trying to find a place to sleep that would go undetected by the police. The organizers pass out candles and offer tea to anyone interested. It is a cold night, and the candle feels warm in my hands. The attendees are diverse and represent the entire spectrum through which a government defines a human being—from undocumented through the citizen. Two people unfurl a quilt on the ground containing the names of everyone who has died in and around Calais while trying to seek safe passage to the UK. Since 1998, 308 have died. We gather around the quilt, and a young woman speaks about the tragedies that have unfolded over the previous days—the drownings and the train deaths—and she shares a message from a survivor of the train accident, from his hospital bed, where he recovers from his injuries. They had just arrived at Calais and were seeking a place to sleep, somewhere they could go unmolested by the police, some place they could rest without harassment, without being told to leave. But wherever they sought temporary refuge from the elements, voices told them to leave, so they went from place to place, bush to bush, throughout Calais and its hidden camps, until they decided to try their luck along the train tracks, a place, they reasoned, the cops would not go. And they were right.

A few Calaisians speak, those few locals who have challenged the rhetoric emanating from town hall, the discourses sowing fear and apprehension among the inhabitants about the displaced's presence in their bushes and fields, hidden within the tightest of spaces. But this woman speaking now is forthright in her conviction it is not the Calaisians who live in insecurity and danger, but the people forced to live in squalor and dirt; they live in insecurity and fear—not us. A young girl takes the microphone and says that although we may have different colour skin and different points of view, we are all human beings and worthy of dignity and respect.

A displaced man takes the microphone and addresses us in Arabic in measured and slow sentences, whose words are translated in French by a translator standing at his side. He fights to keep his composure, overwhelmed, he seems, by the burden of what he has experienced and the challenge of putting it into words. He has grown tired of living in the forests like an animal. He is a human being. The displaced are human beings. "Like you," he says, pointing at the crowd. Like us. "We are not criminals," he says. "Some of us might have taken something small here or there, but it was only because we have nothing, only because we need to survive." He emphasizes this point again and again—we are not criminals—as if specifically responding to a particular message circulating on social media and across news channels, as if trying to make us understand how inhuman conditions can easily lead to immoral actions, demanding we put ourselves in their shoes, their situation and then ask what we would be prepared to do to survive in such conditions. Suicidal thoughts and desperation are common, he says. The waiting kills. We need a solution, he says. This is not it.

A man on crutches takes the microphone and asks to share a poem written by one of the men who died at sea. The poem is an apology. The speaker apologizes to his family for having left them to chase his dream in the UK. His sisters. His mother. But they need not worry about him anymore. He shouldn't have left. He knows that now. He should have sent more money. Tried harder. Did more. He failed, and he is sorry. But all that doesn't matter now; he has found rest. He is dead. And gone.

Auchan

Coquelles lies to the west of Calais's downtown. It's an area of farmland, but the commune does have hotels and a shopping mall, Auchan. The mall is open daily from 8:30 and closes at 21:00 Monday through Thursday, 21:30 Friday and Saturday, and 12:30 Sunday. Auchan is easily reached by motorways and is serviced by several local buses. It has all the stores a consumer could want — a one-stop shopping experience. It caters to all tastes and budgets, all members of the family. Food. Technology. Clothing. Toys. Games. Appliances. Auchan has plenty of parking, too, and if you park at its rear, you can see farmland stretching before you, reaching north to the sea. It's an interesting contrast, as the mall serves almost as a boundary, a border, between Calais and its environs, between the urban and rural, between here and there. Everything looks peaceful and tranquil. The farms have a vigorous quality. They are as picturesque as they are efficient. Different shades of green. Different things being grown. Lines demarcate the land, separating this from that, indicating what belongs to whom. A rural road leads from Auchan to the coast, flanked on the east and west by more farmland. In the evenings, on those rare sunny evenings, the sun takes its time setting, floats over the green farmlands, and sets them on fire with its orange light. It's spectacular. Beautiful.

But these images can mislead. These farmlands are not as vacant and pastoral as they appear. They are not so innocent. Along the roads, CRS (compagnies républicaines de sécurité) vans are frequent, often travelling in groups. These vans are generally responsible for maintaining order, controlling crowds, and preventing riots. Their presence then along these country roads remains curious, as a riot and/or general disorder seem as unlikely as finding a pot of gold at the end of a rainbow, which sometimes do appear around Calais, especially when the sun returns after a brief but heavy downpour. If you train your eyes, however, and learn how to spot certain abnormalities, things out of place, you will understand a different world exists just on the periphery of Auchan, just beyond its glittering lights and among those lush farmlands and in its more secluded and secretive spots. You will see that among those people walking from Auchan towards the parking light, only some get into their car, start the engine, flick on the lights, and drive home to their beds and warm showers. Others, however, mostly men in beaten and broken clothes, will continue walking past the parked cars, towards the fields, and then down narrow pathways before disappearing completely.

This evening, five of us are doing a tent maurade in the fields by Auchan. We have twenty-five tents to give away and will go searching for people in need of one. Dylan, the team leader, lays out the plan in detail. We will split into two teams: One will wait by the car with the tents, and the other will head along the path and ask people whether they need a tent. Once the team has visited a few campsites and taken a few orders, they will message the number of tents to the car team, who will then start to carry them towards the sites. Dylan tells us to remember we will be entering people's living spaces, their temporary homes, and must remain respectful. We should always acknowledge our presence and ask whether we can enter their premises. "The living conditions are not good," Dylan says, "so prepare yourselves."

I am prepared. In this kind of work, you need to dial down the humanity and become slightly more robotic, only a part of an assembly line. You are just a piece of metal performing its duty, without complaint or excuse, for a greater purpose: creating a part. All pieces of the assembly line must work together. Each operation and movement must go flawlessly; otherwise, the end product suffers. And here, our end product is the sheltering of twenty-five people. Our humanity has led us to deliver tents to people on the move sleeping rough under the shadow of Auchan; we need not further display it in the field in the form of visible discomfort and unease. We must continue because the people of Auchan continue; they persevere and remain resilient. There is no time for romance, no time for tantrums about the unfairness of it all; we must become robots to get the job done because until safe passage to the UK exists for asylum seekers, there will always be jobs to do.

From the parking lot, we take a muddy footpath, which at some point in its history must have had some function; today, however, it acts as the main thoroughfare through the camps of Coquelles, its main highway. Sunlight fades, and night beckons. The path is well trodden but slippery due to the recent rains. Men swiftly pass us in both directions. Some listen to music; others stop to chat in Arabic. Garbage and debris decorate the brush and grasses on each side of the path. To the right, the north, open farmland stretches to the sea; to the left, the south, a fence runs parallel to the path, separating the camp land and the more residential areas. Barriers are important in Calais; they help to keep the mess out of sight. Before we see any camps, however, we encounter another entity calling these camps home: rats. The rats of Coquelles are fat and healthy; they seem undisturbed by the presence of humans, for they know these camps will provide them sustenance, and therefore their exposure is worth the risk. And exposed they are.

They run across the footpath with apparent abandon, gleeful even. They have found their paradise.

The first camp is well hidden, tucked between the path and the barrier. Under a blue tarp, a group of men sit around a fire and talk. Dylan says hello and asks whether we may enter their living space. Crates full of vegetables and other foodstuffs sit on the ground. Smoke from the fire drifts into the sky. A man stands and beckons us to enter. We thank him before Dylan explains the purpose of our visit and asks whether there is anyone without a tent. The men around the fire discuss the issue among themselves, and after much debate, they decide they have sufficient tent space to cover all those living there. We thank them for their time and leave them to their fire and dinner.

The pathway rises slightly, meandering past farmland. Trees rise on the north side, providing some relief from the rain and some camouflage from flashlights and coarse voices. Through the trees, we can see the blue tarps of another campsite and a group of men stoking the flames of their fire. A man rises to greet us and beckons us to enter with a welcoming gesture. Forty people live in the camp, he says, and not all have shelter from the elements. Dylan explains we can only provide two-person tents, making it essential people in the camp share them. After much conversation and clarification, Dylan says we can give them five tents and will return with them in ten or so minutes. We text the van team, telling them to prepare five tents.

The camps come fast now. Every few metres, one appears on the left and the right, nestled among the bushes or against the hillside. Some are packed tightly; others are more spread out. From some, music emanates; from others, only the soft sounds of conversation. The conditions are horrible and shameful. They mirror the images one may hold about the slums of Mumbai or Nairobi. But the Global South does not hold a monopoly on acting indifferently to the world's outcasts; here in Calais, just three hours north from the Eiffel Tower and the Louvre, those symbols of Western civilization, men subsist in the mud and cold, among the rats and Auchan's shiny lights.

We have taken an order for five more tents and return to the van to collect them. Bethany and Mike meet us at the pathway's entrance, and we divide the tents among ourselves and prepare to return to the site to distribute them. A familiar face, though, has a different idea. I recognize him immediately: the man from Old Lidl. The man who told me how he felt about Macron and Elizabeth. He is again intoxicated and angry. He is again telling Macron and Elizabeth to go fuck themselves. But when he spots the tents we carry, his attention becomes much more focused and precise. He wants one and grabs hold of the one in Dylan's hand. The man wants a tent and now. Dylan asks him which camp he lives in and explains our system. Nothing doing. He wants this one now. Dylan explains these tents are already reserved for others. He does not care; he tugs more forcefully on the tent. "Fuck Macron," he says. "Fuck France." Bethany asks whether he is staying with anyone, and in response comes more bursts of anger, incomprehensible speech, and a flurry of "Fuck Macron." He pulls on the tent. He wants it. There is no reasoning with him, no talking him down. And why should there be? In the two weeks since I have seen him, what has happened to make him more agreeable to his surroundings? What has changed? His anger and desperation have only increased, becoming more volatile and sharper. Calais purposely breeds this kind of anguish. The police chase these people around the city as if they were vermin; they keep them in a state of perpetual unease and keep them living in the rain, wind, and mud. They make them survive in filth. And this man who demands his tent has endured things no one should; government policies have transformed him into this ball of rage before us. And Dylan, not wanting to escalate the situation further, gives the man his tent, who then shuffles away into the night.

The further away from the entrance, the more camps we encounter. The police, we learn, do not venture this far along the path during their evictions, which explains why hundreds of people are camping along this thin corridor. We pass elevated tarp after elevated tarp, fire after fire. Rats are frequent sights, as are the men who have laid a carpet atop the mud to prostrate themselves and pray towards Mecca. I can think of no image that captures their complete degradation better than praying in the mud, among the rats. This is Europe.

Shoes

We never bring shoes to the distribution because they are the most troublesome item. Most beneficiaries need new shoes, but we can only distribute them to people who need them. If the shoes are broken, if their physical integrity has disintegrated, if they are crumbling and falling apart, they may have a new pair of shoes. If there are holes in the shoes larger than a two-euro coin, they may have a new pair of shoes. If they are two sizes too small or two sizes too big, they may have a new pair of shoes. For size, the order takers must ask the person for permission to touch their shoes to check where their toes are. It's not great to deny a person on the move shoes, but we only have stock for those who desperately need them. For those few people for whom we offer new shoes, the order takers ask for their size and note the description of their old ones, which are recorded on the back of the ticket. The order takers then inform the person to return at a certain time to exchange their shoes, and once the distribution has finished, the volunteer team returns to the warehouse to collect the new ones.

We have returned with the shoes the men have ordered. We set up benches in the field so they may sit and try them on. Bethany carries a clipboard with all the shoe orders, from which she will call out the names and ticket numbers of the beneficiaries. She hands me the ticket for a man named Muhammad, shoe size forty-two. I ask Muhammad to sit on the bench, and I go to the back of the van to ask Kate for a pair of forty-twos. Kate rifles through the crates of shoes and hands me a pair of brown, narrow dress shoes. I am doubtful Muhammad will like these, and my concerns are confirmed when he sees them in my hands and says something in Arabic to the men standing behind them, to which they all laugh. He struggles to put them on. When they finally wrap around his foot, he pushes down against his big toe, and I can see how little separates it from the shoe's end. "Too small?" I ask, trying to mime small with my hands, and he nods, so I return to the van and ask Kate for a pair of forty-threes. These feel sturdier in my hands, a little more appropriate for the terrain he will encounter, and when he slips them on, the shoes wrap themselves nicely around his feet. But when I give him the thumbs up, confirming the shoes do fit, he shakes his head and presses his fingers down on the shoes' tips, near the laces, indicating they are too narrow to accommodate his feet. I ask Kate for shoes the same size but wider. These the man finds too small. The next pair are too large. The next are too uncomfortable. Each preceding pair has some flaw, some issue. I feel myself getting annoyed. I roll my eyes at Kate each time I return to the van, returning the flawed pair and asking for a different one. She searches the crates and boxes for a pair he has not tried. I start taking several pairs with me, and when he rejects each one, with a shake of his head or some gesture underscoring his displeasure, my impatience grows. I take a look at the shoes he had on, that crumbling mess of materials, and wonder why he cannot be satisfied with the slight imperfections of the ones we offer. I check my mounting annoyance and remember where I am, what I am doing, and with whom I am interacting. I remember the men who came to the showers in Belgrade with bleeding and blistered feet, feet that looked as if they had suffered through war. I remember the grimaces and pained sounds they made peeling the socks from their feet. I remember the shoes held together by mere strands. I remember the smells.

My frustration is matched by Muhammad's. He does not care about our intentions, our best efforts. He came to get shoes. We advertised shoes. We told him we would bring him shoes that fit. We did not tell him he would have to graciously accept the shitty ones we are forced to give out. We did not tell him they would likely not fit properly, would do little against the wetness of the places he is forced to live, or would likely not last as long as a good pair of trainers or boots. We did not tell him dignity was conditional upon the supplies we have.

Muhammad has followed me to the van. I show him the remaining shoes we have in his size. He takes each in his hand, feeling the material and construction, and he drops each with a profound level of dissatisfaction. I hand him another pair; he waves me away and begins to walk from the van and back to Coquelles. I am astonished at his decision. He would rather keep the shoes he has than take any of ours. He would rather go practically barefoot than wear shoes that do not fit. What we offer is of no use to him. Even in his present situation, a displaced person sleeping rough in an inhospitable city, things like comfort, appearance, and quality still matter to him. He will not graciously and humbly accept the charity of others, items of clothing usually given not out of any sense of solidarity but as a stand-in for the dump. When I first started sorting through donated clothing, my concern was mainly for spotting obvious red flags, such as references to sex, drugs and alcohol, national symbols, and the sea. As for the item itself and its overall quality, I gave only the most cursory glances. I gave little thought as to whether I would wear such a piece of clothing or what I would think about accepting a shirt or a sweater from someone who only gave the article to get rid of it. If the clothes fit and did not have large holes or dirty sections, we could distribute them without concern. Questions of dignity and self-esteem did not give me pause, since the desperate and displaced should react happily to whatever items they receive. Beggars cannot be choosers, I had always heard. Humanitarianism does not concern itself greatly with confidence and respectability; it worries about whether bodies can still breathe and function and whether they are fed and warm. Vulnerable bodies should be thankful for whatever they can clothe themselves with.

But Muhammad, in his refusal to blithely and blindly accept any pair of shoes thrown his way, has forced me to reconsider people in need because although this man undoubtedly experiences hardship, he remains unequivocally a man who has his idiosyncrasies and likes, his flair and flash, his desire to look good.

I have a begrudging respect for this man, yet I am also ashamed and embarrassed by the shoes we are forced to distribute and ask these men to wear.

Muhammad has suddenly stopped walking and has begun conversing with another man in Arabic. Something this man said has made Muhammad reconsider his decision, for he takes a few steps back to the van's opening and explains in a flurry of body language he wishes to see the white shoes he had dismissed not a few minutes earlier. I hand Muhammad the shoes and watch him walk back towards his camp.

A Drowning

We had planned a cultural event with the people living in the camps of Coquelles. A volunteer from an NGO delivering emergency first aid to displaced people around Calais wanted to take a few large tents to Coquelles to screen a Champions League football match and set-up an area to chill and listen to music. The idea was to flatten, at least temporarily, the hierarchy existing between those who distribute aid and those who receive it. Especially for those of us whose only interaction with the beneficiaries is based on giving things, this event would be an opportunity, and a reminder, the people we serve are human beings who exist outside relationships of dependence and who have interests and passions going beyond which jumpers or jackets they most prefer.

Later that afternoon, however, a story begins dominating our social media feeds. A dinghy carrying displaced persons sunk somewhere between France and England. A rescue mission is underway, but fatalities are expected. We sit glued to our phones as the numbers jump from five suspected dead to eleven to eighteen to twenty-three and to twenty-seven. With each increase in numbers, we debate whether hosting a cultural evening would still be appropriate, given that the tragedy would hit closer to home for the people than for us, that some of them might have known those who perished, and that some of them would attempt a similar journey in the not-too-distant future. The organizers decide we will still go to Coquelles but will first gauge the atmosphere and ask the people what they want. We can still step up the tents, chargers, and screen and then wait outside, allowing them to take their minds off the news, their situation, and us. But then news comes that Gérald Darmanin, France's interior minister, will visit Calais tonight to deliver a press conference at the hospital, where the found bodies have been sent. He will speak about what has happened. In response, the NGOs hastily agree to meet at Darmanin's arrival point and delay his passage to the hospital.

At the protest, a man speaks to the reporter and does not mince his words. His voice, the hammer and the microphone, the nail. We have gathered below the lighthouse awaiting the minister. But this Calaisian wants the journalist to understand he does not belong to any association. He speaks for no one but himself. His anger and disgust at the drownings manifest from him alone. "I am from Calais," he says. "I am a citizen. People must know we Calaisians, ordinary folk, are against the actions of the French police and the French state." As he speaks, a dozen cops with heavy weaponry guard the entrance to the spot where we believe the minister will arrive. Now and then, a police van either enters or exits the space. Calais has no shortage of police vans. They are everywhere. More come and disappear into the dark. With each passing vehicle, we hope to spot the minister, the man who has come to spin the death of displaced people to his political advantage. His narrative is known; he needs not utter a word. The smugglers and traffickers—no attempt, incidentally, is usually made to differentiate these terms—are to blame, as they trick the poor and desperate migrants into believing they can offer them safe passage. The smugglers and traffickers prey on the defenceless and vulnerable, the meek and the puny. The smugglers and traffickers lie to these poor souls about the dangers and perils of the crossing. The smugglers and traffickers provide shoddy equipment for the passage, lifejackets, and dinghies of poor quality, which are prone to spring leaks and crumble in the face of inclement weather, big waves, and powerful winds. The smugglers and traffickers take sex as a form of payment from women if they do not have the necessary funds to pay the exorbitant fees to cross. The smugglers and traffickers are ruthless, cunning, and guile, bad men who line their pockets with money from the world's most vulnerable. They are alpha predators. The hyenas of Calais. They must be targeted, uncovered, and eliminated with the same energy and comprehensiveness given to the pursuit of terrorists. They must be stopped.

This narrative no longer has any effect on me. I have heard it so many times that I have grown numb. Politicians believe they say a thing often enough, if they repeat the same words and phrases ad nauseam, these phrases and sentences will eventually seep into the unsuspecting minds of the casual viewer or listener. The simplest explanation is usually the most popular, the one requiring the least amount of critical reflection on the part of the listener, who nods and eagerly agrees with all they hear, all the reasons and rhetoric, not because they necessarily agree with it but because this explanation requires little in the way of effort. And the politician's story does make sense for anyone who wishes to believe it. It is a tragedy with recognizable victims and villains. There is no ambiguity or grey zones. There are smugglers and the people they smuggle. No more information is required.

The politician, of course, will not disclose, nor will the listener ask about, how government policies—the specific and deliberate aim of treating migrants as an invading species that must be eradicated—create the perfect market for smugglers to thrive. I am not in the habit of romanticizing smugglers and will not ignore the duplicitous actions some undertake to grab the most money from their clients, but focusing on smugglers ignores those holding the watering can that allows these entrepreneurs to grow and flourish. No legal routes exist for these individuals to reach the UK unless they want to spend years in a camp praying they will be miraculously chosen to resettle in a safe country—an unlikely scenario. Critics talk about refugee shopping, the idea displaced persons want to settle in the most developed countries to claim asylum in, meaning, for many, that these persons are not refugees fleeing persecution or war but are economic migrants, looking for the best labour markets to flex their muscles. What these critics fail to mention is nothing in the 1951 Refugee Convention prohibits a refugee from seeking protection in a country further afield; nothing says they must apply for asylum in the first safe country they reach. Regional agreements, such as the Dublin Convention and third-safe country arrangements, posit the contrary, but these accords are mere containment mechanisms. Protection is not their primary goal; management is. They aim to keep the desperate away from the world's strongest economies. These critics also do not mention that the majority of the world's displaced do not seek protection in the world's richest places; rather, they find refuge in the nearest safe place, usually in a neighbouring, poor country. These critics ignore the reality that the harshest and most draconian rules will not stop people from seeking a dignified existence. Calais is one of the most unfriendly places to be displaced, yet they still come. They withstand the evictions and tear gas, the wet weather, disgusting living conditions, and the mud and rats. They withstand having to endure the indignity of standing in line, daily, seemingly forever, for food, water, clothes, tents, showers, anything and everything. They withstand the news of drownings, the suffocations, the deaths by train; they withstand the weather reports calling for rain and heavy winds for the next week; they withstand all of this and still find their way to the beach, to their boat, and push off from the shore, with their eyes on England, only thirty-three kilometres away.

The Hoodie

I am order changing at Old Lidl. A man has exchanged a medium hoodie for a larger one, and I am about to return the hoodie to the van when a young man standing at the table, among dozens of others, waves at me, suggesting he wishes to see the jumper. I hesitate. It's not his turn; his number has not been called, and I do not know whether he has a ticket. He beckons me closer with a slight hand movement. So much is happening at this moment, so many voices, so much movement, and I cannot withstand his smile any longer, his pleas for me to come closer with the article, just let me see and feel it his body says. I crack and break and ignore my better judgment, handing him the hoodie. He smiles and holds the hoodie against his body, noting the size and its look, and caresses the material in his fingers, and its texture produces satisfaction within his smallish frame. He likes it; this is obvious. He wants it; this is even more obvious.

I ask him for it back. My arm is extended, my hand, open. It is wishful thinking. I see it now. He still looks at it. And I can so see it. I vocalize my request, "May I have it back," in the naïve belief my baritone voice would hold some sway over him or would change the course of what will inevitably happen. He shakes his head, and his smile widens. Mischievous. Cunning. He again poses the hoodie in front of his body, as if daring me to admit that, yes, it does look good on him. But this is not the point. He does not have a ticket. He did not arrive on time. He is essentially taking that hoodie from someone who did arrive on time, someone who had been in line before we even arrived, waiting patiently for the best ticket number to get the best items. This man is undermining the fairness of our system. If others sense we are playing favourites and our rules are not equally applied across people, communities, and backgrounds, we lose trust.

My arm stays outstretched, but my mood has reddened. I feel anger rising in me, not so much directed at him, even though he is the one laughing at my stern desire to reclaim the hoodie. No, I am angry at myself. At my stupidity. At my naiveite. At my clear inexperience in the field. Why did I not ignore his plea? Why did my eyes have to rest on his? I should have passed over him and shoved the hoodie back into the van. No, I had to focus on his pleas, his needs. I had to ignore the people around him. I had to play favourites, individualizing a response that had to be collective. I had to be affected by his wish to hold the hoodie and then had to succumb to it.

Fuck. His playfulness is eating at me. He is mocking me. He is taunting me. He thinks little about our rules. This man is laughing in my face. Whenever I ask him for the hoodie, he hides it behind his back, waving it back and forth, he the matador and I the enraged bull. And then he decides. He turns his back on me and lets the crowd swallow him. He has taken the hoodie. He just fucking took it. And what? Do I swallow his intransigence? His flaunting of our rules? He just symbolically spat in my face. Should I take it? I feel my body tighten, as it usually does when I experience embarrassment and humiliation. I want retribution. I want the fucking hoodie back.

I leave my post and follow him into the crowd. Ten-person deep, but I see him, circling through the crowd as if he instinctively knows I am stalking him. He moves swiftly, here and there, darting behind and between the men. I keep my calm, but the rage is making its presence known. It's his smile mostly. The way he treats this as a game. The way he treats me as an overbearing parent. The way he is making me do things I do not want to do. I do not want to be this man. I do not want to be chasing him through this crowd. I do not want to be this enforcer.

Then I see it. He passes the hoodie to a friend of his, who then hands it to another man, and then to another, and soon the hoodie has moved through a half-dozen hands, and I can no longer gauge its movement. I can no longer track it. And it hits me: I have lost the hoodie. It is gone, and there is absolutely nothing I can do. The embarrassment weighs on me. I feel anchored to the earth. He has made a fool of me and has robbed someone else of a hoodie. I return to my post and confess to a colleague what has happened. She shrugs her shoulders and is surprised by my downcast demeanour. "If that is the worst thing to happen today," she says, "consider it a good day."

Erick

We have just given out the last pair of shoes. We always bring more shoes than we need, spares of different sizes and widths, just in case the sizes the men request are too large or too small. So, if we have a twenty-five-shoe order, we may take fifty shoes with us. Because of these spares, we also return to the warehouse with shoes, which can present a problem. At shoe drops, displaced persons not at the distribution earlier sometimes pass and inquire about what we are doing. When we tell them, they invariably show us the paltry state of their shoes and ask whether they can have a new pair. We patiently explain these shoes are only for those who came to the early distribution and have tickets. We patiently tell them the times and places of our distribution. Sometimes, though, these same people see the extra shoes in the van and ask what prevents us from giving them a pair, especially when all the tickets have been collected and shoes remain.

On this occasion, two men stop by, just as we are packing up and putting the benches away and ask whether they could get a new pair of shoes, since, after all, there are clearly shoes left in the van, and no one is around to record how we have ignored the rules just this one time. The two men point to their shoes and show the ravages of sleeping rough in Calais; their trainers are flimsy, having lost most of their structural soundness, and the soles are peeling. Mud covers them from top to bottom, and water can enter anywhere. They need shoes, and we have shoes; this situation, then, should require little compromise or understanding. But

Erick, the shift leader, tells them as politely and respectfully as he can that although they need shoes and we have shoes, we cannot give them shoes. This information perplexes the two men, who struggle to understand what Erick says, not the words but the overall rationale. Erick's argument is twofold. First, although we do have shoes in our van, they should not indicate great supply; we must carefully allocate shoes throughout the year to ensure some remain. We only have a limited supply. Second, we have a system for distributing shoes: The people who arrive first at our distributions and demonstrate the clearest need for shoes receive them. If we break this rule, we lose the trust of our beneficiaries; our methods become unfair. Our rules must apply to everyone equally.

Erick must register the skepticism on their faces, since I do, so he provides an example of a time when he did exactly what these two men are asking of him: He bent the rules. Not so long ago, a man appeared before Erick at the end of a shoe drop, just like this, asking for shoes. The man needed shoes, some remained in the van, and no witnesses roamed about, watching to ensure Erick followed his rules. So, he caved: He asked the man for his size, took a pair from the van, and handed him his new shoes. But just as the beneficiary had finished tying his laces, another man appeared from the shadows and confronted Erick about his decision. This man had been observing Erick from the shadows for a particular reason. Not long ago, he had made a similar request to Erick. He did not have a ticket but needed shoes, and shoes remained. But Erick denied his request, explaining the rules and the philosophy behind them. This man was not happy about Erick's selective implementation of the rules. What kind of game was he playing? What kind of favouritism influenced his decision-making?

The image of this man has since haunted Erick. For every decision he makes, he assumes such a presence is lurking over his shoulder, ensuring he applies the same rules to everyone. So, when the two men tell Erick no other people are about, lurking in the field or hiding behind some brush, there are no witnesses to what he could do, Erick remains unswayed by their arguments because of the image of the man who felt cheated and betrayed by Erick's flaunting of his rules. The men, too, remain unconvinced by Erick's arguments. They cannot understand how we can be so stingy with our goods and how we can be so cold, callous, and, yes, cruel. Erick says sorry, then again, and then one more time. He breaks under the weight of his convictions, the rules we must follow to sustain our operation over the next months. Look at what they make us do. Look at what they make us become.

These men with broken shoes and cold and wet feet look at us with accusing disbelief. I want us to go, to leave, to flee. I want to say sorry four or five more times, get in the van, and go. But Erick will not leave. He needs them to understand why he, we, cannot give them shoes. He explains over and over again our policy, how it's the only fair approach, the only way to treat everyone equally. But when a man with shoes is explaining to a man without shoes why it remains fair for him to go shoeless when many shores are within reach, logic and rationality hold little importance. Fairness means nothing in a world defined by injustice. Nothing can justify a man without shoes, and nothing can mitigate these men's anger towards us and our withholding of their shoes. Erick refuses to see this. He cannot accept these men would view us with such derision and animosity. But the rules are fair, he argues, cannot you see? Cannot you see how it is not us but the context forcing us to behave so…so…so ruthlessly? But these men do not care for our explanations or excuses. They need shoes. We have shoes. But we refuse to give them shoes. This is the situation. A man with nothing has little time for nuance. Perspective provides him nothing.

A week later, Erick and I are standing at the back of the van, watching two men approach. I hold a clipboard with a list of names, and to each name, we will distribute a two-person tent. We have a referral system in place whereby if different organizations come across displaced persons lacking shelter and needing a tent, they can open our Google document, insert the person's details, and give them the time and the place of the tent drop. We do three tent drops a week at different sites across Calais. Since tents are a higher-value item, we do not advertise the tents we have to give at distributions, but if someone asks about acquiring a tent, we can quietly take them aside and put an order in for them. There is, however, one caveat: They must share. Because of our finite tent supply, two people must fill a two-person tent. In volunteer meetings, we have discussed what this policy means in practice and whether we would deny a person shelter if they refused to share. No. The consensus was we would not deny such a person, but we would do everything in our power to fill tents with two bodies. On the Google document, for example, the person requesting a tent must provide their name and that of the person with whom they are sharing. That person must accompany the orderer to the tent drop, otherwise... well, otherwise, nothing. If the person arrives without a friend, we will request, strongly, that they find someone to share with because, as always, supplies are low, and we must maximize our stock.

The two men approaching are older; one appears in his thirties, the other in his sixties. And we are about to ask them to share. There is an indignity to this rule I cannot shake. More so than the shoe rules, more so than any other of our countless rules. Perhaps because I can feel its humiliation more so. The idea acutely registers on my body. I can relate to the degradation of compelling one to share a tiny space. I am a person who appreciates space. Emptiness revitalizes me. Long moments of silence keep me sane and safe. People and their proximity, voices, and opinions can distract me and make me think less of myself and my qualities, attributes, and traits.

The older man has pleading eyes. Erick has just informed him that he and his companion must share the tent because of our limited supply. "Supply" is a word I have come to loathe, and I can see it has little effect on the old man except one of incomprehension, with a splash of disappointment. The people sleeping rough in Calais are usually younger, in the prime of their lives, with the stamina and strength required to withstand the brutalities of Northern France. This older man is an exception, a rare sighting. He has decided to go, even if the odds of a successful conclusion are stacked against him. The search for a dignified life has no age limit.

In French, the older man pleads his case with Erick. He says the tent provides little privacy for two men. He wants privacy. He craves his own space. He does not know his companion so well and would prefer not to share such a cramped space. He asks whether it is possible, please, to have his own tent. Erick looks at me, and I glance down at the paper, hoping an answer may lie there, hoping Erick will convince the old man about the necessities of our system. If Erick were not here, I would have cracked and given this man a tent for his own. I would have broken our rules. I would have. Yet I know this desire to be human in an inhuman setting is not always helpful.

Erick says, "I'm sorry" for around the fifth time, and the older man accepts the verdict with pride. No more pleading. No more arguments. He will accept what he can get. No begging. He will not beg. "Merci beaucoup," he says and turns to return, with his companion, to whatever piece of shrubbery he came from. With the sun's exit, the wind has become more excited, more playful and assured. A confident wind is a dangerous thing.

In the dark, I look at Erick's face, illuminated by the streetlights and passing cars, and how it appears etched by every "no" he has had to say here in Calais. It is a spreadsheet of rejection, of the accumulating toll of denying life's basics to those who need them the most. "I would have cracked," I say, without real reason or aim. My voice is neutral, without clear emphasis. I do not know whether I say this out of admiration or critique. I do not know the point I am making other than the preceding incident was awful for different reasons, and I feel the need to clarify what I would have done if Erick were not standing beside me, if I were leading the tent drop, and if all final decisions rested with me. Erick only says, "Maybe I should have cracked, too."

Tickets

Giving out tickets is a fraught task. At the larger sites, Coquelles and Old Lidl, we give out around one hundred tickets. One team of two or three people will proceed to the site first before the van with the items arrives to distribute the tickets. We do this so everyone has a ticket before the van arrives to ward off potentially chaotic scenes. We try to instill a measure of control in everything we do, but the vagaries of life on the move do not conform well to the parameters we desire. Indeed, states themselves have understood displacement and its effects are phenomena even the most sophisticated technologies and most brutal border policies cannot control completely. The people who know where and when our distributions will take place get to the site early to line up, ensuring themselves the best possible tickets. The first tickets usually go smoothly, but when they disappear from our hands and more and more people start to arrive, the situation can become tense. People in need swarm and encircle you, and you suddenly find yourself with ten tickets left to give but twenty hands demanding one. You hear words like "please." You feel the hands grabbing at the tickets. And despite your efforts to instill some order, barking out demands for everyone to back off, the bodies still come and demand recognition. Teams have had to evacuate when the situation spirals out of control, and our pleas for calm go unheeded.

A tall man from South Sudan approaches the order takers as we prepare to start the distribution. With the tickets given out, people now wait for the goods the tickets promise them. The man shows us his ticket with the number seventy printed on it. "Let me talk to you," he says. "What is the point in giving out so many tickets when those with higher numbers do not get anything of value?" I remember him. He raised a similar point last week when after waiting for almost three hours, he only received a pair of socks, a hygiene pack, and a SIM card. We tell him what we told him last week: We try to give out items to as many people as possible, and every person with a ticket will receive something. Our answer does not please him, since he knows a SIM card is not the same as a waterproof jacket and, a hoodie is more valuable than a snood.

We ignore his further complaints, as we do not have time to argue about the finer points of our distribution model, but I keep my eye on him throughout the process. He hovers around the table and studies what people order as if trying to calculate what may be left when his turn finally arrives. I watch his reaction whenever we run out of an item and remove its picture from our catalogue. He converses with another person waiting, and I imagine they discuss how they would improve our system to make it fairer so people do not have to wait three hours for only a pair of socks. Frustration takes him each time we remove another item from the catalogue. He shakes his head and studies our movements, trying, it would seem, to understand how we cannot understand the cruelty of our system—forcing people to wait and watch as items they need disappear from the catalogue. As I check off each ticket, and the numbers I call out climb and climb, anxiety enters my body. I watch him watching us and pray, selfishly, that my colleague beside me will call out his name. But no such luck: He towers over me and looks over the remaining items with a touch of exasperation bordering on anger. I read his body language. His body has stiffened, and even the sighs he releases at the paucity of items remaining do not seem to soften his stance. He speaks through each gesture, and I feel his annoyance. It is sharp to the touch. Piercing. At the catalogue, he shrugs and shakes his head. He points to a t-shirt, then to a tarp, and then to a pair of socks. I sigh, internally, the socks, of course, the fucking socks. They are an embarrassment. Made of the cheapest, thinnest material imaginable, these socks barely reach the ankle and do next to nothing to protect or warm the foot. We were supposed to distribute them in the summertime. We had put in the order in time and did all the necessary paperwork, but because of the vagaries of shipping, they did not arrive until the fall. So, in late November, we are distributing them. In weather approaching zero degrees Celsius, we give displaced people socks that would barely keep their feet warm in a cooler-than-normal summer night.

I know how he will react when I put the tucked socks in his hand, especially since the sock illustration on our catalogue suggests a thicker, more robust pair, something that could withstand Calais's weather. Confusion will pass along his face while he fingers the material and determines what he holds. Incredulity will follow perplexity. After pulling the pieces apart, the two socks will rest in his hand and bear his inspection. Anger will then follow skepticism.

I tell him he can also have a scarf, but he points to the one around his neck. He has come to the distribution to find things he lacks, not to stock up on supplies. "Nothing else?" I ask, hoping he may select something else to compensate for the paltry socks I am seconds away from putting into his hands. But he shakes his head and waits. I relay his order to the volunteer in the van. Since the sock box rests close to the entrance, I ruffle through it, wishing by some miracle someone might have accidentally packed a thicker pair among the smaller ones. But no. There is nothing except the puny black socks.

My colleague hands me the goods, and I try to hide the socks among the other items so he may not see them until he is away from the table and may not see the point in returning to the van to vent his anger and frustration about them. He instead places everything on the table and organizes them so that they are easier to carry. And then it happens: He spots those so-called socks hidden within the t-shirt and investigates them, holding each one by the fingertips. The socks hang in front of my eyes. He does not say a word. No need for words exists. His argument hangs there for all to see. The socks confirm something for him, which requires no elaboration. They confirm something for me, too. He has waited over two hours for these socks. Imagine that. But he does not press his case further. There is nothing else he can say. No, he must accept our socks with frustration and gratitude because where else will he receive socks in Calais?

Vomit

I have this bad habit: I eat too fast. I don't know why, but I have never been able to savour my food, to enjoy the simple pleasure of eating. As a boy, I would race through meals to return to my video games or go outside to play. Yet as I have aged, my body has had increasing difficulty taking in so much food so quickly. My esophagus rebels and pushes the excess load back up into my mouth. In a word, I regurgitate. Over the past couple of years, this regurgitation has taken on a more serious and sinister quality, and, at times, I have choked. My eyes watered; my breathing became more laboured and wheezier. Whatever propelled the undigested bits back into my mouth had suddenly weakened, and, instead, the bits took up residence inside my throat, making it increasingly difficult to breathe. Most people who die from choking do so alone. They do not want to cause a fuss or become the centre of a commotion, so they excuse themselves from the table, go to the bathroom, and politely choke to death. I can relate to the impulse. I do not like eyes on me, particularly concerned eyes, ones that judge and intervene. Whenever I have had a meal in a group and have felt this sensation take me—this choking—I always politely excuse myself, careful to not let anyone notice my watery eyes and laboured speech, and find refuge in the closest private space. I then take my index finger, shove it in my mouth, and tickle the back of my throat.

At the warehouse, all the different associations eat lunch together at 12:30. A member of the group preparing the meals steps into the volunteer area and rings a vintage farmer's bell to indicate lunch has been served. We fill our plates and then find a place to sit among the tables and couches, or if it is nice outside, a rare and special happening, we may find a plastic chair and take a seat under the sun.

I don't do any of this. I take my plate and disappear into the warehouse. I find a secluded spot under shelves loaded with banana boxes of joggers and beanies. The boxes climb to the ceiling, resembling a kind of box mountain, a gargantuan peak of donations. I find a cardboard box full of winter boots and sit. I do this because I like the solitude. I need to recharge after a morning filled with social interactions, of receiving and giving orders, debating, strategizing, organizing. I also do this because I do not trust my body not to misbehave in front of an audience. I do not want the attention, the concern. I do not want to be saved in case I clutch my throat in a desperate attempt to find my breath. I would rather be alone.

Forkfuls of rice and curry do reach my lips in an orderly fashion. There is a desire not to rush, an attempt to savour each taste and texture. But old habits die hard, as they say, and soon I have lost all mindfulness of the experience, and the forkfuls come in a manic fashion. Behind me are boxes of SIM cards, and above sit boxes of toothbrushes and bags of soap. A pair of trainers has fallen from its hopper. The ladder has not been put away. The floor could use a sweep. How sure can we be the waterproof trousers are waterproof? How can we fit all our donations in this small space?

The blockage is noticeable, and it is already too late. I stand and pace. Thick and thin waterproof jackets. Snoods. Beanies. Gloves. Boxes and boxes. The rice is lodged and will not shift. Some bile has found its way to my mouth, and I swallow, only adding to the mess. My eyes water. Joggers. Size 39 trainers. Boots and boots and boots. Oxygen has gone. When I open my mouth, an alarming emptiness fills it.

I walk, briskly, to the warehouse's back entrance, not to the front, with those tables full of concerned, good people. No, I want to be alone. I pass a few stradlers, those workers wishing to wait for the line to whittle down before they went for their lunch. I pass women and men sorting clothing. Our eyes meet, but nothing out of the ordinary strikes them. I have made sure of it. A moment of recognition. A nod, maybe. A passing grin. There's nothing of concern happening here. Just a man walking, a man they have seen before. I am not out of place. I belong here, and now here I am walking to the back warehouse door. No one can fault me for wanting to take the back door. It's perfectly reasonable, nothing suspicious or untoward. My pace has quickened, though. There is this creeping urgency. My need to breathe. My need to expel this substance stuck inside me.

The outside is impressive in its ugliness. There are containers and piles of palettes. Old caravans have been transformed into offices. Tall grass and mud and puddles. Bins for cardboard, recycling, compost, and garbage. The other day, I threw a bag full of used shoes in there, and their smell was violent. Things have been painted, giving an illusionary sense of colour and warmth. But these are grey days, and I need to vomit. A woman on a forklift passes me. I need seclusion. For what I must do. No prying eyes. No concerned voices. Do not touch me. Do not look at me. I got this. Understand?

I need to wipe my eyes. Everything is watery, blurry, but I dare not touch myself, lest there be questions, worry, and concern. There is little time. I need to rectify this blockage, this absence of air. Among the cars parked in the field, the warehouse's makeshift parking lot, I stick my finger down my throat. It's not a violent plunge; all it takes is a mere tickle, a touch or two, a soft circling of the throat's interior. It's playful, almost sensual. The result is instantaneous and glorious. My body heaves. My abdominals go to work. All of my parts coordinate to expel the substance from my airway. There exists a wonderful choreography to the expulsion, but the movements need not be memorized. Everything is innate; the instructions are written on the organs and muscles. And in the flash, the substance is gone, and I feel reborn.

On the ground, the rice lies splattered against some dirt. With my boot, I kick some mud over the remains as if I were hiding incriminating evidence. In a way, vomit is a kind of evidence. I have vomited in Calais, and I feel no shame or remorse. I do not instruct myself to eat slower or to eat more mindfully. Vomiting in Calais feels almost necessary. An act of rebellion. It is a human response. I have responded to a human need. I wipe the saliva from my mouth and take a deep breath. The air feels good in me. The sun has broken through the clouds; a renewed freshness comes and revitalizes the scene. Things can get done in such weather. Around the corner, men of colour line up for their lunch, hidden behind a few stores among tall grasses, out of sight.

3
Sarajevo

January and February 2022

On the stairs leading up to the Museum of Crimes against Humanity and Genocide 1992–1995 are the words "Here the dead speak"—and they do. Opened in July 2016, the museum displays a vast collection of artifacts and video testimonials from the survivors, as well as the killed, of the war that destroyed Yugoslavia. The museum is transparent in the war's brutality. Little is left to the imagination. This is what happened: ethnic cleansing, genocide, mass rape, pogroms, torture, concentration camps. Each personal belonging resurrected from the mud and amnesia and now protected behind casing reminds the visitor behind every dead person—approximately one hundred thousand of them—stood a human being. In one casing sits an old backpack and piece of rope. Beside the objects is an inscription explaining their significance. On July 11, 1995, the Serb army took Srebrenica and began to round up and detain the city's Bosniak residents. When it became clear the Dutch peacekeepers, or NATO, would do nothing to prevent the Serb army's provocations, fifteen thousand other Bosniak men fled the carnage through the forests, hoping to reach territory Tuzla—an area controlled by the Bosnian government over one hundred kilometres away. (In the next few days, the Serb army would kill approximately ten thousand Muslim men and boys at Srebrenica.) This exodus would become known as the Death March. These Bosniak men and boys walked for days through undulating terrain and over landmine-covered grounds. The Serb army pursued and attacked them. Thousands were killed. Many more died from their wounds, hunger, or sheer exhaustion. Others, though, once they realized the Serb forces had surrounded them and their fate was either death by bullet or death by surrender, decided to take their own lives. One museum casing shows the rope one man used to hang himself from a tree branch in the forests of northern Bosnia; his backpack was found underneath his hanging body.

The museum's messaging is simple but effective: Unless we remember the brutalities of war, we are doomed to go to war again and again. Perhaps the most poignant room in the museum is the one where visitors get to write messages about how the museum affected them and then tape their messages to the wall. The room is colour. Messages adorn the walls on green, blue, pink, orange, yellow, and red paper. It's spectacularly bright and vivid. It's like people took cans of paint and threw the liquids against the wall. Each message is a splash of colour. There is no uniformity. No consistency or pattern. Just colour. On the paper are written messages of peace in dozens of languages. In English, some read "Love is greater than war," "We should share love, not war," or "Learn! Never repeat!" Yet even though visitors have proclaimed the importance of love, the feeling has had difficulty resurrecting itself in post-war Bosnia and Herzegovina. And although no more bullets fly or bombs explode, for the returning refugees, war still rages—a war over memory and accountability.

Between 1989 and 1992, the UNHCR estimates approximately 2.3 million people fled their homes because of the collapse of

Yugoslavia; of these, six hundred thousand came from Bosnia and Herzegovina. For those Bosnians reaching Western European countries, particularly Germany, Austria, and Sweden, the receiving governments granted them temporary protection, not refugee status, and each country differed in terms of the rights they granted to the displaced. On the more restrictive end of the spectrum, Germany refused to convert the Bosnians' temporary status into permanent residency, limiting their access to the German labour market, and provided few integration measures. Sweden, on the other end, almost immediately granted Bosnians permanent residency, allowed them access to the labour market and the education system, and offered integration opportunities. In 1995, 130,000 Bosnian refugees were resettled in the US. In the same year, the warring parties signed the Dayton Accords, which ended the violence but did little to provide a framework for reconciliation or nation-building. The peace agreement froze the conflict instead of solving it. The country was split into two autonomous regions: the Republic of Srpska (Bosnian Serbs) and the federation of Bosnian and Herzegovina (Bosniaks and Croats). The question of refugee return featured prominently in the accords, yet because animosity between the ethnic groups continued to exist, many Bosnian refugees, as well as those internally displaced, feared returning home to where they could face persecution. This reality did not stop some European countries, particularly Germany, from pressuring refugees to return. By 2005, ten years after the Dayton Accords, Germany had repatriated the majority of its Bosnian refugees, since the country had rarely given permanent residency to them. The UN estimates of the more than two million people the war displaced, half have returned to Bosnia, but many have refused to return to their original homes.

For those who have, some must live next door to the people who drove them away. The museum shares many stories. A Bosniak man named Mirsad returned to his hometown of Hranča and felt surrounded by the ghosts of the past. The Serbs who set fire to his home and property and killed his brother still live in the town, and few have faced any consequences for their actions. They avoid Mirsad at all costs, and Mirsad fears testifying against them for fear of retaliation. So, there is neither justice nor reconciliation. The ghosts appear here and there, demanding attention and reverence, but the past remains buried in an unmarked grave, unremarked upon. But despite the silences, disavowals, and forests swallowing the homes the displaced abandoned thirty years, as if trying to erase all unpleasant memories from the historical record, the ghosts will not go so gently without having their pain acknowledged, without having some equilibrium restored, and without having their former lives as fully formed human beings, free of bullet holes, remembered and honoured. As Mirsad said: "Imagine how hard it was for me when I took my children to school and I realized that they were going to that gym hall where I was held captive, and where my brother and other people were killed. It's inhumane. It's impossible not to feel fear there."

As much as the museum's colourful messages may speak of "never again," the war they reference has never ended; the legacies of its violence and displacement still scar the beautiful green mountains of Bosnia and Herzegovina. This geography knows displacement. Its forests have offered cover to millions. The overland routes Bosniaks took thirty years ago are now being followed by the displaced from Afghanistan, Iran, and Syria. They hike over the same terrain, follow the same footsteps. They have similar hopes:

protection, security, and a future. The forests care not who they shelter, nor should we—since anyone can become a refugee.

In Sarajevo, I volunteered with an organization providing humanitarian aid to asylum seekers passing through the city to Western Europe. Here are a few of their stories.

Kamran

The community of Ilidža sits under Mt. Igman at the western limit of Sarajevo. It has a cozy, village feel, especially in the wintertime. The volunteer house is not hard to find. You go straight over the bridge, past the police station, past the Kozman supermarket, a little further, and turn left at the mosque. It's a few houses down, on the right. You know you've reached it when you see a white van. The house is nondescript, blending into the others, and nothing about its appearance would give you the impression that within its walls is an organization distributing clothing to hundreds of displaced people a week. There are three floors, including the basement, where volunteers pack the orders for the day's distribution.

We take orders over the phone, load the van, and distribute the items across the city, including two temporary reception centres: Blažuj for single men and Ušivak for families and unaccompanied minors. Some messages are in English while others are in French, Pashto, Farsi, and Arabic, and for which Google Translate becomes an irreplaceable lifeline. Most of the conversations begin with something like "Hello sir, please help us. We need warm clothes." The writer then elaborates on his and his friends' position: "We are going on game." The expression "going on game" among people on the move expresses their choice to try and cross a border irregularly. Most will head to the north of the country, around Bihać, and attempt to enter Croatia, and from there, it's only another few hundred kilometres to Slovenia and the Schengen area, with fewer border crossings. In the messages, people on the move explain how border police at Croatia or Slovenia or Italy had stolen their supplies while being pushed back over the border.

The European Center for Constitutional and Human Rights defines pushbacks as a set of state measures used to force refugees and migrants back over a border soon after they crossed it without providing them any opportunity to apply for asylum or to challenge the pushback order—which can have devastating consequences. In November 2017, Madina Hussiny, a six-year-old girl from Afghanistan, was hit and killed by a train in Serbia after Croatian border guards had refused her and her family entry. The previous night, the Afghan family of fourteen, had crossed irregularly into Croatia but were soon apprehended by Croatian police while resting in a field. Although the family had indicated to the police they would like to apply for asylum, the family were instead driven to the railway line and ordered to return to Serbia. The train struck Hussiny shortly thereafter.

Four years later, in November 2021, the European Court of Human Rights ruled that in pushing the Hussiny family back into Croatia, the state had violated several articles of the European Convention of Human Rights, especially the fourth article of Protocol 4, which prohibits the collective expulsion of aliens from a signatory's territory. Croatian authorities had played a role in putting the six-year-old girl in the path of the locomotive.

Despite the light Hassiny's case has shone on Croatian pushbacks, little evidence suggests Croatian police have curtailed them. In October 2021, just a month before the ECtHR's verdict, the German public broadcaster ARD, along with several other European media outlets, published the results of their monthslong investigation into the collective expulsions carried out by Croatian police at the Bosnian border, indicating the prevalence of the practice as well as the violence usually involved.

Michael and I arrive at Blažuj on an unseasonably mild day in January. We park the van on a side street beside the M17, the city's principal throughfare, and step out into the afternoon sun. Mountains rise before us, covered with snow and skinny conifers. Blažuj itself is nothing special—a few restaurants, gas stations, mechanic garages, and companies. It's a place to pass through, not one to linger and savour the sights. But what makes Blažuj unique and what has brought Michael and me here today is what cannot be seen at first. Someone passing through the suburb, for example, would not know that hidden in the valley between the two mountains, away from the eyes of the locals, stands a temporary reception centre for migrants, a nice euphemism for a refugee camp, administered by the International Organization for Migration (IOM).

I look at the order sheet and count the number of Blažuj orders—twenty, comprising about ninety people. Demand has skyrocketed recently, and we have had difficulty matching it. We are distributing items to around four hundred people a week. Supply always seems to be dwindling. One day, we run out of sleeping bags; the next, it is backpacks. In our WhatsApp conversations with people on the move, we must manage their expectations and always be transparent about our effort "to try" and fill their exact order. Most of the time, however, we must replace a sleeping bag with a blanket or a hat with a snood.

The beneficiaries arrive after completing the fifteen-minute walk between the camp and our distribution site. We would distribute outside of the camp if we could, but the IOM has denied our requests, so we must settle for this less-than-ideal location beside the highway. I ask each of them their name and order number and check their names off the list while Michael rummages through the mound of plastic garbage bags in the van, looking for the right order number and correct number of bags. I ask them whether they would like some tea, and for those who do, they inevitably ask me about shoes while I am pouring their drink from the thermoses we brought. Shoes are a highly sought-after item, of which we have next to none, especially in men's sizes. They point to their feet. Some are in flip flops; others are wearing shoes whose structural integrity has deteriorated beyond repair; others still have poor quality ones unsuitable for life on the move, especially for traversing the mountains of Bosnia and Herzegovina. I tell them we do not have shoes to give.

In a lull during the distribution, Michael tells me how more and more displaced people have left Sarajevo's centre and moved into the camps, as 90 per cent of our distributions now happen here at Blažuj. Michael cannot explain this shift, but it may be due to the camp's relative superiority to sleeping rough in squats or hostels during wintertime in the city centre, a space that has not been set up to accommodate people on the move. I watch some guys walking back to the camp, bags in hand, and wonder how long they plan to stay in camp before moving on. I wonder what factors they must juggle before deciding to head out into the mountains of Bosnia and push forward to Croatia in the north. Among the guys leaving, I also see a familiar face returning, carrying his opened bag. I can tell from the manner in which he walks and his rigid body language that something about our order has left him unimpressed. He drops the bag at our feet, opens it, and motions for us to look through it. "There's a problem," he says. Michael asks him to explain what the problem might be while I look for his order number to see the items he received.

His name is Kamran, and he says we have not provided him a backpack, even though the order list provides no indication he asked for one. Michael tells him in calm and direct sentences we did not receive an order for a backpack, an answer that propels Kamran to reach for his phone and open WhatsApp. Michael and I check the distribution phone and can see backpacks were mentioned, but we did not promise Kamran we would bring one. This does little to assuage Kamran's frustration; he keeps repeating that "This is a problem, a big problem," since he, from what we can gather, is going on game soon and will need something to carry his belongings. There is a chaotic, frantic energy about Kamran; his movements are fast but unhinged. Being on the move and undocumented propels one to adopt a constant vigilance, defined by hyper-defensiveness, to stay alert and on guard from the many dangers lurking in the forests.

We agree to bring him a backpack tomorrow. He nods while still talking about the problem. The problem. He pulls from his bag a pair of boots we managed to find for him, one of our last pairs. They are brown, ugly, and inadequate for his journey ahead. But they are all we have—the last of his size. He stuffs his feet into them. They are too small, and he keeps muttering, "problem... problem... problem." With the flip-flops he had on, he takes one in each hand and tosses them into the sky. "A problem," he says. "A big problem." The dark blue flip-flops sail into the sky, flipping and contorting under the blue canopy, looking as if they could fly forever over the mountains and beyond Bosnia. Before long, however, their momentum stops, and they hang momentarily in the air, suspended like some big and ugly blue bird, and like all things, they tumble back down to earth, landing harmlessly in the snow.

Kamran joins his friends by the pedestrian underpass and lights a cigarette. Michael and I debate whether to claim his flip-flops. "Let us wait until he is gone," Michael suggests, and I agree. I want to do nothing to suggest his outrage was somehow unjustified.

Javid

Europe has sophisticated machinery in place to prevent pushbacks. The Council of Europe—the continent's leading human rights organization, including forty-seven members—provides numerous guarantees against them. Beyond Article 3 of the Convention, which prohibits states from returning individuals to where they may be tortured or experience inhuman or degrading treatment, Article 4 of Protocol 4 to the Convention explicitly forbids expulsions. In *Sharifi and Others v. Italy and Greece* (2014), for example, the Court ruled Italy had violated Article 4 when it returned thirty-two Afghan nationals, two Sudanese nationals, and one Eritrean national to Greece without hearing their individual accounts. Moreover, since the Italian authorities failed to investigate how the Greek state would apply their asylum legislation in practice, the collective expulsion of these individuals ran the risk of chain refoulement, in which they would be deported from Italy to Greece and then to their country of origin, where they could experience degrading or inhuman treatment. Moreover, the Court ruled the Dublin system—the EU's mechanism for determining which member state is responsible for examining an asylum application—must be administered in a way compatible with the Convention. The returning state must ensure the destination country offers asylum protections to ensure the people concerned are not returned to their country of origin without assessing their claims.

I think about these court cases while talking to Javid over WhatsApp and organizing the following day's distribution. Javid has contacted us for some clothing but has not specified the type of sizing he needs. I ask him for clarification. He responds not with a precise order of the clothing he wants but with a story about his recent pushback from Croatia: The police beat him, he lost his left eye, and he needs treatment. I take a moment to digest what I have just read. He lost his eye. They beat him, and he lost his left eye. I write I am so sorry to hear what happened to him and tell him to go to camp to see a doctor. I pause before I hit send and think about what I am encouraging Javid to do: register at a refugee camp. Camps are symptomatic of a sick and dying international protection regime. The default response to refugees has become to stick them in camps and make them wait. But I also know Javid will find no other free medical services outside the camps, as visiting a clinic or a hospital in the city centre will require paying. I weigh the available options and decide to tell him to go to camp to seek treatment, which I do, followed by another sentence about how sorry I am about what happened to him.

Another message comes, three or so sentences long. Javid thinks little about my compassion or my "sorry's." His frustration is palpable. I feel it in his words, breathing fire into his sentences. Javid wants something concrete and tangible from us. He wants his vision—his sight. He needs to see, and he needs us to see how much he needs to see. The game does not care if he cannot see the traps laid for him. There is no special treatment, no shortcuts for men and women and children with limited sight. The mountains, forests, and rivers do not disappear for him. They remain whether he sees them or not.

I need my vision, Javid writes, and then posts a link to an Instagram video. It's the news. A woman sits at a desk and speaks in a language I cannot identify. Below her flow sentences written in the Arabic script, but I do not think they or her words are, in fact, Arabic. At the bottom right of the screen, I locate the only English word on the screen—Iran—and conclude the broadcast is in Farsi. The program then switches to a live feed of a man wearing sunglasses. The shot is close, centred on his face, with little background details visible. He must be on his phone. He must be Javid. He must be telling his story. I do not understand anything of what he says but can identify two words because of their proximity to the English ones: Bosnia and Croatia. Javid speaks in a calm and measured tone. He never gets agitated, nor does he raise his voice. His volume is consistent, as is his flow. Stutter, he does not. I find it remarkable he has managed to reach such a large audience in Iran to tell his story, whereas in Bosnia, he must contact a group of volunteers for information about how to find treatment for the eye he lost at the hands of the Croatian police. I wonder how the story will be spun within the Iranian media, as a cautionary tale for other Iranians thinking about making the perilous journey west or as a propaganda piece about Europe's hypocrisy concerning human rights.

Another message from Javid. He is in camp and has already visited the doctor but was unsatisfied with the treatment. What should he do? Over WhatsApp, I contact the Danish Refugee Council's office in Sarajevo, the only NGO in the city that does medical referrals for people on the move, and explain Javid's situation. The NGO sometimes arranges hospital visits for people on the move, but their reply is quick and unambiguous: They only make referrals to the camp doctor and suggest Javid return to the doctor he saw and request further treatment. My message to Javid is also unambiguous: The only free treatment you can expect is from the camp doctor. Please consider visiting them again. I do not say I am sorry.

Nima

The clothing we give provides a lifeline to people on the move. They give a little extra protection for the journey they are about to undertake. A hat. A pair of gloves. A thick jacket. These items can become essential in the mountains of Bosnia when the nights drop below zero and the snow rises past the ankles.

Our van would not start yesterday, perhaps due to the cold, so we had it towed to a mechanic's shop for repairs. As a result, we could not distribute all our orders and instead only distributed those in the Old Town in our car. We told the rest, those staying in Blažuj camp, we would bring their things tomorrow and apologized for any inconvenience. These things happen in a grassroots operation such as ours. You have to be flexible and take every obstacle in stride.

I am loading the car with Blažuj's orders. There are twenty. And they all fit. Barely. I have checked the list to make sure I have packed all orders, one through twenty, and have included all the bags for those orders containing more than one. I disregard all the orders above because those were delivered yesterday to the Old Town and, thus, are of no particular importance. I pay them no mind. They do not concern me. Outside of my remit as they are. I am relieved by this fact. One less thing to worry about. This aversion to matters beyond my immediate responsibility has always formed an important part of my philosophy. Stay in your lane. Keep your eyes straight. Do not deviate from the path. Do not meander. Keep yourself safe.

I check the phone to double-check the beneficiaries have received our message about the new meeting time. A message from Nima. Please send the location. I go to Google Maps, find the location, pin it, and then send it to him. I do not linger on the name too long, as Martin and I must get ready to go. We have a distribution to do. People are waiting for us. They need the things we are about to give. A sense of satisfaction warms me, despite my best intentions in preventing the feeling from materializing. But it is there: This is good. This is needed.

Martin greets each person and asks for their number while I dig through the car to locate the correct bag or bags. We are getting through the order. The distro is going well. I then hear Martin greet Nima and ask me for order twenty-two. My heart quickens, and the anxiety rushes. There is no order twenty-two; the highest is twenty. Twenty-two was delivered yesterday in the city centre. Why is Nima here? Why is he standing in front of us demanding clothing that should have been delivered to him yesterday? Why is he here? He shouldn't be here.

I need an explanation. I grab the order sheet and search for an answer. And before long, I see it. It's there in plain sight. I see it as clearly as I see Nima standing in front of me. Under order twenty-two, someone has written in pencil "Blažuj." The order location was changed. Martin apologizes to Nima. We have forgotten his clothing. We didn't bring his order. Nima is first confident we have misunderstood the situation. "I messaged you yesterday, and you told me to come here." He seems certain this clarification will straighten the matter because how could it not? He has followed all our instructions. We promised to have his clothing. He is here. We are here. What could the problem be? A feeling of self-hatred arrives as I watch Nima slowly realize what we are telling him: We forgot his clothing in the warehouse. The look of disappointment clouding his face is unmistakable. Forlorn. Despondent.

Martin and I tell Nima if he can wait thirty or forty minutes, we will drive back to the warehouse and collect his order. Nima shakes his head. "I go to game," he says. He points to the remaining bags sitting in the car, at the orders we have remembered to bring, and asks if we have just one hat to give him. "No," I say, "those orders are for other people," cognizant of the cruelty of my words. Nima no longer displays any emotion. He is stoic. Perhaps throughout his journey, he has become accustomed to experiencing disappointment, so much so that whenever it greets him, he knows not to get too upset, since that is no way to act towards a friendly face. We pleadingly ask him if he could wait just a little longer so we could claim his clothing. I am desperate for him to acquiesce to our demands. I need to right this wrong. I cannot bear thinking about whether the clothing we forgot could be the difference between a successful journey and an unsuccessful one. But he says, "No, thank you" and walks away.

Ghesra

"They robbed me of my youth," Ghesra says, drinking his tea. Around him are the two big bags of clothing Alice and I have brought him and his two companions. They look so minuscule compared to Ghesra, who is built strong and sturdy. "They made me miss my mother's funeral in Iran. I couldn't go back to see her one last time. Three months ago, my brother also died. They took this from me." Ghesra looks at me, and I am not sure what he wants. I can give him my ear. He may have it. Beside me, Alice is telling him she can't imagine what that must have been like. I am glad she is speaking because I do not have the strength to offer platitudes.

It's a beautiful, unseasonably warm day. Sunlight is bountiful. Spring is in the air. Winter's excesses seem, at least for the moment, to have passed for the year. The mountains' snow has begun to melt. A sense of rebirth flows through the air. Everything feels fresh and new. Somewhere, something is on the precipice of blossoming. The temperature is pushing ten degrees. I feel like removing my winter coat. I feel like changing into shorts. I feel like putting on my running shoes and running away, someplace with rivers, shade, and plenty of places to hide. Ghesra is dressed for the mountains. His coat is thick and puffy. It looks as if it could withstand a charging bull or a volley of bullets. He wears a toque and skiing pants. He is ready for whatever nature throws his way. His body language, however, betrays such confidence. He is shaky. His foundation has cracked. A current of unease flows through his body. He is tired and unshaven. His body carries the weight of a decade on the move. Whatever he has experienced and seen has imprinted itself on him. His body is a shrine to brutality—to the unambiguous effect of a border on human skin.

"I once made it across the border to Croatia," Ghesra says, "and applied for asylum in Zagreb." He looks at Alice and me before continuing, as if internally debating whether to say the next sentences. The sun is high, almost right above us, and reveals marks and scratches once hidden by the dark. "They took me back to the Bosnian border and beat me." I never know what to do with the stories of violence I hear in the field. Rage is a counterproductive, albeit understandable, response, as are the empty platitudes that occasionally drop from my mouth about how I can't even imagine or about how sorry I am. I find the best way to handle such situations is to become a turtle. Whenever a distasteful story presents itself, I retreat into my big, beautiful shell and listen from a safe position. But I do listen. I listen actively. I grant my interlocutor the respect their story deserves. I let them borrow my ear, but I cannot let the story slip further into me. Nothing bypasses my shell.

Ghesra is speaking. "And they laughed when they beat me," he says. "That was the worst part. How could they laugh while beating another human being? How could they?" Alice tells Ghesra if he wishes, we can make a report about the violent pushback he experienced. Ghesra says he gave an interview to Italian and German journalists after the pushback and let them take photographs of the bruises along his leg and arm. Alice explains we are not journalists, and we take the reports for advocacy purposes—to inform the EU about the illegal practices occurring at their borders. "They already know what's happening," Ghesra says, his frustration boiling. "The European Union knows what's happening, and they don't do anything." He descends into a barely comprehensible rant about the hypocrisies of the West, about human rights, about Iran, and about how Western governments prop up regimes with deplorable human rights records because they need their oil. He is only emotion now. His valve has opened. And out it comes.

He is correct about the EU. They do know what's happening at the Croatian-Bosnian border. Court cases and journalist accounts have unambiguously painted a picture of an extralegal space in which police officers can beat and apprehend people on the move until their heart's content. And as much as the EU speaks about the importance of human rights, the right of asylum, and the prohibition of refoulement, the group's priorities lie with border management and the cessation of irregular migration. Croatia wants to join the Schengen Zone (and it did in 2023), so the country must prove to Brussels it can stop the flow. It is the EU that funds Croatia's entire border control apparatus. In the EU's list of priorities, protecting the human rights of the world's displaced falls well below stopping irregular migration.

Ghesra apologizes for his outburst, but we assure him he has nothing to apologize for. He finishes his tea, thanks us for the items, and picks up his two bags of clothing. Alice tells him to message us if he needs anything else, and he and his friend thank us again, waving as they walk away. I hope never to see Ghesra again, not because I fear experiencing another of his outbursts, even though they do make me uncomfortable despite my best attempts to mitigate their effect, but because if I never lay eyes on his face again, there is a chance he might have made it to wherever he aims. If I never see him again, it means he moves. It means he has kept going. If there is movement, there is hope. And it's a peculiar wish to never see someone again, especially when that desire does not stem from a place of hatred and anger but a place of good, but I reiterate: I never want to see Ghesra again.

Nazir

Our relationship with the people we serve is not without its bumps. People become frustrated when we run out of an item they need, especially if we suggested we might have it for them. We try to be as transparent as possible with people. We never promise anything, only explicitly saying we will try to fill their order. This approach is not to avoid any accountability on our part; if we could promise an item will be in the box when that person's order comes around, we would. But since we serve dozens of people on any given day, it can become difficult to predict whether some items will remain when a particular order arrives. Disappointment, then, is almost inevitable. Sometimes, people understand our position; sometimes, they do not.

I am filling an order for a man named Nazir. He has asked for six sleeping bags, but I know from how the item has flown from the shelves this morning I will be unable to fill his order. I message him over WhatsApp, telling him how sorry I am, but we do not have any more sleeping bags left and can provide blankets instead. I sit the phone down and pack the items Nazir requested we do have. A few minutes later, I check the phone to see if he wants blankets instead of sleeping bags and see he has not taken the news very well. He accuses us of lying to him and then calls us a donkey, and although I am not sure where Nazir is from, I know in both Arabic and Farsi, to call someone a donkey is an insult. A donkey is someone who lacks intelligence and common sense. A donkey is a stupid person.

My instinctual response to the insult is laughter. I tell my colleagues Nazir did not take the news about the sleeping bags well and show them the message. They shrug it off and continue packing the orders. I find the insult curious. My parents used to have donkeys, and they might have been many things, but stupid was not one of them. I remember how they would escape from our property and run wild in neighbouring farms. They got loose constantly and would force us to strategize ways to keep them locked in. Their personality was unpredictable; they could be affectionate, standoffish, and, yes, stubborn. But they were never boring.

Nazir's comment does not strike me as insulting at all. I instead find it, as I tell my colleagues, more complimentary. I get the laugh I want, but part of me wonders whether my joke is inappropriate. Why have I felt the urge to fixate on Nazir's comment? Why not just move on? Did I think Nazir overreacted in his response? Was he not entitled to his anger at our inability to fill his order? I try to imagine Nazir sitting in the camp day after day, waiting for an opportune moment to journey north to Croatia. Maybe he has decided to make the trek once he has a sleeping bag. I have also wondered about the decision-making process among people on the move, about when and how they decide to try to cross a border.

The factors they have to consider must be multiple. And maybe, for Nazir, everything has aligned for today being the most favourable moment to depart north, and all he needs is a sleeping bag.

The more I think about Nazir's insult, the more I wonder whether Nazir is justified in his anger. He has asked for a sleeping bag before and was met with the same response. And today, if his order number had been one or two and not eleven, he would have received a sleeping bag. Should we have specifically set aside a sleeping bag for Nazir, since he had asked for one before? Perhaps. I don't know. We try to be fair and consistent in all our decision-making, but sometimes that proves impossible given the day-to-day realities a grassroots organization like ours faces. These excuses do not help Nazir, and I do think he can feel frustrated with an organization that does not help when it says it will try.

I do not expect gratitude from the people we meet. If you work in solidarity with someone, you do not expect them to thank you, and you should expect them to express their disappointment and even anger when you fail to deliver. I can feel annoyed with Nazir's comment and deflect his anger by turning it into a joke if I wish, but I must remember the distance separating our positions: He is there, and I am here. I am the one who helps, and he is the one who needs. I can laugh at his anger, but he must wait for a sleeping bag. All his hopes and dreams could, potentially, rest on a sleeping bag. Everything for him could depend on something as banal as a sleeping bag. I do not know the journey he has endured from his country of birth to Sarajevo, but I know mine, and they are not equivalent. If I want to go to Croatia, I can. I do not need a sleeping bag. I can go by car, bus, or plane. I know border officials will judge my worthiness by the quality of my passport and not the content of my character. What separates me from Nazir are forces beyond our control—histories of colonialism and exploitation—and by sheer luck, they have benefited me and cursed him. I can laugh if I want, but if the situation were reversed, and the god of luck had bestowed on Nazir the gift of Canadian citizenship and me the citizenship of whichever country he flees, I know I would express my anger if I had been repeatedly denied a sleeping bag from an organization that claims to help people on the move. If all that separated me from a refugee camp and the chance to fulfill my dreams was a sleeping bag and Nazir denied me one after I had been patient these last few days, or even weeks, waiting for one, I would call Nazir a liar. Maybe even a donkey.

Going on Game

"We are going on game." I hear this expression almost daily in the field or on the phone with people on the move. They justify their need for a particular item by using this curious phrasing: "I am going on game tomorrow. I need a sleeping back." or, more ominously, "I just returned from game, and I no longer have my jacket." Generally speaking, the expression "going on game" expresses the choice of a person on the move to try and cross a border irregularly. In Bosnia, going on game usually means travelling to the north of the country, around Bihać, and attempting to enter Croatia. The phrase intrigues me, especially its origins, which remain mysterious. Every national group, regardless of language and cultural differences, seems to use the phrase in Bosnia, as it has become an almost universal sentiment, intelligible in dozens of languages. While working with people on the move in Belgrade, however, I never heard the expression and in Calais, only a couple of times, which only adds to the intrigue. In Bosnia, however, the expression is everywhere.

For me, the phrase rings too cavalier, too soaked in a feeling of nonchalance. Games have winners and losers, sure, but they are fun, light-hearted affairs. The consequences of losing are never life-threatening. The worst is disappointment or maybe anger if you do not take losing well. Here, in the Balkans, however, people die while on game. People die on the border of France and the UK, Türkiye and Greece, and, yes, Bosnia and Croatia. In this game, the stakes are high.

Here is another, more ominous, reading. "Game" also signifies the flesh of any wild animal, and the term is often used in the hunting context. People with guns hunt game. So, in this sense, and somewhat macabrely, "going on game" can accurately describe in the eyes of the men and women manning the borders of Europe the metamorphosis of people on the move into a kind of goose or duck that may be hunted for sport. Among the border guards of Fortress Europe, people on the move become game.

In my more optimistic moments, though, I like to think that "game" is used as a verb, not as a noun. In English, and according to *Webster's Dictionary*, to game something is "to manipulate, exploit, or cheat in (a system, a situation, etc.) slyly or dishonestly for personal gain." Conventional thinking frowns upon people who cheat. We honour and celebrate those who follow the rules and do not cut corners. In matters of immigration and asylum, people who do not follow the rules and who do not wait their turn in line are demonized and chastised as cheaters who game the system for their benefit. Yet if the system is unfair to begin with, can it still be considered cheating to not follow its rules? Asylum has become increasingly impossible to reach in Europe. European countries routinely breach international laws regarding it. Pushbacks have become an all-too-common response to people seeking refuge. Legal routes are evaporating. To game the system becomes a way to respond to an unfair one. To go on game, then, means trying to find safety in a world increasingly hostile to it. I always hope they are successful. Most of the time, however, they are not.

The Spanish Speakers

We receive a message from a man staying at Delijaš camp, about a forty-minute drive from Sarajevo. He is with fourteen other people and would like to know whether we can bring them some clothing. None of us have ever visited Delijaš before, so we do not know the state of the camp or the people's needs. Alice contacts a colleague at Caritas with knowledge about the camp, and she suggests the need there is not strong. Nevertheless, we decide to visit and see for ourselves, so at the end of our normal distribution, Martin, Pierre, and I throw the bags in the car and set off for Delijaš.

We leave the relatively straight roads of Sarajevo and Ilidža and ascend into the mountains of the Republic of Srpska, the Bosnian Serb enclave, which, along with the Federation of Bosnia and Herzegovina, comprises the country of Bosnia. Among these mountains, almost thirty years ago, Serb snipers aimed at Sarajevo below and laid siege to the city for four years. Serb flags flutter from lampposts, as national sentiment has not dwindled in any of the country's parts, even flaring in recent weeks with Srpska's threat of leaving the federal army and other state-level institutions.

Many fear that the Republic of Srpska aims to secede from the country, potentially to join Serbia or to form its own independent country. Many more fear a return to war. Before long, we are back in Bosnia and Herzegovina.

The mountains are breathtaking. Snow still covers the tops of some, stubbornly refusing to melt from this unseasonably warm winter. I am amazed at how quickly Sarajevo fades away behind the mountains. There is no suburbia in Sarajevo. There is the city and then the mountains. Nothing really in between. You'd be forgiven for thinking you were hundreds of kilometres from any kind of major metropolis. Houses sit upon mountain slopes, and smoke rises from their chimneys.

Martin takes the turns slowly, as the local drivers pass him with ease. "Four years ago, my ego wouldn't have been able to handle that," he says. I am glad he is now four years older. We are driving south along the M18. I am on the phone and looking at Google Maps. In a few kilometres, we are meant to turn left onto a road Google has ominously termed "Unknown Road." And when we do come upon it, the isolation the name evokes is laid bare to see. The one-lane road winds and cuts its way through the mountains. Martin does not pass twenty kilometres an hour. Now and then, an old beat-up car shoots at us from around a blind bend, and Martin must quickly guide us to the side of the road.

There are few signs of civilization. A few old bus stops appear, but I cannot imagine a public bus navigating these roads. According to the phone, we are only a few kilometres from the camp and the town of its name, but it's hard to believe given the geography in front of us. Then on our left, we see what appears to be a camp.

Rows of buildings sit perched on the side of a mountain. They look new but ordinary. Fences encircle the structures preventing easy access as well as escape. Surveillance cameras catch and record every movement. The isolation of the camp shocks me. I cannot fathom how any displaced person could have ended up here unless they were transported. No person would come here on their own accord. Who are the people staying here? How did they arrive? Where do they hope to go?

Upon passing the camp and heading to our meeting point, a mosque just a few hundred metres away, we pass a group of about fifteen people walking along the road. Men and women. Young and old. Their presence is peculiar in such an isolated spot, but we think they must be locals out for a Friday afternoon stroll and do not think further on them as the mosque's minaret comes into view, and we park the car just opposite it.

I am typing a message to the group, saying we have arrived, when a police car stops in front of ours, blocking any possible exit. Two officers step out and instruct us to do the same. They want to see our documents, both personal and organizational. They want to know what we are doing here. Alice and others have spent many hours navigating Bosnian bureaucracy to make our work legal in the eyes of authorities. They have filed all the proper paperwork, gathered all the necessary documentation, and even hired a lawyer to ensure everything we do is to the letter of the law. All that work will be put to the test now.

One officer inspects our passports and white cards, a piece of paper further explaining our presence in the country. He records the details on his notepad while his partner flips through the legal documents Martin has given him, papers explaining what our organization does and, importantly, that we have a legal right to do so. The officers are polite and respectful. They do not unduly intimidate or interrogate. They differ from the police I met in Belgrade and Calais; their behaviour does not drip with arrogance and entitlement. The officers only want to know where we are coming from, whether we come to the camp regularly, and whether we are distributing any food. Their fixation on food is somewhat perplexing, as they confirm us several times that we are not giving any food to the people we will meet. We assure the officers we are only distributing clothing. They want to know where the clothing came from, and we tell them they are donations. They make a few more notes, converse with each other in Bosnian, and then return our documents. We wave to them as they settle back into their car and drive away. We are legal.

The locals we passed on the road approach the mosque. They hover near its entrance, just across the street, by a few benches. I snap a few photos of the mosque on my phone, trying to fit the minaret and a mountaintop into the frame. I wonder from how far and wide the faithful come to pray here. A man breaks away from the locals and saunters towards us with his phone. He does not look like a local, or what I have come to identify as local in my brief time in Bosnia. He looks South Asian. He looks like others we have met outside the Blažuj camp. He sidles up to Martin and points to a message on his phone. "Are you Hussein?" I ask from the other side of the car. He nods and smiles, relieved to have found us, and then waves for the others to join him. I am amazed. These men and women are not locals but displaced people themselves, who for some reason unknown to me have found themselves in a camp hidden deep in the Bosnian mountains. These people look nothing like Hussein, nothing like the others from the camps. And I critique myself for adopting an ideal of what a refugee should look like—someone not like me. I have grown so accustomed to meeting people from areas of the world where war has become normalized, a natural part of life, that when I meet someone who does not fit my expectations, my whole understanding crumbles. But it's good. Let it fall apart.

The group is also not speaking Arabic, Farsi, or Pashto, but Spanish. I wonder if they are Venezuelans. Yet what would a group of Venezuelans be doing in the mountains of Bosnia? Could they be from Cuba? When I was in Belgrade, I heard some Cubans had applied for asylum there. I wonder how they all know one another. They all speak cordially to one another, suggesting a close relationship, perhaps one dating back to times before now, before the mountains of Bosnia. I want to ask them where they come from, how they ended up here, isolated and alone, and where they plan to go next. But I don't.

Beyond their clothing items, we have also brought a suitcase full of thermoses, which we distribute when we have enough of them. Hussein tells them, in English, they can take one if they wish. They seem happy by the news, as each searches through the suitcase searching for a thermos. I find it so surreal to be distributing thermoses to Spanish speakers deep inside Bosnia and under the shadow of a minaret. But such disruptions to the regular flow of images and assumptions are good and healthy. Hussein asks me whether we will come again, and I tell him because of the distance, we will not be able to make this distribution a regular occurrence. He thanks us all the same, as do the Spanish speakers after selecting their thermos. We watch them return from the direction they came, along the road, towards the camp and its fences and cameras. For how much longer they must stay there, I do not know, nor do I know their final destination.

A Pushback

The two men from Senegal take a seat beside Michael and me. We have asked them to join us today at a restaurant close to Blažuj camp because they mentioned in one of our WhatsApp conversations they have experienced a pushback. We want to take their testimony and use it for advocacy purposes—to show the EU and the European Council pushbacks continue to happen regularly.

While working on the phone, volunteers become attuned to looking for hints of pushbacks in their conversations with people on the move. Sometimes, people directly tell us of their experiences of having the police beat and rob them at the EU's borders, particularly the Bosnia-Croatia one. Other times, however, they are less direct and use phrases hinting at a pushback. One such phrase I am always looking for is "I lost everything." It's an evocative statement, simple yet intriguing. I want to know more. The sentence could encapsulate their reasoning for departing on such a journey in the first place; more so, however, it speaks to something lost on the move, something taken without permission by those who operate beyond the scope of the law.

If we suspect someone has experienced a pushback, we send them a message explaining the process of providing a report. We ensure they understand their testimony will not improve their present situation, get them refugee status, or safe passage to Croatia,

Germany, or the UK. We tell them we will use their story only for advocacy purposes to make Brussels and Strasburg implement changes punishing pushbacks. We tell them their story may help make the border areas more humane places for all displaced persons. If they agree to share their story—many do not—we arrange to meet them.

Jacob's interview has taken a few weeks to arrange. He was unsure at first and then was sick, but at last has finally appeared and with a friend, Samba, who was with him during the pushback. We exchange pleasantries and order coffees. Jacob explains he would feel much more at ease speaking in French than in English, and we agree but ask Jacob to speak as slowly as possible. Michael, luckily, has a better grasp of the French language than I do. Before we begin the interview, Michael again explains the process transparently. As volunteers, we quickly become skilled at managing expectations, and Michael reiterates their testimony will not improve their situation but may help, in the future, bring about lasting changes to border policy in Europe. Jacob and Samba say they understand and consent when Michael asks if we may record the interview.

There are questions we are supposed to ask about the pushback that took place. We need details about the date of the pushback, where it occurred, how many displaced persons were involved, whether women and children were present, how many police officers participated in the pushback, from which country, and what exactly the officers did to the displaced persons. But as Jacob and Samba tell their story, I soon realize how difficult it will be to filter their story into boxes to be checked, into a simple narrative of a pushback. The men unleash information upon us. They want to begin their story with their arrival in Greece, not with the pushback, as if to focus on the forced return would only provide a snapshot of their experience and not the entire story. Upon arriving in Greece from Türkiye, they applied for asylum and waited five years for a response. They waited in Lesbos, in Moria camp. They had their movements curtailed and their right to be in Greece interrogated at every turn. Their black skin granted permission to locals and the police to question their presence anywhere outside of a camp. The racism they experienced was intense and unwavering. Jacob speaks about the exodus of millions of refugees from Ukraine and shakes his head when he alludes to the stories circulating on social media and news agencies of Nigerian foreign students in Ukraine being denied entry into Poland. He speaks about the selective empathy and double standards of Europe's and the West's solidarity with the displaced. Being a refugee has nothing to do with skin colour, Jacob says, looking disappointed such an obvious statement needs articulating.

The Greek government rejected their asylum claims. The men decided to leave for the mainland and crossed into Northern Macedonia and then into Serbia as a larger group with the help of smugglers. In the Serb border town of Preševo, however, Serbian border guards, who were quickly reinforced by the army, apprehended the group. They fired shots into air to prevent the group from fleeing, and soon, forty displaced persons, Samba and Jacob among them, were loaded into trucks and returned to Macedonia.

We ask the men whether they tried to apply for international protection in Serbia and asked the border guards they met for international protection. Under European law, all border guards must determine the particular circumstances of an individual's case before they can deport them, especially if they ask for asylum. Samba smiles at our naivety and uncheckered belief in the rule of law. Samba, too, knows what the law says, but in his many years on the move, he has painfully and unambiguously learned what the law says and how it is applied are two different things. There is no point, Samba says. If you do, they immediately return you. And if you don't, of course, they immediately return you.

The men then recount the stories they have heard from friends and other people at the camp about the endemic violence at the Croatian-Bosnian border. I have become far too familiar with these stories: the summary deportations, beatings, robberies, and deaths. Jacob and Samba will travel to this border next, and their dread is obvious. They know all too well the threats that follow them as they cross borders under the cover of night. They know the violence the game presents. On their journey to Serbia, they had to leave a friend in Macedonia because his foot had swelled, and he could not walk anymore. Just the other day, another friend of Jacob's drowned in a river while trying to cross from Serbia to Bosnia. Yet the ubiquity of violence does not lessen its corporeal threat. I see the anxiety on the men's faces as they talk about Croatia and about what awaits them at the border. I see the fear. Yet these men will continue on their journey no matter the costs because—and this is what many in the West do not understand or refuse to—the life they desire in Europe is worth the risk. The men have not disclosed why they left Senegal, and we have not asked. Jacob says he left due to personal troubles and nothing more. But whatever the reason, whatever compelled them to leave their country of birth, must be strong enough to motivate them to persist. I would personally never judge anyone for leaving one place to seek a better life in another, but if the reason these two men left Senegal years ago was purely economic, then they would have returned home by now. I cannot imagine anyone suffering the humiliation and hardship for years on end, as these two men have, if their only motivation was money. No. Something far more existential and urgent pushes them onwards to Europe. No matter the toil the game has already had on them, they will not go back. No matter how much the international protection regime has failed these two men, they will not go back.

Airplanes

On the morning of my last walk to the volunteer house, I pass the northern terminus of Sarajevo International Airport. In a few days, I will be sitting inside the departures area, awaiting my flight that will take me from Sarajevo. Through the barbed-wire fence, I can see the runway, which stretches a few kilometres to the terminal building. At the southern end is where Bosniak soldiers built an underground tunnel during the siege of Sarajevo, in which people, as well as goods, travelled from the besieged city to freedom. But the war is thirty years old now, and the tunnel has become a museum. Around 8:45 a.m., a plane ascends from the runway and lifts into the sky above me, the fence, and the city. The barriers on the ground—mountains and gates—hold little sway over the plane's movement as it glides across the sky as effortlessly as a bird. The letters on the plane's side remain blurry, but I think it may be going to Istanbul, or maybe Frankfurt, or maybe Vienna. Sarajevo International Airport has few international departures throughout the day. In any event, the plane, as well the passengers it carries, is leaving Sarajevo. And from the sky, as I know from personal experience, everything on the ground seems insignificant. The items are not threatening. Playthings. They look like children's toys to be used by precocious and imaginative little tykes. Pick up a car. Pick up a man. Have fun. But as the plane flies higher and higher, the roads, buildings, and people all vanish and are replaced by clouds and the blue sky. For those on the plane, the ones enjoying the miracle and privilege of flight, of having all their worldly threats disappear, they begin to feel, or at least they should, as free as a bird.

4

Samos

April and May 2022

At the height of the Syrian refugee exodus in 2014 and 2015, communities on the Greek islands summoned their strength and helped those fleeing arrive safely to their shores. As asylum seekers continued to arrive, however, humanitarian fatigue and antipathy set in among the same communities, angered as they were that other European nations refused to share the burden. The 2016 EU-Türkiye deal effectively closed the Aegean route; Brussels paid Ankara billions of dollars to stop asylum seekers from travelling to Europe, forcing them to pursue even more dangerous and clandestine ways of reaching the continent. Pushbacks by the Greek authorities also became more common. A June 2020 Amnesty International investigation of pushbacks from Greece to Türkiye uncovered twenty-one pushbacks over three months. Human Rights Watch has repeatedly revealed how the Greek coast guard returns migrants to Türkiye. The coast guard will often transfer them from the dinghies upon which they travelled to motorless, inflatable rafts and set them adrift near Turkish territorial waters. Authorities have been accused of removing the engine or fuel from boats and then towing them back to Türkiye, as well as puncturing inflatable boats. Pushbacks have become so widespread in Greece and Europe generally that many have argued they have taken on a systemic character, becoming a national policy rather than isolated incidences. Even though pushbacks violate European and international law, even the EU, at times, has tacitly accepted them in the name of border control.

In early 2020, Turkish President Recep Tayyip Erdoğan opened the Turkish border, allowing thousands of migrants to head towards Greece because Brussels had failed, according to the president, to honour its part of the 2016 agreement. In response, Greece suspended its asylum procedure, and the Greek police, army, and special forces, along with support from FRONTEX, used tear gas and rubber bullets to push the people back into Türkiye. On one occasion, the coast guard fired at a rubber dingy approaching the shore by sea. Instead of reprimanding Greece's reaction and its flagrant disregard for European law, the Commission lauded the government's reaction, with the president calling Greece the "shield" of the EU. At no time did the Commission emphasize the importance of not using excessive force against asylum seekers, nor did the organization mention that it violates EU law for a member state to suspend the reception of asylum applicants unilaterally.

On July 7, 2022, the European Court of Human Rights found the Greek coast guard guilty of conducting a pushback when it towed a boat carrying twenty-eight Afghan and Syrian refugees back to the Turkish coast on January 20, 2014. The migrant boat capsized, and eleven people died. As punishment, the Court ordered Greece to pay 330,000 euros to the applicants. European Home Affairs Commissioner Yiva Johansson also told the Greek government pushbacks must immediately stop and that continued EU funding is predicated on human rights law being respected. Yet these consequences seem unlikely to deter states from committing pushbacks.

On the Greek island of Samos, at the height of the European refugee crisis, approximately seven thousand asylum seekers lived in a sprawling informal camp sitting perched above Vathy, the island's main city. The conditions were deplorable. There were no services. Sanitation was nonexistent. NGOs offered a handful of services in Vathy, including laundry, psychosocial support, and some education classes. Other volunteers removed the rubbish in the camp to prevent it from turning into a landfill. Tensions between the camp and the city were high. In the fall of 2021, however, the authorities closed the informal camp and transferred its residents to a brand-new refugee camp, euphemistically known as a closed controlled access center (CCAC), located at a ten-minute drive from Vathy, up in the mountains.

"You can still see the camp," Frank says, pointing to the right. He has just picked me up from the airport, and we have begun to descend the hillside towards the Aegean. The view of the Bay of Samos has come into focus, with Vathy sitting at its terminus. Frank is a coordinator with the NGO I am volunteering with on Samos. "Do you see all the white?" he asks. I scan the horizon, across the bay and over the town, and before long, my eyes lock onto a patch of white squares incongruously situated among the green of the mountainside. They look like solar panels, but they are not. They are the camp's remnants. "It was supposed to come down last fall," Frank says. "But I guess they ran out of money." I find it fascinating the camp's skeleton still stands after all the hoopla the town's inhabitants made about its ugly sight and the deleterious effects it had on Vathy. Perhaps it was not the camp itself but its residents that the town protested so much against.

The number of asylum seekers living on the island has dramatically dropped—from ten thousand to four hundred. The drop, Frank explains to me, can be attributed to a variety of factors. Many former residents received refugee status yet decided not to stay in Greece. Others who were rejected clandestinely moved north. Yet the main reason for the low numbers is the fewer arrivals. On the surface, fewer arrivals could mean less demand for reaching Europe's shores, and fewer people risking their lives on poorly made boats with lifejackets that may or may not work. Dig a little deeper, however, and the real reason becomes clear: Greece has become exceptionally difficult to access. Since the 2016 EU-Türkiye agreement, Turkish authorities have worked hard to keep asylum seekers from crossing the Aegean. Greek border authorities meet those who do make it through. Instead of allowing asylum seekers to ask for international protection, the Greek authorities push them back towards Türkiye. The ubiquity and ruthless effectiveness of pushbacks at the Greek-Turkish border are the likely reasons for the steep drop in arrival numbers.

Frank explains the NGO's philosophy over coffee. Arrivals to Samos have built protective armour around themselves due to their difficult journeys. The NGO aims to break through it offering opportunities for refugees to envision a future. It focuses on fostering responsibility, structure, and initiative through its community volunteer program. Frank then outlines the asylum process for Samos. An applicant's country of origin greatly influences their chances. Palestinians are almost guaranteed asylum, while Afghans' prospects improved after the Taliban's

2021 takeover. Single Syrian men face more scrutiny. African asylum seekers' success depends on their country's situation and individual circumstances. From 2016 to 2020, asylum decisions could have taken over a year due to backlogs caused by the EU–Türkiye agreement. The EU has since invested in expediting the process. Now, applicants receive decisions faster. Those granted asylum can relocate within Greece, although many move on to other European countries. Rejected applicants can reapply or become undocumented, often attempting to reach Western Europe via the Balkan route.

We talk about how volunteers should behave within the camp. How a volunteer should interact with the displaced people they meet has always caused me considerable consternation. My experiences in Serbia, France, and Bosnia and Herzegovina taught me to keep my distance and remain professional. Friendships cannot form when the power dynamics are so skewed, as inevitably crutches form, and volunteers are asked to perform duties they have neither the skills nor the expertise to do. In this way, volunteers can do more harm than good. So, in the field, I keep my shield up. I disclose little personal information, and when someone asks about my nationality and about how things are in Canada, I give the most perfunctory and dull of answers. I never ask the people I meet about their stories, about the reasons they left or about their hopes for the future, because such a question could trigger a storm of emotions I am in no way qualified to handle. If people introduce these topics on their own accord, I actively listen and offer sympathetic platitudes, but I never take the conversation anywhere. They always steer the car, as it were. It is not that I feel each person I meet is fragility personified, breaking at the slightest nudge, but that it is better to err on the side of caution.

Frank respects and understands this approach but worries that its extreme form, completely isolating yourself from the people you serve, can do more harm than good. Volunteers, he reasons, are likely the first people displaced people meet that treat them as humans first. On their journey here, smugglers see them as a lucrative source of cash, whereas governments treat them as pests needing control or elimination. They have to keep their defence mechanisms sharp and their hands as fists. The road forces them to act vigilant and put survival before solidarity.

At the camp, though, where threats of physical violence become somewhat neutralized (psychological violence, not so much), arrivals need something to extinguish that nervous energy, the never-ending anxiety of the road, something to dull the blade. A friendly face is one such mechanism to cool the fire. Through daily interactions and the programs the NGO offers, Frank hopes to show arrivals some people care about what happens to them and how they are treated, and that cannot be done by volunteers acting cold and distant. Volunteers cannot become a crutch for an asylum seeker to lean on; boundaries are still sacrosanct. Yet for volunteers to redirect an asylum seeker's frustration and restlessness into something productive and constructive, relationships are essential. Stark power differences will always remain between volunteers and asylum seekers, and true friendships will likely never materialize them. But for NGOs to help build the skills and capabilities of asylum seekers while they wait in a camp, a certain degree of respectful cooperation is mandatory.

Frank tells me the organization has designated about twenty asylum seekers as community volunteers, each given certain responsibilities. Kai from Sierra Leone, for example, runs the sports program. Omar from Sudan is in charge of all things construction-related. Sayem from Afghanistan likes to take pictures. Nurul from Bangladesh ensures the chai point is fully stocked and running smoothly; if someone wants a cup of chai, they go to him. Rahman from Iraq is a cook, responsible for all meals the volunteers eat. Though not an official role, Ahmed, a young, brash man from Egypt, likes nothing more than to annoy the volunteers. And there are the children—Amena, Alina, and Yassen—who keep the volunteers on their toes. These are some of their stories.

Amena, Alina, and Yassen

The camp sits atop the highlands of Samos, about a ten-minute drive from Vathy. A narrow winding road ascends the mountainside, leaving Vathy's tourist shops and coffee houses below. It zigzags its way up and then over the slope, arriving at farmland and not much else. Here, you are away from everything. It's a stereotypical rural scene. Rustic and bucolic. The pace of life is slow. Everything seems to meander. You may see one or two people walking in the opposite direction, down towards the town, or someone riding a bike in the same direction. Nothing seems particularly odd about this, save for the appearance of the travellers: They do not look like the island's inhabitants. And you may think nothing of the sighting until just over a knoll or two, you see from where those people came. The sight of the camp is striking. It sits incongruously among the landscape and brutally rises from the soil and stone, violently making itself known. The camp seemingly consists of an endless series of grey buildings and containers that undulate over the hills. High fences and barbed wire surround the camp. Gates open and close. CCTV cameras record. Men and women patrol the space wearing vests with the words "private security." At night, lights illuminate the space, and eyes watch for forbidden movement. Curfews are strictly enforced. Residents cannot leave camp after 20:00 and cannot return after 21:00; if they do, they sleep outside. When I first saw the camp, I associated it with a penitentiary, a place where only the most hardened and dangerous criminals would reside—a prison far enough removed from civilization that ordinary folk would not have to worry about an escapee wreaking havoc on themselves or their loved ones. Criminals, however, do not reside here; asylum seekers do.

Security is thorough. Guards check your identification, ensuring you have permission to access the camp, and then record your name and the organization for which you work. You are then led into a room where any bags are placed on a conveyor belt to be checked for contraband. You then remove all valuables and metal objects from your pocket and proceed to walk through a metal detector. Once you are cleared and deemed safe, a guard will then open the camp's main gate and direct you inside. All guards wear indistinguishable uniforms and take their job seriously. Rarely does a smile pass by their lips. Their "hellos" are listless and inert. Yet for their professionalism and the seriousness in which they conduct themselves, they often have little to do. They check in and out residents and wander around the camp ensuring everyone is acting according to rules and regulations. Over hours, you can often see the same pair of guards walking back and forth along a row of containers, talking to one another. Some smoke; others wear sunglasses. They rarely talk to the volunteers or the camp residents. They just walk and watch. And collect a paycheck.

The volunteers are about to leave for the night. We have closed and tidied up the community space and the laundry room and are saying goodbye to the residents, those who cannot leave the camp once the night falls. Yet I have somehow found myself in a game with two little girls. In front of me stands Amena, a girl from the Democratic Republic of Congo (DRC), who arrived here on a boat with her mother last fall. She is a self-charging battery, a child of never-ending energy and precociousness. In one moment, she has me pushing her in a toy car across a stony pathway as she steers in an unwieldy way. In another, she steals my cellphone and somehow manages to select a song on my Spotify playlist that is, let us say, inappropriate for a child. In another, she climbs atop my shoulders while I input data into the laundry spreadsheet and demands I carry her about. We communicate in a mixture of English, French, and body language, but all is usually for naught. She would not heed my instructions even if she completely understood me.

At this moment, however, Amena has a ball in her hands and is trying to throw it over my head, beyond my grasp, to Alina, a girl from Afghanistan, who arrived on the same boat as Amena and who stands behind me, imploring Amena to throw it high. Alina is not as demanding as Amena, but what she lacks in being omnipresent, she makes up for in mischievousness. She can busy herself with drawing or sketching, and one would get the impression she could never cause any trouble or drama. A perfect child. Yet on occasion, that veneer drops, and a cunning grin replaces her once-studious focus. An example. For two days, we had trouble locking our van doors, which meant anyone, regardless of age or driving experience, could open a door and hop in. Once the children found this out, they snuck into the van at every opportunity. Once they saw the volunteers would try their hardest to remove them from the van, the kids realized they had discovered a truly wonderful game: Annoy the volunteers. Although Amena and Yassen, a boy from Gaza, also participated, it was Alina who truly revelled in this game. Whenever she saw me coming for her, to pull and lift her from the van, she would shriek in delight, her face dripping with pure joy. After struggling to get her out of the van and then focusing my attention on removing the remaining ruffians, I could see Alina from the corner of my eye running around the van, opening the passenger side and hopping back in the van. It went like this for ten or so minutes — my removing a child only to have them reappear in the van seconds later. It would eventually take the work of three volunteers to keep each child out while locking the van doors from the inside.

The ball goes sailing over my head and spins under the camp lights. Alina catches it and laughs with great glee. She likes having me, the big and tall man, in the middle. Alina positions the ball behind her head, launches it into the night, and screams, "Amena catch." And Amena, in her little pink and purple flip-flops, moves her body to track the trajectory of the ball, tracking its movement across the sky, her eyes big with focused anticipation, and reaches her cupped hands out into the air, where the ball lands within. This pattern continues for a few minutes, until Emilie, a volunteer coordinator from France, announces it's time for the volunteers to leave.

I say my goodbyes, but the girls are not having it. Amena latches onto my backpack and tries to prevent my movement, pulling and pulling in a futile effort to stop my forward momentum. Alina grabs Liam, a volunteer from the Netherlands, and tries to prevent him from moving towards the gate and the outside world, to the town below, where people are enjoying wine, food, and good conversation. The gate approaches. It's just ahead. The guard has unlocked it and has readied to let us pass, as it is he who dictates who comes and goes. Even though the girls must understand on some level the gate exists for them and not for us, that all gates inevitably open for us and close for them, they still hold out hope they might slip through the cracks holding onto our backpacks and they may gaze upon what exists just beyond. But we know better, and we must unhook their little hands from our backpacks and prevent their little bodies from sneaking through the opening. We tell them they must stay here, but we will see them soon. Sorry, we say, but you must stay here. You cannot leave. You cannot come with us. The children raise no great protest. They know they belong in here and we out there. Nothing more needs to be said. Amena and Alina do not ask why they cannot cross the fence. Experience has taught them they must remain inside and under the barbwire until someone, some man or woman they cannot see and will never know, tells them they can leave.

It's the Easter holidays, so the handful of children living in the camp are on holiday. Ordinarily, they would spend their day in school, either a Greek public one or one run by an NGO on the island, but these weeks, they spend their leisure time harassing volunteers. Amena is a legend in the camp; a little body of boundless energy, she can rattle even the most chilled of volunteers. I have tried to keep my composure with her and not let my frustration transform me into a brute. Word around the camp is her home situation is not the greatest, home being the tiny container she and her mother share with other people. Amena hides when her mother walks past the laundry room, and when her mother finds her, the little girl follows her mother's words as if gospel. I do not begrudge Amena's mother for leaving her daughter in the care of volunteers, since what is our purpose if not to relieve some of the burden of existing in a refugee camp? I am also skeptical about the castigation and judgment thrown at Amena's mother for being poor at the job, from both volunteers and residents alike, because I do not know how it is to be a mother in a refugee camp. I cannot judge what I do not understand. I cannot fathom what the daughter and mother have endured on their journey to Samos or what they have left behind in hopes of securing a brighter future in Europe.

But Amena is exhausting, and she has pushed me to the edge several times. She craves attention and stimulation. She bounces into the laundry room, eyes instantly drawn to something she can take or use. She grabs a blue marker and starts colouring on the white stickers we use to create laundry cards. Or she bolts to the washing machine and fiddles with the settings or tries to open the door. Or she steals the white-board-marker cleaner, goes to the storage cubbies, and starts erasing the numbers indicating which number belongs to which order. Or she tries to steal my phone from my pocket (which she has done on occasion). Or she draws on my shorts or arms. When the laundry room is not bursting with activity, I indulge her brazenness and pay her the attention she so craves. She wants to learn and take charge. Her eyes study my movements as I remove the finished clothing from the washer, stuff them into the bag, and then fill the machine with the next dirty clothes. I feel her focus when she watches me add powder and detergent to their rightful places and set the machine to the correct setting. For the next order, though, Amena is right next to me, demanding to do it all herself. She removes the clothing from the washer and adds the next bag. She puts the powder and detergent in place, although she is forced to ask for my assistance opening the detergent bottle, much to her disappointment. Her concentration is remarkable, a far cry from the child whose attention could latch onto anything. She is careful not to spill any detergent and double-checks the washer's settings with me. The routine seems to fascinate her, the order of everything, and she has become singularly focused on getting something done. All her energy has been directed to one task, and she moves from one step to the next.

In one hand, Amena carries the finished bag of clothing and in the other, her blue marker. I point to the space, and she shoves the bag in without problems. I tell her to write forty-two on the white space above the cubicle. She hesitates. I try again in French, but again, she looks at the white space and then at me with confusion. My request has perplexed her. She stays motionless for a moment longer before repeating the number and placing the marker's end on the white. What appears looks nothing like the number, just a bunch of squiggly lines forming crude shapes. She is mocking me, I think, another one of her cunning attempts to get under my skin or achieve what she desires. The other day, for instance, I heard her take a tumble outside while playing with some of the other kids. She then stumbled into the laundry container, howling uncontrollably. Tears fell from her eyes; her face was all distorted. She emitted such a horrible sound. And it continued without apparent end. The crying and sobbing only seemed to intensify, and those horrible sounds penetrated deep into my mind and started rattling around, frustrating and unnerving me, so I gave Amena my cell phone, something she has always craved, and the effect was instantaneous: She stopped crying and offered me a little smile.

This episode replays in my mind while I watch her write those nonsensical lines. This again must be some trick, some ploy to get what she wants. I erase what she has written, and she protests as if I have destroyed something she has worked hours on. I show her the number tag attached to the bag, clearly indicating forty-two, and tell her to copy that number onto the white space. She studies the number, looks at the white space, and then stares again at the number as if internally debating how to reproduce that number. Her marker touches the white space, and although she stares at the number forty-two, what she writes looks nothing like it. I erase the number again, and the same episode repeats itself. She wants to reproduce forty-two, but try as she might, what she reproduces is a far cry from it. "Show me," she says. I try to take the marker from her hand, but she does not let go. "No. No," she says. "Show me." I take her hand and help her guide the marker across the white. We struggle to write a four and then have more difficulty with the loops of the two, but we are finished; we have something resembling the original enough that anyone could recognize the number as forty-two. Yet Amena still peers at the order number and then the one on the whiteboard, comparing and contrasting the two. Something still seems to irk her; something is out of place. Something is not right. A shrieking and halting "no" rips from her mouth, and in a flash, she has erased the forty-two and has returned to recreating the number as she fits. Her creation again looks nothing like the number, and I am curious about why she sees the number this way and cannot dutifully copy what is right before her. She is satisfied with her work and puts the cap back on the marker, signalling the end of the job. I do not correct her anymore. I give her the number as she sees it. Yet as Amena returns to busying herself with other things, doodling and begging for my phone, her number, and its incorrectness, draw my glance every few seconds. It begins to terrorize me. I cannot put it out of my mind, nor can I accept its existence among the correct numbers — the ones that look like how I know numbers should look. And I know that as soon as Amena leaves, as soon as some outside noise or commotion draws her attention and sends her running from the container, I will erase her number and write the correct one.

Yassen takes my hand and leads me away from the football pitch. He is five, from Gaza, and has known mostly camps for his short life. He has exceptional football skills, including an accurate and powerful shot that embarrasses goaltenders twice his age, and a smile that could allow him to get away with murder. "Come eat," he says, leading me to the Arabic-speaking area of the camp. The sun has set on this third Tuesday of Ramadan, and it's time for the Muslims of the camp to enjoy iftar, the breaking of the fast. I try to politely refuse, not wanting to interfere in such an important tradition or to consume the resources of people who have so little, but as I see the set table and the men now waving me to join them, I know to decline at this point would be rude. The community has prepared a feast: marinated fish and salad, some pasta and pita. I have seen the small kitchenettes of the containers, the meagre space and resources one has to cook, yet I am always amazed at what people can do with so little. Food appears on my plate, and Coca-Cola fills my cup. There is no evidence of want or lack. Talk is abundant and light. Laughter follows many sentences. The dinner is a mirage, tricking me into thinking I could be in Damascus before the war or in Gaza during its never-ending war. To refuse would break the spell. To decline would signal to them that what they have as refugees is too precious to waste on a man of privilege. They must save every morsel for themselves and their children.

My vegetarianism is also an issue. I fill my plate with salad and pasta and hope that Hossein, the gentle giant from Gaza sitting beside me, will not notice I have not included any of the fish. He does and motions me to take one of the headless fish sitting in the sauce. This I will not do. I cannot sacrifice my vegetarianism in the name of being of respectful guest, and I do not think my hosts would want me to either, as my lie would again highlight the gulf between us: Instead of a group of people inviting me, another person, to break fast with them, my falsehood—my willingness to betray a part of myself to satisfy their desire to satisfy me—would present in sharp relief their status as charity recipients in my mind's eye. I must not offend my hosts, for they have nothing, and I have everything. And although this is true to a degree, we are separated by a great amount of power and privilege, I do think my guests would take my lie as a sign of disrespect, since I would be willing to deny a part of myself out of pity for them.

I turn to Ahmed beside me, a skilled ping-pong player from Syria and someone who speaks some English, and ask him if he could explain to everyone I do not eat meat. Hossein takes the information in stride, aims his spoon away from the fish to the potatoes lying around them, and proceeds to drop a few on my plate. I thank him and take a bite. The old taste of fish still hits me, and I struggle to eat each potato, but I do not stop. This is an acceptable compromise, something I can do.

A young man, slender and light on his feet, sits next to me and introduces himself as Muhammad from Iraq. When I say I am from Canada, he sighs and says, "The dream of every refugee." Muhammad has been on Samos for almost four years and has experienced rejection after rejection. He thinks he is now the camp resident who has spent the most time on the island, a depressing distinction. His desperation creeps into the conversation as he asks me whether I think it would be easy to be smuggled into Canada from the US. I am reticent to offer my opinion on the matter, since I know how dangerous the attempt can be, especially in the winter months: Asylum seekers have frozen to death on the American-Canadian border. I do tell him Canada is not the promised land for asylum seekers as it may appear from the outside. I talk about the third safe country agreement between Canada and the US, which stipulates that asylum seekers crossing from the US into Canada may be returned there without having their cases heard. I explain Canada has something called indefinite detention: Canadian authorities can detain irregular migrants or failed asylum seekers indefinitely, forever, for a host of reasons. People have become so desperate in these detention centres, after years of waiting for a resolution, that they have taken their own lives.

My warnings do not dissuade Muhammad. He has convinced himself of Canada's hallowed status. Canada has never deported anyone arriving without papers, he says, with complete genuineness. I wonder how someone who has lived the past four years in a refugee camp could be so naïve about the utter disdain states have for people arriving at their borders irregularly. He must believe in Canada because the alternative is too awful to fathom. It's the Janus-faced nature of faith: hope versus self-delusion. I tell him although authorities may struggle to send him back if his home country proves uncooperative, that does not mean they will free him. Never underestimate a state's cynicism. They would rather him rot indefinitely in a detention centre than release him to the world. A sense of foreboding clouds Muhammed's once carefree demeanour. Some of my words have sunken through, but by providing these warnings, have I not just done the work of deterrence for the Canadian state? I have become a border crossing. I would like nothing more than for him to get refugee status in Canada, but he should be aware of the risks involved. I had to fact check his rose-coloured narrative about Canada and its alleged benevolence. It would have been irresponsible of me to let him travel to the country without telling him truth. He deserves to make his decision with as much information as possible. Muhammed understands what I am saying: I do not want him to harbour any misconceptions about Canada. Yet his look devastates me because I know I planted doubt where hope once grew.

Sayem

Sayem was a minor when he left Afghanistan and became an adult in Samos. In the old camp, he had a difficult time, fell in with the wrong crowd, and started to self-harm. Little by little, though, he came back from the dark. He takes photos of the camp and its residents with Frank's DSLR camera. He has a natural photographic talent, as he effortlessly makes striking portraits of people full of detail and poignancy. Personality flows from him. His English is basic, but he still makes everyone laugh. He volunteers in the laundry room and barks the finished order numbers in lightening speed, challenging anyone recording them on the laptop to keep up. In English class, he sometimes confuses the letters "i" and "e" but does not let the mistake deter him from answering the next question and the next. Sometimes, though, Sayem will disappear for a few days to hibernate inside his container as if allergic to sunlight.

Sayem sits beside me in the laundry room, looking at his phone. He wears a purple t-shirt, and his arms are exposed. Along his arms live the scars of his self-harm. They are the marks a rake would make along a patch of dirt, long, skinny marks. I would never ask anyone about their scars or about why they exist. I would never inquire about the reasons why they took a blade to their own body. It is too obtrusive a request, too pushy and none of my business. When I see Sayem's scars, I can only feel relief they are older and have somewhat healed. I have read a primary motivation for someone to self-harm is to gain a measure of control over internal emotions. Some past trauma has seized their attention, and the awful event replays over and over again. They cannot escape the memories of the barbarism they suffered. The images are vivid. It is as if they are there again. Reliving it. Over and over again. Nothing can stop the projector from playing the scenes. Nothing can draw their attention away. They crave a measure of control over what they feel. So, shift the focus. Put it on something immediate. Something close. A leg or an arm. A razor is within reach and a bit of pressure. And clarity arrives. The past vanishes, replaced by the sensation of the razor's edge.

I know nothing about Sayem's journey to Greece or the traumas he might have endured. But I understand the camp's penchant for making people wait creates a conducive atmosphere for dwelling on past pain. With an incredible amount of time at one's disposal, punctuated by meals and maybe the occasional visit to Vathy, an individual has ample opportunity to focus not on the future, since it remains unknown, but on the past and its violence. The refugee camp becomes a warehouse of trauma. It is stored there, locked away behind gates and fences, since there remains no outlet to purge the pain, no valve to release it. For days, months, and years, people sit with what has happened to them without reprieve. There is time for every brutal little memory to dance across someone's consciousness. The onslaught is unrelenting. Few distractions exist. Any hope of a future is beyond their control. And without hope, there is only a past that will never go away. With all this time to dwell and the past's attack so ubiquitous that one cannot get a moment's rest, a blade can provide a useful distraction.

I am thinking about his scars when Hamza, a young man from Somalia, walks in and speaks with Sayem in broken English. He points to Sayem's scars. I do not know whether they have discussed this topic before or Hamza has just noticed them, but Hamza seems concerned about the young Afghan's scars. They communicate mostly in body language with a few English words thrown in. I understand Hamza is asking Sayem to confirm he no longer cuts, since "it's not good" in Hamza's words, but Sayem brushes Hamza's comments away with a wave of his hand, focusing instead on the game he plays on his phone. But when Hamza's pushes the issue further, unwilling to let the topic die with Sayem's disinterest in discussing it, the teenager only looks at Hamza and says, "You don't know. You don't know." Hamza looks at me for meaning, as if I could decipher Sayem's words. Although I think I understand him, I don't dare articulate my thoughts, choosing instead to input another laundry order into the computer.

Sayem has lost his best friend on the island, Tariq, a fellow Farsi speaker. From Afghanistan originally, the burly man had spent many years on the move, Greece and beyond, with the singular goal of getting permission to stay in Europe. He now has it. As much as we are happy for him, we are equally concerned about Sayem. Tariq had taken Sayem under his wing and guided him through life as a refugee in Greece, the way an older brother might. Sayem is in between asylum applications, having been rejected and not yet starting a new one, and because he has no legal standing to remain in Greece, his body effectively illegalized, he must ask for permission to leave the camp, only heightening the isolation and claustrophobia he must already feel living there. Given Sayem's history of drug abuse and self-harm, we worry Tariq's departure may cause him to revisit self-destructive practices and revert to his old ways.

However, we feel Sayem has turned a corner and has developed the coping skills needed to withstand the mental onslaught of living in a refugee camp for an extended period. He has found things that provide pleasure. He has hobbies and a community of volunteers who like him. The Monday after Tariq leaves, Sayem visits me in the laundry room, and we shake hands and ask how the other is doing. He sports a stylish new haircut that suits him, and I tell him as much. My comment seems to please him, and he flashes me a smile. I do not see him for the next two days, but I do not worry. He misses his English class on Wednesday, which does not concern me, as most students have been absent recently, even though Sayem has proven to be one of the more dedicated ones. Just the previous week, he promised me he would come to my class, but when I went to the container to prepare, I noticed him sitting among the students of my colleague Liam's class. He had gone to the wrong class. After the class finished, I joked with him, asking, "So, you think Liam is a better teacher than me?" Sayem got the joke and said, "No, no. You are the same." I told Liam to stop stealing my students, and we all laughed.

On the Thursday after Tariq left, I am working in the laundry container. It is busy. I am registering newcomers while taking and returning orders. Sayem enters, and although I am relieved to see him, I am not in a socializing mood. We shake hands and exchange pleasantries. I feel him fade into the background, standing and watching me. Hovering. Does he want something to do? Should I delegate? I am speaking to a French-speaking woman from the DRC, a new arrival I think, and asking her whether she has a laundry card. She presents her asylum card, but I tell her this is not the card she needs. Sayam interjects, knowing how our system works and having taken more laundry orders than I have, and explains in a not-so-subtle way she needs a laundry card and holds one up as an example. It's not a problem, I tell her, we can make her a new card. I search for a French-language card in the basket when I think I hear Sayem say we don't have any left, which I know to be false. Sayem brushes past me and out the door, ostensibly to go search for more. "Sayem," I call, "we have them," but he is gone.

I put Sayem out of my mind, focusing on the many tasks at hand, until Emilie returns from lunch full of exasperation. "I've had it with teenagers," she says, dropping her keys on the table. Sayem, she tells me, visited the lunch container while everyone was eating. He told a few jokes that fell flat and soon realized no one was paying much attention to him. Everyone was engaged in other conversations, other things. Sayem decided to put the spotlight back on him. He took Emilie's keys from the door and locked everyone in the container. Well, they all paid attention to him now, as they shouted at him through the window to open the door. Emilie, who suffers from mild claustrophobia, yelled at him to stop playing childish games and open the door immediately. Sayem, though, enjoyed the power he yielded and savoured his newfound ability to make people wait for him. When he did grow tired of his shenanigans and gatekeeping became a depressing chore, he released his captives, who went on with their day, except for Emilie, who took further opportunity to chastise and reprimand Sayem for acting like a child. Sayem left the scene upset and wanted to show Emilie, and by association the organization, he did not need them anymore. He was done. Finished. Whatever slight he felt the organization had inflicted upon him would be returned in kind. Sayem did not need us. Inside his container, he found all his clothing with the NGO's emblazoned logo, as well as his volunteer card, and returned them to Emilie. He announced his resignation from the organization, and it must have felt momentarily good. I know nothing about what it feels like to be a teenager trapped in a refugee camp, and I wouldn't presume to know the specific reasons that led Sayem to hand over his volunteer clothing and credentials. But I do know something about acting impulsively and rashly. When I was younger, I would react impetuously to every perceived insult or attack. I would sever all contact. Blow the whole fucking thing up. I felt great joy in renouncing my attachment to any organization and person and imagining their great anguish for making me do this. They would realize how much they needed me. I never enjoyed something as much as watching a bridge burn.

Emilie did not question Sayem's decision, nor did she try to persuade him to stay. Having grown tired of his antics, she accepted his resignation without thought. And like that, as if the previous months had been a mirage, Sayem was no longer a volunteer. In the laundry container, we agree Sayem might have just been letting off some steam and was probably just reacting poorly to Tariq's departure. Perhaps in a day or two, Sayem will realize he overreacted and ask to return as a volunteer.

A commotion erupts from outside. Loud voices spread across the camp. Something is happening. Emilie and I exit the container and turn towards Chai Point, the NGO's command centre, where people can get a cup of tea, socialize with others, or print important documents from the computer. Chai Point is a community space; it brings people together. On the picnic tables outside the office, people play checkers and cards; children draw and play Jenga. It is a dynamic place; the walls are painted in bright colours, so different from the overwhelming grey characterizing the rest of the camp.

Two camp residents are attempting to escort Sayem out of Chai Point. But he's not having it; he wants back in. Something or someone has infuriated him, something or someone inside the office. And he wants at it. He is walking rage. The residents struggle to contain him; he is uncontrollable and beyond appeasement. He keeps shouting and pointing at Chai Point. People tell him to calm down, but he will not. People tell him to walk away, but he will not. The scene has attracted the attention of other camp residents and the camp's private security officers, who get on their walkie-talkies and start relaying what is happening to their colleagues. They do not intervene; they just watch, like the rest of us, Sayem descend into violence. Ahmed has his arms on Sayem shoulders and begs him to calm down, as he seems to say the worst has not yet happened and that Sayem can still walk away from this, if he would just go to his container and calm down, if he would just go away. The young Afghan puts up his hands as if to indicate he understands and he will remove himself from the situation. He says, "No problem. No problem." But this is not the end. Something has snapped within him; his anger will no longer be directed inwards upon his own body. No. He will send it out to the world.

In a flash, Sayem has a rock in his hand and throws it through the window of Chai Point. The projectile scatters the people inside but not before hitting Nurul in the knee. He clutches his wound while two residents help him walk from inside Chai Point to a bench just outside. Henry, from Cameroon, a giant of a man, approaches Sayem, not with aggression but with calm, his words painted with disappointment and sadness. "Look at what you've done," he says, pointing at Nurul, who still holds his knee. "You've hurt your friend." Sayem sees Nurul sitting on the bench in obvious discomfort, and for a moment, a look of regret passes across the young man's face; concern for Nurul momentarily breaches his anger. "No problem," Sayem says again. "No problem." But there is a problem, and Sayem knows he has done something irrevocable. Part of him knows what has been done cannot be put back together. Everybody is staring at him. All eyes are on him. Dozens of people have watched him transform into rage. We have all experienced his deterioration, the peeling back of the Sayem we know, the boy with the mischievous smile, the boy with the camera hanging around his neck, the boy with the scars, until all that remains is this enraged stranger. Who are you? Where did you come from? Were you there all along? Henry says it again: "Look at what you've done." Sayem raises his hand to the sky, to Nurul, as if asking if he is okay, as if asking for his forgiveness.

From behind a gate, three police officers arrive and surround Sayem. Their aggression matches Sayem's, and soon the officers have the young man up against the fence and handcuffed. Two officers lead him away while the third tells everyone to go about their day. One private security guard, among the many who sat back and watched Sayem explode, now springs to action and directs all spectators away from Chai Point. Emilie and others go with one officer to give a deposition of what transpired. I return to the laundry container and register the clothing of a man waiting patiently. Sayem's things are still sitting on the table. His volunteer identification rests atop his volunteer shirt. In the photo, he is smiling.

No argument within Chai Point triggered Sayem's wrath. It had already been triggered. This is what happened. He finds a hand rake volunteers have used to plant flowers. The tool is metal with three thick tines, perfect for separating soil. I have seen it lying around the camp and have always been careful not to let it slip into the hands of the children. Sayem understands the rake's potential, beyond its more utilitarian purpose, which is why when he enters Chai Point, he does not utter any threats; he starts swinging. He first hammers at the window until it breaks into pieces and then sets his attention to the open laptop sitting on the table, and with a few potent hits, the screen breaks and goes dark. People call on him to calm down, but nothing distracts him from his work breaking things belonging to the NGO that has wronged him. A young man tries to disarm Sayem but instead gets scratched by the rake's tines. A minor injury. An accident. Sayem does not aim his wrath at people, only things associated with the NGO. Objects and tools. He will later say his anger that day became too much to swallow and too big for his body to contain. He could no longer hold it himself; it weighed too much, so he decided to share it with the camp, his world.

Authorities decide to remove Sayem from camp. About what will happen to him or where he will go, they do not care. He is a disruptive presence that must be banished. Excised. Once again, forces have expelled him, casting him adrift into the world. Unmoored. Displaced once more. In front of the camp, just next to the gate where asylum seekers must queue to enter, stands an ATM. When we leave the camp that afternoon, we see Sayem sitting beside the machine with his suitcases. I wonder if those are the same suitcases he took with him when he left Afghanistan. Sayem sees us approach him, but he does not register our presence. He only sits back against the machine with his head tilted towards the sun. The young man looks at peace, resigned to his fate. Emilie asks whether we can call anyone to pick him up. Is there anyone he can stay with in the city? Her questions remain unprocessed, just floating beyond his comprehension. He only smiles at her and says, "Thank you." Emilie keeps asking whether she can do anything, something, but Sayem smiles at her and repeats the words "Thank you." I cannot tell whether Sayem mocks Emilie with his thanks, as if blaming her for what happened earlier, and is now sarcastically telling her she has already done enough. Or maybe he is genuinely thanking her for all she has tried to do for him over the previous months while admitting to her and to himself that all that effort could not overcome the violence such a camp can inflict upon a mind. "Thank you, Emilie." We leave him sitting outside the camp, next to the ATM, surrounded by suitcases, with a little smile still etched across his lips.

I believe in the work this NGO does. The opportunities they provide give camp residents something meaningful to do while they wait for their asylum cases to be resolved. The work conjures up a future for themselves away from these fences and the hardships they fled; it lessens the brutality of waiting. Yet after one, two, or three years of waiting for a decision to restart life, even the hardiest and most resilient of people can begin to crumble. All the classes in the world cannot compete against the fences of a refugee camp, against its soul-crushing nothingness. Time becomes a torturer. It does not stop for those trapped in legal purgatory; instead, the seconds, minutes, and days keep ticking away, ripping their passions from them. They watch time float by, outside themselves, just beyond the camp, where life continues. Time is no longer an opportunity to search and seek experience; the camp transforms it into something of which residents are both inside and outside. Time still has much consequence. Its effects can still be seen on faces and skin. Yet for all its consequences, residents have nothing to show for the time they have experienced. Waiting has emptied time of its significance. One unremarkable day follows another. Time without opportunity deadens the soul; it kills all internal sparks. Sayem reminded us that behind the docility the camp tries to engender among its residents, a person still rages against the unnaturalness of their cage.

On my way back to my apartment, I run into Hasan, a young man from Djibouti. I hear him before I see him because he always shouts "Hey Canada" whenever I cross his path. He has a bombastic personality, loud and unmistakable. Many times in the laundry, I heard his voice sailing across the camp long before I saw him saunter past. He has an energy difficult to contain; it shoots from him and affects everyone in his path. He is infectious. Today, however, a more sombre mood has taken him, as he has heard about what happened to Sayem. His body carries a sadness. No jokes or smiles come. But as much as Sayem's news troubles Hasan, it does not surprise him. There is nothing original about the story. His nonchalant response tells me such outbursts are to be expected when a person has his body and soul humiliated daily. "The camp is no good," Hasan says. He taps his head once, twice, as if showing where it aims its attack and inflicts the most damage. "That wasn't Sayem," he says, and I agree. What we saw today was the camp's spawn—a child raised on neglect, humiliation, and degradation. And inevitably, the boy will turn his wrath on the father who created him, who took away his light and replaced it a bunkbed and shitty food, day after day after day.

Samos has two ports, one on opposite sides of the bay. The one furthest from the city centres welcomes the Blue Star Ferries, Greece's flagship ferry operator, which connects all of the islands in the Aegean. The second one sits in the city proper and is much smaller. Tourist boats from Türkiye often dock there, as do coast guard vessels. Beside this second port's entrance is a popular fishing spot. Locals bring comfortable chairs and a rod and cast their line into the Aegean blue. Others fish from the spot, but these men do not have poles and chairs. Instead, they sit cross-legged on the ground and bait their line with pieces of bread. Without a rod, the fishermen just toss their line into the sea and move it around to the best of their ability. Among these men are camp residents, who have taken the camp bus to the city centre to enjoy some time away from the gates. Perhaps, fishing is something they did in their own country; maybe, it holds no nostalgia at all, just something new to break the monotony. The first time I saw Rahman fishing there, I had to double-check my eyes had not deceived me. But it was him, a community volunteer from Iraq, dressed in his hoodie and jeans and sending his line out into the water. He looked out of place sitting on the water's edge in the early morning sunlight. I had only associated Rahman with camp activities: chopping onions and eggplants, washing dishes, serving chai, sweeping the floor, or playing ping pong. But here he was outside the camp's fences, sitting on his own accord, and doing something that brought him an obvious amount of joy. I didn't wish to disturb him, so I just waved in his direction and left him there in his solitude.

Two days after Sayem's outburst, I am walking back to my apartment and pass the popular fishing haunt. Sure enough, Rahman is there, casting a line out into the sea, but beside him also sits Sayem, eating an apple. He looks at peace. Gone is the anger that had driven him to pick up the rake and throw the rock. Nothing heavy seems to weigh on him. He could be any teenager hanging out with friends on the waterfront, looking for ingenious ways to pass the time. He watches Rahman adjust the line and is about to offer his advice about how to manoeuvre it when he sees me approach. His smile disappears as he rises to his feet and shoots out his hand. I have intruded upon his moment and will remind him of things he had momentarily forgotten. I have broken the spell. I am the teacher, and he is the misbehaving student who now has some explaining. How fast his visage changes, from playfulness to an intense sombreness. I ask him how he is doing and if he has caught any fish. He brushes away my question, my little icebreaker, and asks about the camp and about how everyone is doing, a not-so-subtle question about the welfare of Nurul and the other residents who met his rage. I tell him everyone is fine and that everyone misses him. He says he is sorry about what happened and tries to explain his outburst. From the English words at his disposal, he tells me about how bad the camp is for his… and he cannot find the word and instead points to his head. The camp became too much, too heavy, too cumbersome. Like trying to swim with a boulder tied around your ankles. No matter how hard you swim and how much effort you exert, you will only sink further and further into the abyss, the coldest and darkest parts. I try to tell Sayem he does not need to justify his actions, at least not to me. We all understand the situation. He tells me he misses taking photographs with Frank's hefty DSLR camera, and his words evoke memories of him walking around camp with it slung around his neck. He would point and snap at any scene or image that took his interest, anything that struck him as visually interesting or spoke to him personally. The camera became an extension of his vision, a tool to explore his artistry, his world. Although I did not always see the potential in the scenes he shot, he did; he saw how objects, shapes, and light spoke to one another inside his frame. Things that I could not see, he did. His photos transformed into a window showcasing his world, a peek behind the curtain.

But now, Sayem is without his camera and community. At the moment though, fishing as he is under a shower of sunlight, the loss does not seem so great, as he exists outside the grey walls, among the nondisplaced. Before I leave him, Sayem tells me a decision has arrived concerning his asylum application, and I tell him I hope for a positive answer, for what else can I do but hope Sayem may finally have an opportunity to restart his life because the alternative may prove to be too much even for someone as strong as he.

Kai

Kai is from Sierra Leone and is the NGO's sports coordinator, which means he is the closest thing to God at the camp. He is responsible for organizing the football tournament, putting together the teams, and ensuring everything runs smoothly. Residents take football seriously, so Kai becomes the man people go to about questions, concerns, or anything sports-related. He lays out the rules of the matches, discusses the importance of respect and professionalism, and warns of the consequences if anyone should breach those rules.

He is a Manchester United fan, and when he met me and discovered my name, he immediately began attaching the surname "Lingard" to it, Jesse Lingard being a famous Man United player. I had never heard of him. I would always hear "Jesse Lingard" before seeing Kai. Working in the laundry room, I would hear the name come bellowing from outside.

Before the tournament began, I would watch him supervising practice matches between the residents. He was like a hawk surveying the ground below for any prey or, in Kai's case, players who played too aggressively or were too reckless with their tackles. Kai would point out to me potentially troublesome players, and when that player did cross the line, he would give him a stern talking to. Everyone, no matter their nationality, respected Kai and his role as a neutral arbiter, which is why they always came to him to plead their case about a suspected foul or about being taken off the field too soon. The football pitch can become tense, and without a stern yet fair hand to guide the proceedings, a match can quickly devolve into fighting, which would reflect poorly on Kai and the NGO. During a game, security guards always hover around the pitch, anxiously waiting to see whether a dispute may turn into violence.

The first game of the tournament tests Kai's resolve. To maintain a level of neutrality, Kai neither plays nor referees; he keeps score and watches the game unfold to ensure everything goes according to plan. As soon as the whistle blows to start the match, both teams complain about the referee's ineffectiveness, complaining about his missing a foul or calling a clean tackle a foul. It's an entertaining match until chaos erupts. One player receives a nice pass and cuts between two defenders; the defender desperately tugs on the attacker's jersey, who then proceeds to elbow the defender in the face. The referee does not hesitate; he rushes to the guilty party and shows him a red card. A melee ensues. Players from the penalized team surround the referee and vehemently protest, and I wonder what their argument could be, since the foul was obvious and flagrant. But rumours spread across the stands and among the spectators that the foul was only half the story and that a few seconds before the offending incident, the victim committed a similar act against the aggressor, which the referee missed. So, the players confront the referee and demand to know why he has only decided to penalize their team. The captain is the angriest of them all, even though he is not the offender. He screams and shouts at the injustice of it all, the clear-cut favouring of one team over the other. He is confrontational and combative. Things get more heated, more tense. Bellicosity is in the air. But Kai, who has been in the centre of the commotion since it erupted, faces the captain and does not waver in supporting the referee's decision. He is calm but direct and never undermines the referee. The decision will stand, and that is that. Tensions continue to rise. Combustible. A single spark could engulf the entire pitch. Nearby, private security guards watch the drama with great anticipation, almost hoping the situation devolves into a brawl so that it would give them something to do.

I return to the laundry container and tell Emilie about the goings-on, almost as a way to process the unfolding drama. Emilie does not concern herself with the story's details—the drama and intrigue—but the potential for escalation. She knows the consequences of any violence. Emilie races to the pitch, with me close behind.

Kai has things under control. The players on the penalized team have removed their jerseys in protest and continue milling about the sidelines, pleading their case to anyone who will listen, but nothing can be done. The captain decides his team will not play in such, in his mind, stacked conditions; instead, they will boycott the remainder of the match. The other team, meanwhile, remains on the pitch and just passes the ball around, not wanting to involve themselves in a situation that has gone so spectacularly well for them. No need to tempt the gods that have smiled so favourably on them. The captain still huffs and puffs from the sideline; one moment it looks as though he has accepted the outcome and has resolved to focus on the next game, but then a rage takes him, a quick reminder of the injustice that just transpired, something he will neither forget nor forgive, and then he goes marches again, towards the referee and Kai, bellowing out his case for all to hear. But Kai just bats him away, as if he were only an infant throwing a tantrum, needing only to be left alone to calm down. If Kai could send him to his room, he would. Emotions finally cool, and when the final whistle sounds, I approach Kai and say how extraordinary it is for the first match to end in such a way. All the tension, emotion, and drama. He just smiles his infectious, beaming smile and agrees the proceedings got a little tense, but it is okay. High emotions are to be expected, he says. Players want to win; they take the match seriously. His composure amazes me. Just minutes before, a brawl seemed almost inevitable, but Kai steered everyone back to if not a sense of calm than a sense of the repercussions if the controversy spiralled out of control. What happened does not bother him. He only pities the match ended in such a manner, since it had been such a quality one before the furor.

Kai is the definition of grace under pressure. Nothing rattles him. He has a firm but fair hand, which people respect. They see him as the wise judge who can deliver justice impartially. He is so well revered that soon he will travel to Chios to help the NGO's team to prevent fights from breaking out on the pitch. The secret, Kai says, is to explain the consequences of infractions beforehand. Get all the players together and spell out in the clearest possible detail the repercussions of every transgression. What penalty will lead to an injection from a game? What penalty will lead to a complete prohibition from participating in football matches? Consequences help to diffuse any possible violence on the pitch. Know the rules and know what happens if you break them. I have trouble visualizing Kai delivering his stern warnings to players about the repercussions of violence. He is calm, direct, and serious. People believe him because he is telling the truth.

I have only ever seen Kai upset once. We are about to leave for the day when he comes racing towards us. He carries a lot of anger. I almost do not recognize him. "You need to do something about this guy," he says. His finger points to someone back towards the pitch, beyond our sight. "We have a match starting soon," Kai says. "He cannot do this." What happened was this. There is a special area of the camp for unaccompanied minors, boys and girls under the age of eighteen. In the name of their protection, their movement is strictly curtailed. They live in a cage within a cage. They can only leave their designated area without permission and supervision for three hours a day: 16:30 to 19:30. The football pitch is a camp highlight, so some minors want to spend their free time playing football on the grass. For this week and last, though, Kai has scheduled football matches during this period, something the entire camp has known about and agreed to. Minors deserve to play on the pitch as much as anyone else, but no one from camp management told us they would be starting on this day just before the match's start.

After the minors were released from their cage, a man from camp management approached Kai and Liam, standing on the pitch watching the players warm up, and said the minors may have the pitch to play. Liam and Kai did not protest the notion but maintained they could not use it now, since there was a match that had been planned for some time. Kai himself said to the man the minors were welcome to use the pitch, just not now. The man did not take the news well. He ignored Kai, completely denying his presence, even though he is the sports coordinator, even though he has been organizing sporting events before this camp was built, back in the jungle, where residents did not have a pitch to play on. Instead, the man directed all his focus to Liam and demanded to speak to someone higher up about allowing the kids to play. This slightly infuriated Kai because it was based not on what he said, since Kai spoke clearly and directly as he always did, but on who he was: a Black asylum seeker from Sierra Leone. Based on these characteristics alone, and not the content of what Kai said, did this man deem in his mental calculus Kai was unworthy of his regard and respect? And this disrespect Kai could not stomach. Respect orients Kai's worldview; if you give it, you should receive it. This is unconditional. He believes actions have consequences. What is right will prevail, if not in this world, then in the next. Kai once told me he believes in heaven and hell because justice is not of this world alone, and if you escape punishment for your deeds in this world, you will not in the next.

The man from camp management broke the rules of respect; he did not return what was given. This disrespect is what so angers Kai when we see him retell the story to Emilie. He is almost shaking, the rage evident in his eyes. The man disrespected him. He took all the work Kai did preparing for the tournament and cast it aside as if it were rubbish, items of trash not worth further reflection. Kai and his arguments were not worthy of this man's time, so fetch me someone higher with whom I may speak.

Emilie does go to speak to someone, and the match resumes, and the minors are asked to play at another time, which they are fine with, since they never asked to play during the match. None of this drama was necessary. The man was drunk on a false sense of self-importance. Because these men and women with walkie-talkies have an authoritative role in the camp, implementing rules and maintaining order, they believe the power they wield is due to their greatness. Give a person a measure of power, and they will begin to believe great things about themselves.

Ahmed

Ahmed did not make a great first impression on me. Early twenties and full of bombast and arrogance, his behaviour could be difficult to predict. When asylum seekers still lived in the jungle, Ahmed had a reputation for getting into fights over the smallest of infractions. He treated each slight, however minor, as a great insult towards his honour and would meet each with a disproportionate retaliation. Emilie and Frank say his behaviour has improved over the months and years; he is calmer now and less prone to naked aggression. Yet to my eye, he still possesses a wild energy difficult to control and direct to more worthwhile tasks. When you are young and on the move, defense mechanisms quickly become honed and weaponized. You are ready for anything.

Ahmed sometimes visits me in the laundry room, not because he enjoys my company per se but because of the laptop on which we record the laundry orders. When the work is slow, he will go on YouTube and find videos of his favourite football player: Liverpool defender Virgil van Dijk. I am not much of a football fan, but when I watch clips or highlights from the World Cup or Euro Cup, it's for the goals. Big and spectacular goals. Individual efforts. A sublime free kick. A mesmerizing display of passing. A beautiful header. I don't watch for the defense, but defending and van Dijk's greatness at it spellbind Ahmed. His bluster and bravado go to mute while he watches the Dutchman play. He studies him and what makes him great. At first, I don't see it. I don't understand what Ahmed sees. But highlight after highlight, I understand what makes van Dijk special. It's his grace under pressure. An attacker burls down on him at full speed, yet the man stays focused on the player and the ball at his feet, tracking his movements and anticipating his next move. He jogs almost at an angle backwards, keeping the opposing player in front of him so that he may have the best position to block that player from passing him. The way he counters the attacker's aggression with such gracefulness is beautiful to watch, making it seem all so easy. Whatever the player chooses to do to evade van Dijk's presence, the defender responds and skillfully neutralizes the threat. After every highlight, Ahmed shakes in head in admiration.

Van Dijk is also built like a hockey player and uses his weight to win battles for the ball. Smaller bodies seem to ricochet off his and then go tumbling to the ground. His tackles are perfectly timed, always poking the ball away first before upending the opposing player and avoiding the referee's wrath. He also commands his players on the pitch, especially on the defensive end, directing them to go guard an uncovered player

I see the influence of van Dijk on the way Ahmed plays defence. He mirrors the Dutchman's movements and positioning. He has his vision. Ahmed can defend. His body becomes a magnet for the football, hitting his thigh, torso, and foot but never his hand. Whenever a ball comes perilously close to the net, Ahmed is there to clear it from harm's way. Each of his tackles is perfectly timed. Like the Dutchman, Ahmed is built like a boulder. He is strong and agile. I have watched him pin players against the wall encircling the pitch, like the boards of a hockey rink, and easily muscle the ball away from him and fire a pass up field. The strategizing and fluidity of the football pitch concentrate his mind. He appears studious, meticulously analyzing the play unfolding before him. What will his next chess move be? All other troublesome thoughts go away for the match's duration. Ahmed's blistering eyes stay fastened to the events around him, never straying or wavering. His concentration is absolute. And his teammates respect the quality of his play because they listen to him when he barks out an order or he points to an opposing player who is running about unguarded. Spectators see it, too. After every nice tackle or block, they shout, "Eh van Dijk."

Ahmed is not always so graceful on the pitch. Arguments do sometimes erupt, and Ahmed enjoys directing his rage towards the referee, who in his mind cannot make a correct call. "Eh, what foul, ref?" is one of the young Egyptian's favourite phrases, as is "Eh, ref, that was a foul." Ahmed, of course, has never committed a foul in his life yet is routinely subjected to them. Once, a teammate of his substituted for him, and Ahmed came and sat next to me in the stands. In a voice that should have been lower in volume, Ahmed declared without a hint of discretion the referee was garbage and did not know what he was doing. Whether or not the referee was garbage was debatable; what was not in question, however, was his hearing, as he heard Ahmed's opinion of him, walked right up to Ahmed, and flashed him a yellow card.

Ahmed's Achilles' heel is tobacco. He smokes regularly. Friends and acquaintances are always giving him their small bags of tobacco and paper so he may roll a cigarette. Ahmed is that friend who always bums. A cigarette is usually balanced between his fingers; a trail of ash follows him around. The habit, as to be expected, has taken a toll on his physical endurance. Even though his economy of movement lessens the expenditure of energy, his smoking still wreaks havoc on his stamina. After only ten or fifteen minutes on the pitch, he asks to be substituted.

Ahmed finds peace in football, in its rhythms and rules. But the realities of camp await him whenever he is not on the pitch. Throughout his stay in Samos, authorities have rejected Ahmed's claim for asylum several times. They have judged him unworthy of protection, even though they know he will not return to Egypt, and they have neither the energy nor the resources to deport him. They want to test his endurance, to make his existence in Greece so harsh that he may consider returning to his Egyptian village. They submit him to examination after examination. How desperately does he want his papers? How many years is he willing to sacrifice at the camp? The waiting proved too much for another, older Egyptian, a friend of Ahmed's, who chose to return voluntarily to Egypt after three years of waiting. Voluntary return is a program managed by the IOM that facilitates the self-deportation of asylum seekers. They arrange the necessary paperwork and even provide financial aid to help the asylum seeker return and then reintegrate into their old life, the one from which they had spent years fleeing. Choosing self-deportation does not mean the asylum seeker was lying about the reasons they fled—that is, they did not face persecution or hardship in the country of birth. Rather, their choice only reinforces the degrading conditions of those facing an eternity of legal limbo. Interminable waiting pushes a terrible choice on a displaced person. It is sometimes better to go back to danger and uncertainty but have a degree of autonomy than waste years in a refugee camp. A refugee camp is a repository of waste——wasted talents, skills, ambitions, and dreams. It is a museum of dashed hope.

Ahmed will not go back. He remains at the mercy of camp authorities and the bureaucrats deciding his fate. And for some reason, they have said he cannot leave the camp. The system has denied him permission to leave, only for those essential appointments in the city, like with his doctor, lawyer, or psychologist. Each resident is at the mercy of what the computer might say on any given day, about the arbitrary whims of a system prioritizing control over all else. The camp, of course, is not a prison, not in the technical sense. Residents are free to go if they so choose, but those who leave without authorized permission cannot return, leaving them at the mercy of the streets and undocumented status. Unless Ahmed wants to take his chances on the move without any resources or any real legal protections, he will do as he is told: He will stay behind the camp's fences and barbed wire.

It's Saturday, and the camp is quiet. I am in the laundry container, hoping people come and retrieve the forty or so laundry bags I washed. I have sat them outside because they would take up too much room in the container. The multicoloured bags look like a patch of marshmallows. Today, the coordinators have organized a beach day for all the community volunteers, an afternoon full of swimming, eating, and general merriment. As the temperature has risen throughout May, many community volunteers have suggested a beach day, time away from the boiling camp to lounge on one of Samos's beautiful beaches and float on the Aegean. Ahmed led the charge for a beach day, even though he cannot swim, something he admits with great embarrassment. He wants to learn. The shame eats away at him for lacking this skill most seem to possess. Beach days would allow him to practice and become more comfortable in the water and move within it as gracefully as he does across a football pitch.

But when Ahmed enters the laundry container on this Saturday morning, it's not with the enthusiasm one would expect on Beach Day. He is listless and despondent and sinks into the chair next to me. A lethargy has gripped him. His usual boisterousness has departed, leaving only a shell. He tells me camp authorities will not permit him to join the others at the beach this afternoon. He scratches his leg and rubs his hand through his hair. He is becoming edgy and unwieldy. The prospect of being imprisoned in the camp weighs on him. He fidgets in his seat. His anxiousness sparks my anxiety. I tread lightly. He wants a cigarette. He tells me about the medication the doctor has him taking. He does not like doctors. He once hid in the laundry container when his doctor arrived at camp to avoid seeing them. He shows me the pills the doctor has him taking, which I recognize, from personal experience, as a kind of antidepressant. I wonder whether the situation he finds himself in may better explain his depression than his brain's chemical makeup. He hates taking them. They make him feel tired and lazy—not great for football. The doctor watches Ahmed take them, making sure he swallows. A friend of his hides the pill away under his tongue, pretends to swallow it, and then spits it out as soon as the doctor is far from sight. Ahmed will practice this. He's moved to another topic.

He wants me to call Frank to find out why he cannot leave. There's no answer. But I tell Ahmed that Frank will hopefully resolve the issue. He will try his best. His absolute best. "You see this life, Canadia." This is what he calls me: Canadia. He has a habit of calling volunteers by their nationality. Liam, from the Netherlands, he calls Dutch, with whom he always seems to have a problem. "This Dutch boy is no good," he often says. Or "This Dutch boy is a big problem." He is half-joking, half-serious. This

Dutch boy has done a few things to cross Ahmed. During a football match against another NGO, Ahmed and Liam were teammates, and Dutch allegedly made a few poor decisions, which cost the Egyptian a victory. The Dutch boy also forgot to bring Ahmed's favourite jacket to the laundry in the city to be washed. Ahmed's opinion of you can quickly change.

I ask Ahmed if he has seen Dutch this morning, hoping to take his mind off the beach and direct it towards one of his favourite pastimes: criticizing the Dutch boy. He does not bite. "This life is hard," he only says, looking at his fingernails and then at me. "You see my life, Canadia." He grins. "You see how hard it is." He then looks at me. "I could cry but what would be the point?" These situations require a delicate balance between embracing and distancing. I want to validate his experiences and rally with him against the unjustness of his present circumstances, against his effective imprisonment, but I worry that outrage without results will only worsen the situation. Ahmed needs more than cheerleaders for his cause; he requires real solutions, which I cannot provide. I do not get to share in his anger to the same extent because the bars surrounding Ahmed do not surround me. I am not trapped on a Greek island. Volunteers provide a canvas on which asylum seekers can express themselves without consequence or judgment. We listen, but we also leave. If we provide too much emotional support or become too invested in their cases, we risk evolving into a crutch for asylum seekers to support themselves. And if that crutch suddenly disappears, the asylum seeker may fall hard. Yet my reactions to Ahmed's words cannot be cold indifference; there must also exist a level of humanity in my response, a sense of connection. Ahmed should feel his words have reached me. I can only show I have heard him.

His words have reached me, and his story will not become lost in the recesses of my mind. He has affected me.

Ahmed does not go to the beach today.

The People's Clothing

When the authorities closed down the jungle campsite in September 2021 and transferred its inhabitants to the new camp outside of city, a debate emerged among the various NGOs in Samos about whether they would agree to go and work in the camp. Some thought that by doing so, they would legitimize the camp's existence and subsidize work that should be done by camp management and those bodies funding them. Other NGOs felt withholding their services from the camp would not incentivize camp management to do more; from their experiences working with authorities on other islands, the coordinators thought they would let the conditions deteriorate. Authorities believed they offered asylum seekers nothing more than a bed, a roof, and some food. No laundry, no classes, no programs, no support. Our NGO believed if they did not go to the camp, residents, not camp authorities, would suffer. When I first arrived, I was skeptical of the NGO's argument to stay, since it was subsidizing work that should be done and paid for by camp management. They were supporting the functioning of a refugee camp. Take their laundry service. We wash the clothes of all camp residents, between four and five hundred people on any given day, with only eight washing machines, which were not provided by camp management. No. The NGO relocated the machines from Lesvos, from another one of their projects. Camp management provides no support to the laundry centre—no funds for detergent, powder, plastic bags, tags, or any of the other little things necessary to keep the project going. On some mornings, we arrive to work to find black bags full of blankets left on the doorstep by camp management. We are expected to wash them. At other times, some random camp worker appears with clothes a family has left behind and wants us to wash them, regardless of how many orders we have to finish for the camp residents. Their sense of entitlement angers me, especially since they provide nothing to the project. The laundry project has become theirs, just another camp appendage, to be used whenever they need something washed. I asked Frank one day what would happen if they just stopped their laundry service, if they took their machines and left. Would the resulting tension—of people not having the ability to wash their clothes—force the camp's hand? Would they buckle and buy washing machines? Frank did not equivocate. They would let the residents suffer, he said. He has worked in Greece too long and seen too much to believe camp authorities would replace any machines they took. He knows the callousness of Greek authorities to asylum seekers runs deep. I remain skeptical. I cannot fathom how a refugee camp, especially one as modern as this one, could forego having a laundry station. It just did not seem realistic, but I soon realized I had underestimated the indifference of camp management.

Now and then, crackly voices sound from speakers situated around the camp. They usually inform a camp resident they are requested to visit camp authorities. Could so and so from Cameroon please report to the office? It reminds me of high school when an administrator's voice would break the monotony of a class and request the presence of some teenager at the office. I would secretly wonder what the kid had done or what had befallen them for the office to request their presence. Was it good or bad news? Would they receive a punishment or a reward? A similar internal questioning must reverberate through the asylum seeker as they make their way to the camp offices, although with much greater consequences. The absolute worst that could happen to the high school kid would be suspension, for maybe a few days. Not a minor sentence, to be sure, but not a decision that would steal years of the kid's life. The kid would return to school. We would see them again walking the halls and talking with their friends. The asylum seeker walks to the office with much greater anxiety because most of the time, their presence is requested to provide an update on their asylum case. Within a few minutes, they will know whether the Greek authorities believed their tale of suffering and granted them asylum or whether their story had too many holes or question marks, leaving them undeserving of protection. In a few minutes, they will know whether they have been awarded Greek ID, the first step to getting a refugee passport, or whether they must apply again for asylum, sacrificing more months, maybe even years, of their life for their dream of Europe.

On other occasions, the crackly voices only announce more mundane news surrounding the camp. Because of the camp's multicultural nature, they repeat the message in several different languages, all staticky and difficult to understand. I can barely make out the messages spoken in English. One particular message grabs the camp's attention, as the words are spoken in English, French, Arabic, Somali, and Farsi: The camp has a problem with its water supply, and until further notice, authorities will be rationing water, opening the taps for two two-hour slots, one in the morning and the other in the evening. Emilie and I laugh at the absurdity of the news, especially considering we have eight machines full of clothes that have suddenly stopped working. We remove the sopping wet clothes from the machines, ring the excess liquid from the fabric to the best of our ability, and leave them drying in the sun. As we work, we try to think of a plan about how to continue providing our laundry services without water. Camp authorities are typically opaque and nonresponsive when asked when the water might return, and residents keep dropping off bags, maybe hoping beyond hope the water shortages have not affected the laundry. Emilie rings another NGO assisting displaced people in Vathy that has an underused wash centre at their disposal. This NGO was responsible for washing the camp residents' clothing before the new camp opened and asylum seekers still lived in the makeshift cape. Since that camp has closed and the asylum seekers have left the city, their washing machines sit silent most of the week.

After much discussion between Emilie and the other NGO, they let us use their wash centre on the days they are closed. We arrange the logistics of getting the bags from the camp to the city centre, washing them, and returning them, all within a relatively short timeframe. Organizing the pieces does prove to be a headache, but we craft a plan, which involves me doing the laundry at the wash centre. The plan seems manageable because we assume the camp cannot go without water for an extended period. One or two days maximum. Nothing more. Residents will need to shower, use the toilet, cook their meals, and clean their containers—all of which require water. Going beyond a day or two would throw the camp into chaos; residents would rightly protest their shoddy treatment and demand authorities please return the water. Yet one day and then another passes, and no news comes about when the water will flow freely again from the taps and showerheads. A voice sometimes emerges from the loudspeakers telling everyone the brief window when water will be available and to use it wisely. Residents then go running to their containers to shower or clean dishes. Rumours swirl about the cause of the shortage; some say it's an engineering issue, and others say the spring the camp sits on has run out of water. The camp's indifference to the problem is striking. It's a collective shrug of the shoulders. Where is the urgency? The embarrassment? I imagine what would happen if Vathy stopped receiving water, if the townsfolk suddenly had none for their showers, cooking, and cleaning, what would happen if their demands for an explanation and then for a solution were met by cold nonchalance, what would happen if after two weeks no water poured from their showerheads or taps? Heads would roll. The local government and city officials would beg for forgiveness, and some would not survive the fallout. There would be consequences. Restitution.

Whether or not the camp has water does not trouble the private security folks. The lack of water does not jolt them from their game plan. Rules and regulations must still be adhered to, which makes our jobs even more difficult. Every laundry bag we take from the camp to be washed in Vathy must pass through the X-ray machine, and the same must happen when they return. The sight of volunteers placing dozens of blue, pink, and green plastic bags filled with dirty clothes upon the conveyor belt to be scanned for contraband must be absurd to any passerby, anyone who does not work at the camp. Our work attracts a crowd of private security and police officers, whose working relationship has never been made clear to me. Once upon returning the laundry to the camp, something on the screen catches the eye of a police officer, who then instructs the private security officer to go rummaging through the bag to find the suspect item. He unties one green bag and goes digging through its contents, passing his hands through the warm, clean clothing of one resident. His search is thorough; his fingers reach every nook and cranny of the bag. Watching him hunt within the bag fills me with anger. I understand the logic of checking bags, the arguments around safety and security, but there is something obscene about how much attention this man gives the green bag. His thoroughness disgusts me. His sense of importance repulses me. He must feel he is doing his job well, keeping the camp safe from whatever he imagines could be smuggled within the folds of a t-shirt or pair of jeans. Yet it is we who are doing his job. It is we who have found a solution to the laundry situation, who are dragging the laundry bags into town. Before, when security forced us to scan every item we either bought or had delivered to the camp, including boxes of sugar and even baguettes, we would joke about how security had finally foiled our plot to smuggle drugs inside baguettes. I am not laughing now. When his search finally finishes, when it yields nothing prohibited or threatening, he ties up the bag, hands it to me, and thanks me for my patience. It's all I can do to keep my veneer of professionalism from cracking.

At the day's end, Liam and Zahir, a volunteer from Afghanistan, cart thirty-five bags of laundry to security while I finish some work in the laundry container. The afternoon sun is particularly brazen today, and most residents have sought refuge in the handful of shady spots. I have only been here a month, and I already feel the camp's atmosphere weighing on me. It's the colour of the place. The awful greyness of the containers, the whiteness of the pebbles, the shiny silver of the fences and gates—all create a heavy monotony. It's the colour of a hospital waiting room, some sterile place, devoid of life. It's the colour of purgatory. The sunlight brings this dullness cruelly to life, revealing the camp's nothingness. Although I could wax romantically about how the residents' unique personalities enliven the camp or about how the camp cannot destroy the passions and hopes of each guest, it's hard not to succumb to the idea of the camp as an extralegal space that transforms human beings into only an assemblage of molecules and organs that must be kept alive. But the residents, of course, do rebel against the camp's logic; there are small acts of resistance and larger critiques of the system. One Somali asylum seeker said to me, "We came here for asylum, not food or shelter." Another young man from Djibouti more bluntly put it: "We are rats in a cage." But the crushing monotony of the place tempers even the wildest souls. The Djibouti man said to me: "Outside in the city, life happens. You forget about the camp. You forget about your problems. You have freedom. Inside is nothing. Inside you only have time to think about rejection after rejection. Inside is control."

Liam has returned with a single cart carrying a half-dozen bags. He looks annoyed. "What happened?" I ask. His fingers begin to untie a bag. "They say we cannot take camp blankets outside of the camp." He must be joking, but I know he is not. Yet I ask again. "You cannot be serious." He looks at me. "Private security phoned camp management to ask whether we could take blankets out to wash, and they said we couldn't." I do not understand. "But we have taken them out before." Liam just shrugs. "Don't they know the camp has no water?" He nods. "Well, how the fuck can we wash these blankets without water?" I say this too loudly. Sitting a dozen metres from me is Kai, who hears my profanity-laced tirade and laughs. "Jesse Lingard," he shouts. "You must follow rules and regulations. Rules and regulations." I laugh too, as the absurdity of the situation is too much and shout back: "Kai, I have been smuggling out blankets to sell on the streets of Vathy for the last months, and they have finally caught on." We are both laughing hard now. "How much did you sell each for," Kai wants to know. "Three euros," I shout. Kai is unimpressed. "You should have asked for five at least."

It is weeks before the water returns.

Fadi and Nurul

Ahmed has me by the arm and pulls me into Chai Point, where people can enjoy a cup of tea, print or photocopy some documents, or socialize. Tonight, however, the room has transformed into a dance hall. Music blasts from the interior, and moving bodies fill the space. I had seen the commotion unfold and did my best to give it a wide birth, as I have always tried to avoid such social eruptions, but Ahmed keeps pulling me towards it. "Come on Canadia," he insists. I follow and prepare myself for the blasts.

A dozen or so people have crammed inside and have succumbed to the beats of the Middle Eastern music blaring from the speakers. At the centre of the commotion is Fadi, a young man from Syria. A circle has formed around him, as if drawn by his energy, and the spectators clap and sway, watching as Fadi contorts his body to the music's beats. He has his shoulder-length hair in a bun, and a cigarette dangles from his mouth. Sweat drips from his forehead and stains pop up over his shirt. But this perspiration results in no shame on the part of Fadi because here in this makeshift club, sweat is expected. It's the body's reaction to exertion, a way cooling mechanism to prolong activity. If you are not sweating, you are not doing it right.

Fadi and his brother have been on Samos for three years. They arrived in Greece after public attitudes towards Syrians had turned hostile. Humanitarian fatigue had set in among the Greeks, who wanted a return to normalcy. Attention had turned to other crises and other wars; some governments declared Syria safe to return. So, Fadi and his brother waited and waited, watching as many received their identification papers and left the camp and Greece behind, but they did not grow desperate. They persevered until word arrived he and his brother had received asylum. And tonight, we celebrate.

I find myself in the circle watching Fadi dance. His joy is electric and propels each one of us to match his energy, to mirror his movements. Even though the onlookers, the fellow revellers, have no personal cause to celebrate, as their fate still resides in the decision-making of some mysterious bureaucrat, they shout and clap for Fadi. Some have known him for months, even years; some have just met him. But they are here to sip from his joy because they must believe soon they too will be dancing to celebrate displacement's end.

Everyone dances, and everyone takes a turn to jump into the circle's centre and to interpret the music in whatever way they see fit. Fadi even points to me to jump into the fray, but I politely decline with a hand over my heart and a slight bow. I just keep the beat. Images of Fadi flash through my mind. He smokes cigarettes while playing goalkeeper in a children's football match. He helps others with their English work. He tackles a rival player on the football pitch. He chops onions and eggplant in the food container. He prints and photocopies documents for fellow Arabic speakers. He answers questions from new arrivals. And now he dances.

The intellectual part of me knows Fadi's journey has only just begun. One struggle has ended; many more await. But for these brief moments, I quiet those lines of argument and lose myself in this moment's beauty. Outside the security guards watch us, I know, but they are not welcome in here. I am grateful to be a part of this ritual of coming back to life—this act of resurrection.

Hilal and his wife, a couple from Syria, have also received word the authorities have given them asylum. Hilal is a teddy bear, a big, burly, and cuddly fellow. He is quiet and keeps to himself but can cook a delicious meal. I would see him in chopping vegetables, choosing spices, and preparing rice. He speaks the language of the kitchen and has the enviable ability to see disparate ingredients and immediately grasp how they would taste together. During Ramadan, he would set to work hours before the sun set, transforming those ingredients into a wonderful iftar meal the whole team enjoyed. Hilal keeps his emotions hidden away, at least from what I have seen. You can never ascertain the mood gripping him; even life-changing moments have difficulty budging his stoic exterior.

Emilie and I are working in the kitchen when Hilal enters stealthily, appearing in the doorway as by a magic trick. Something seems different about him this morning, as a little grin has crept across his face, betraying his typical emotionless countenance. When he tells us he has received refugee status, his grin explodes into a smile and gives Emilie a big bear hug. His happiness is genuine, and the relief relaxes his large frame. I shake his hand and congratulate him. But as I do, Nurul enters, sees the commotion, and understands its significance. He turns to Hilal and asks whether he got asylum. The big man nods and smiles. The look now taking hold of the Bangladeshi is a mixture of pleasure and pain. Hilal's news brings genuine joy to the man; there is happiness in his smile. Yet behind Nurul's congratulations and handshaking lies something less savoury: disillusionment and disappointment. Samos has been Nurul's home for years now, and each second he has lived on the island, he has wanted to receive the news Hilal just announced. Emilie sees Nurul's efforts trying to be happy for Hilal while managing his own emotions—keeping those waves of hopelessness from spoiling Hilal's news. His time will come soon, she says. Nurul nods as Emilie and Hilal exit out the door.

We are alone. Nurul suddenly has his arms around my body, embracing me in a desperate hug. His touch takes me by surprise, but I return the gesture. I know what he wants: comfort. And permission. It's okay to feel heartbroken for having to wait another day in camp while a friend gets a new lease on life. It's okay to carry conflicting feelings: to be sad and happy at your friend's news. Your time will come, Nurul. Hang on a little longer. Before long, we will be celebrating your news. Before long, you will be far from here. I say all this without speaking. In the laundry container, we hug in silence.

Aegean Ghosts

One hundred years before Amena, Sayem, Kai, and Ahmed crossed the Aegean searching for safety, the islands were the site of another episode of mass displacement: the 1923 Greek-Turkish population exchange. The Ottoman Empire fell apart during the first twenty years of the twentieth century. Nationalist movements in Serbia, Greece, and Bulgaria clamoured for independence, and as violence and instability spread throughout the empire's hinterlands, its previously ethnically mixed populations became decidedly not. In the Balkans, the independence movements forced many Muslims to flee to Anatolia. The Balkan Wars of 1912–13, and the subsequent outbreak of the First World War, encouraged Ottoman authorities to relocate troublesome non-Muslims also to Anatolia, joining other Muslims fleeing the Christian ascendancy in the Balkans.

Greece saw the First World War and the evaporation of the Ottoman Empire as an opportunity to reclaim land lost since the 1453 sacking of Constantinople. The war would fulfill the nineteenth-century irredentist agenda of Megali Idea, the Great Idea, in which Greece would take Istanbul and much of Anatolia. With the Paris Peace Conference underway, and the Allied powers eagerly carving out the remaining pieces of the Ottoman Empire, Greek forces landed in Izmir and occupied the surrounding region. The 1920 Treaty of Sevres granted Greece administrative powers over large swaths of the Anatolian region. Although Sultan Mehmed VI had signed the treaty, he controlled less and less of Anatolia, losing political sway to the resurgent nationalists, led by Mustafa Kemel, who desired to create a modern Turkish nation-state.

Despite the growing strength of the Kemelists and the waning support of the Great Powers, the Greek forces continued to press into Anatolia, committing atrocities against the local Muslim population as they marched. In the summer of 1922, however, the Turkish forces convincingly stopped the Greek advance, pushing them back to the coast, and committed atrocities against the local Christian population in retaliation. As the Turkish army advanced, Christians fled their villages towards the coast and then crossed the Aegean into Greece. By the end of 1922, well over one million refugees had arrived in Greece from Anatolia, unleashing a dire humanitarian crisis.

In response to the crisis and the ongoing conflict in Anatolia, the League of Nations started peace talks in Lausanne. The talks resulted in the Convention of 30 January 1923 Concerning the Exchange of Greek and Turkish Populations and eventually in the solidifying of the modern borders of Greece and Türkiye. Article 1 of the Convention defined those individuals to be included in the exchange: "Turkish nationals of the Greek Orthodox religion established in Turkish territory" and "Greek nationals of the Moslem religion established in Greek territory." The Convention continued: "These persons shall not return to live in Türkiye or Greece without the authorisation of the Turkish Government or of the Greek Government respectively." Christians in Türkiye and Muslims in Greece had no say in the matter; authorities mandated their displacement. It was absolute. Those who had fled with only the clothes on their back could not return. The population exchange should not be understood in contemporary terms as repatriation; the displaced would not be allowed to return. The break was perpetual, forever.

Hellenic communities had lived in Anatolia since antiquity and Orthodox Christians for centuries. For these people, the exchange represented nothing but exile from their homelands, a ripping of roots from the ground. The Muslims of Greece, similarly, experienced the expulsion as a traumatic severing from their homes, especially since most had not been affected by the hostilities between the two states. In total, approximately 1.5 million people were forcibly exchanged.

Although the agreement might have saved lives in the short term, its segregationist ethos has had long-term ramifications. The agreement solidified the nation as a repository for a single people and a single identity and hardened national identity (and citizenship) as a prerequisite for belonging. Nation-building fears alterity because it undermines the formation of a distinct identity; to formulate a national identity, nations need social and cultural boundaries that separate themselves from others. National legends and myths rarely incorporate diversity into them, and those left out of national mythologies—minority groups—often find themselves outside the nation looking in. Nations represent a people, just one. The unmixing of Greece and Türkiye in 1923 cemented a mistrust of cosmopolitan and multicultural alternatives.

The agreement's legacy can be seen in the hostile treatment people like Amena, Sayem, Kai, and Ahmed receive as they enter Greece from Turkiye. Yet people still cross the Aegean looking for safety. They flout the nation-state's rules in search of sanctuary. There is nothing new about their movements and goals. Not in 2022, 1923, or 1823. What has become novel is the lengths to which the nation-state's representatives will go to enforce these borders and how much of their souls they will sacrifice to protect the sanctity of the nation-state project. Borders are new; movement is not. That desire to control the movement of people still haunts the contemporary Aegean.

5
Nicosia

August 2022

An arrival centre in Nicosia, nestled on the sleepy side street of Perikleous in the capital's old walled city, has assisted asylum seekers in finding a foothold in Cyprus since 2019. About three hundred newcomers seek help at this unassuming centre every week, but during the off-hours, silence reigns, save for the purring of kitty cats slumbering in pockets of shade. Tourists do not give Perikleous much attention; of far more interest is the next street over, Ledras, which is filled with restaurants, souvenir shops, and ice cream parlors. Its terminus is also a checkpoint, a border zone between the island's southern Greek portion and the Turkish northern one, a stark reminder that Nicosia remains the only divided capital city in the world. On weekdays, however, the number of asylum seekers waiting outside the centre on Perikleous outnumbers those tourists sauntering towards Ledras for a Starbucks and a scone. Contemporary forms of forced migration meet historical ones in Nicosia.

Cyprus, the tiny island nation in the Mediterranean, has become an unlikely hotspot for asylum seekers. After Austria, it has the highest ratio of asylum seekers to citizens in the EU. As of December 2022, close to thirty thousand applications, made over several years, were still awaiting adjudication. The influx has strained Cypriot services, with a lack of staff and political will to process applications faster. Arriving asylum seekers proceed to Pournara refugee camp, where they officially apply for asylum, a process that can take several weeks. Officially built to shelter one thousand people, the camp easily houses twice that number. The conditions are overcrowded and unsanitary. On its outskirts, an informal camp has emerged, reminiscent of the tent-and-tarp camps of Calais and Greece.

Yet displacement is not new to Cyprus. Division and forced migration mark the island's modern history. On August 16, 1974, a ceasefire was declared between the southern and northern belligerents, and the UN drew a 180km line splitting the island into two parts. This "Green Line" acts as a buffer zone between the Greek and Turkish Cypriot communities, a temporary solution that has lasted for almost fifty years.

Nicosia itself bears the scars of this division. As the last divided capital in Europe, some of its streets end in stacks of barrels and rolls of barbed wire, a stark reminder of the conflict that displaced hundreds of thousands. Patrolled by the UN, the Green Line is only a few metres wide in some parts and several kilometres in others. Nicosia bends to the line. Walking along it becomes nonsensical; straight lines are nonexistent. Greek and Turkish Cypriots live so close together in some areas they can hurl insults over the wall with expectations they will be heard. The UN estimates the 1974 invasion resulted in two hundred thousand internally displaced persons: 165,000 in the South and 45,000 in the North.

Today, new asylum seekers from Cameroon, Nigeria, the DRC, and Afghanistan arrive in Cyprus, seeking peace and a chance at a new life. Many take a flight to Istanbul and then catch another plane to Ercan airport in the Turkish-occupied north. From there, they walk into Europe and apply for asylum. The Ledras checkpoint is one of the least dangerous EU border crossings for these newcomers. In the shadow of Cyprus's unresolved history of displacement, the centre offers pieces of hope to these refugees, grappling with their own histories of forced migration and trying to restart their lives on this divided island. Here are some of their stories.

Patrice

The centre works to protect the dignity of its members. It provides services for new arrivals, such as CV writing workshops, barber services, and help with applying for a labour card, but the real draw is the market, where people can shop for the groceries they need as if they were in Lagos or Kinshasa. The caveat is they only have 840 points to spend, or the equivalent of 8.40 euros. They must choose which items are essential and which are superfluous. A loaf of fresh bread costs one hundred points, or one euro. A glove of garlic is twenty-five points or twenty-five cents. A package of spaghetti is seventy-five points or seventy-five cents. Some of the more expensive and in-demand items—such as bread, rice, cooking oil, and flour—have a limitation of one per person. Dignity is predicated upon agency, that is, the ability to act, which involves making choices, however constrained.

Patrice must choose. He is a young man from the DRC, and this is his first time at the market. I explain the system in my halting

French while he scans the items, already making mental calculations. I hand him a basket and ask whether he would like a calculator to help with the additions. He declines and moves to the shelves. Watching him shop, I wonder what I would buy if I only had 8.40 euros to spend at my local supermarket for the week. None of my shopping has ever been so dire. Patrice studies the items on the shelves, notes the prices, and decides what is and is not essential—decisions about which I know nothing.

Patrice puts his basket down at check-out. Judging by the number and type of items he has, I know he has gone over his allotted points. The centre uses iPads for check-out, and each item on the shelf has a corresponding button on the machine. The volunteer only needs to press the button, and the pad does the rest. After I tally Patrice's bread, pasta, oil, sardines, milk, flour, shampoo, soap, and toothpaste, the machine tells me he has gone several hundred points over and must return some items to the shelves. His look is one of shock and despondency. He is surprised and disappointed so little could cost so much. He evaluates the food and does more calculations. At three hundred points, the oil is expensive, and if he were to put it back, he still would have points remaining. Patrice brushes away my suggestion, insisting the oil is essential, and although it costs a lot, the quantity, one litre, will last him months.

He hands me his pasta packages, but he is still over. He sacrifices a few tins of sardines. Still over. Then goes the oil. Throughout the process, Patrice can only laugh while I remove each item from his pile. How he sacrificed his pasta and oil so quickly suggests he possesses neither the tools nor the power to cook the spaghetti. Many members will select items requiring the least effort to prepare because they have nothing to cook with wherever they stay.

After the subtractions, Patrice has an extra one hundred points to spend. He analyzes the shelf and asks what he can get with the amount. Packaged croissants. Instant noodles. Instead, Patrice returns with four drinking boxes, which at twenty-five points a box do give one hundred points, but he has not seen, and I have failed to indicate, the little sign on the shelf, underneath the neatly stacked drinking boxes, saying members can only take two per person. Upon telling Patrice this rule, in my "so sorry" voice, which I have perfected over the previous months working with displaced persons, he sighs in frustration and returns two boxes to the shelf.

This adding and subtracting go on for another ten minutes, almost reaching the point of absurdity, until he reaches 840 with his selection of a small piece of chocolate, worth ten points. His final order looks nothing like the one he first brought to checkout. There are more packages of noodles and tins of sardines and less pasta and cereal. Yet despite the disappointment Patrice must feel about how little 840 points can buy, he still thanks me, again and again, as he places his food into a shopping bag.

Jacob

Members cannot share their cards. A friend cannot shop for a member, even if they are sick. Although such a rule may seem draconian, it helps control who shops at the centre and when. Exchanging cards leads to chaos and confusion. Generally, the system works well, but contentious moments arise, especially when we have evidence of a card being used when the member claims they did not. Whenever someone shops, the volunteer checks the member's card to verify they are shopping the correct day and have not visited the shop that week. At the beginning of every week, Marina, the coordinator, prints the shoppers' list, which contains all the week's shoppers and the day they should visit. When a member hands their card to a volunteer, they check the list, find the member, and then cross off the name. If a member arrives and has already had their name crossed off, it means they have already shopped and cannot do so again.

Jacob hands me his card, takes a basket, and heads towards the shelves. Judging by the confident way he moves through the shop, I know this visit is not his first. His card says this visit is his final one, which means I should confiscate it at the end of his shopping. Members can only shop for four weeks. I look for his identification number on the printout to verify this is his day to shop. But I notice his name has already been crossed out—he has already shopped this week. I search for his number on the iPad, and it reveals he did his final shop on Wednesday, two days earlier. I call Jacob over to the counter and explain since he shopped on Wednesday, he cannot do so again today. His reaction somewhat surprises me: I had expected him to acknowledge his error and go about his day. He is adamant he never visited the shop on Wednesday; this is his first shop of the week. I double-check his name against the sheet and iPad, but each suggests he did visit us on Wednesday. I gently ask Jacob whether he gave his card to a friend to shop, but the man flatly denies the question—the accusation—and maintains he has not visited the shop this week. Jacob never loses his cool. He explains his case in precise wording, each sentence succinctly linking to the next, which contrasts wildly with my own, as I stumble from word to word, trying to convince Jacob my refusal to let him shop has nothing to do with him personally but with the centre's rules. I show him the printed spreadsheet with his name crossed out, the iPad, and the record of his Wednesday shop. All this fails to placate Jacob because he believes what he says: He did not shop on Wednesday, and it is our mistake. I feel like ripping up the sheet and imploring him to take what he needs. I want to apologize for accusing him of lying because I do not believe he is. I hate this role of gatekeeper I must enact. But I know such an impetuous course of action would only result in the shop's quick disintegration; the shelves would soon empty, and the doors would become forever locked. The rules exist for a reason—to assist as many people as possible within the budget we have. It's not for me, a short-term volunteer, to question the shop's logic, its modus operandi, because it must continue to function long after I leave.

I ask Jacob to wait a moment and go look for a more experienced volunteer to ask what to do. I find Fadi, a volunteer from Denmark via Syria, at the registration desk and explain the situation. He is businesslike in his appraisal of Jacob's case. Was his name crossed out on the list? Yes. Was there a record of his transaction on the iPad? Yes. "So, that's it then," Fadi says, shrugging his shoulders. "But he is adamant he did not shop on Wednesday," I counter, "and did not give his card to anyone else." My argument does not persuade him. With great calm and precision, he explains we must trust the checks in our system, and since Jacob's case failed both, we have to respect that; otherwise, we risk compromising the entire project. Fadi says no more, and I understand I will have to relate the bad news to Jacob and experience another difficult conversation.

Humanitarian work involves more denying than granting. Volunteers become good at saying "no." We become robotic in our body language as well in the words we use: "I am sorry, but"; "I understand, but"; and "I can't imagine, but." Learning to say no to people in need is difficult. We have to harden ourselves to pleas of mercy. We have to drink a little cement. Such a transformation is necessary in the field regardless of how hard the task. We perform a specific service, and to step outside our particular remit is to invite disaster. Once we take it upon ourselves to make exceptions for each person we meet to say "yes" when we should say "no," we jeopardize the entire operation. Rejecting the pleas of another does become easier over time; repetition births a sense of normalcy even to the most outrageous of situations. Yet upon my walk back to Jacob and his empty bag, I feel one hundred pounds heavier, the decision weighing me down, punishing my shoulders, back, and hips, until I want nothing more than to flee.

I want to grant Jacob permission to shop, but I cannot. Jacob senses my decision when I ask to speak with him. Positive news requires little explanation, very few words; negative news, though, involves deep conversation. Jacob's eyes do not leave my own. I have his complete attention. His concentration is mine. I tell him how sorry I am, but we cannot help him because, according to our records, someone with his card visited the shop on Wednesday and took his weekly allotment of items. Jacob does his best to swallow his mounting frustration, since this is the fourth or fifth time he will tell me no one using his card visited the shop on Wednesday. "I know, I know," I reply, in the most sympathetic and voice I can muster, "but our records indicate otherwise." I do realize the total and utter disrespect my previous statement casts towards Jacob: I am calling him a liar in a diplomatic way. Insults have never sounded so pleasant. Jacob's breathing remains controlled, as perhaps he senses how little sway he holds here and how pointless it would be to waste energy trying to convince me he is not a liar. I tell him how little money our organization has to buy food, so it must be distributed in the fairest way possible. We cannot allow people to shop twice a week. For a moment, Jacob's calm demeanour breaks, and anger bubbles to the surface. "I did not shop this week," he says. And I want to say I believe him, but if I do, if I validate his claim, then what possible reason do I have to forbid him from shopping? Our conversation moves in circles. I feel dizzy. I want this to end. "I'm sorry," I say again, "but according to our records, somebody using your card did shop this week." Jacob looks at me hard. He is a shield, yet a crack of understanding does break through, weaknesses emerge, soft spots, as he seems to accept, however reluctantly, that he will return to his shelter emptyhanded, wherever and whatever that may be. I wonder about the decisions and experiences that have led him here, to stand in front of me, a volunteer of great means, and to have his request for food denied. "So, I cannot shop today," Jacob says, summarizing what has taken me several minutes to say. I confirm: "No, Jacob, you cannot shop today." He looks again at the shelves and then at me. "So, where can I do my shopping?" The question renders me speechless, as all my answers are predicated upon the ability to support oneself. If you do not have money, where can you do your shopping? My impotence frustrates me. Gatekeepers who deny access should have alternatives, but I have none. Jacob expects an answer, I sense it, but he receives none from me, only the useless phrase "I don't know." With that, Jacob turns and leaves the market and vanishes into the streets of Nicosia.

Claire and Fabrice

Sometimes, we make mistakes. A Cameroonian mother pushes her stroller into the shop; the baby is sound asleep. She hands my colleague, Brit, her card, positions the stroller to the side, out of the way, and grabs a basket to shop. The woman's name, Claire, has been crossed from the list, but Brit has difficulty conveying this information because Claire only speaks French. My attempts also prove futile, since my French lacks the nuance and subtleties to explain the situation. Claire disappears into the hall and returns with her husband, Fabrice, who speaks some English. Fabrice denies he or his wife shopped this week, and we then find Marina to sort out the situation.

Marina is direct. She arrives at the point without pause. After Marina hears the case, she tells the family someone with their card shopped this week, and they cannot. Yet something about the card, identification number, and the young family in front of her compels Maria to investigate further. While she searches the Excel sheet, Clare checks on the baby, and Fabrice paces the shop's floor. Maria concludes the mistake is ours—a mix-up with the registration numbers—and the family is free to shop.

My relief at the passing confrontation is only momentary. The family has filled their basket with at least a half dozen packages of Sumolena flour. Our rule says one per person. I gently explain to them the rule, but Fabrice is adamant he and his family deserve the extra flour because he likes none of the other food on the shelves. "I don't eat any of it," he says in French. Not the pasta. Not the sardines. Not the tuna.

I find Marina again. As if expecting more drama from the family, she brushes past me without even hearing the issue, but she sees it soon enough: the basket full of flour. "No," she says, "you can only have one per person." I tell Marina that nothing appeals to Fabrice, but she's not having it. "Look how many you have taken." She removes the flour from the basket and counts each one: one, two, three, four, five, six. Fabrice, though, does not back down and asserts he and his family deserve the extra flour because there is nothing else he can eat. "Je ne mange pas ça," he says, pointing to this and that item on the shelf. "I don't eat any of this," he repeats in English, in case we did not understand his French. "I understand," she says. "But we can't give so many to one family because we need to make sure everyone can have some," she says, trying to placate Fabrice with compassionate logic. But he wants to respond and say that if he cannot buy anything with his points, what good are they? Marina negotiates with him. "Six Sumolina is too many," she says. "You can have three. One for you, your wife, and your baby." According to our system, infants only count as half a person, so, technically, their baby should not be entitled to a whole package of flour. Marina has made a small concession. Before Fabrice can respond, though, Marina sees the five bags of rice hidden under the cooking oil in the couple's second basket. But instead of admonishing the couple for again exceeding the limit, she returns two bags and tells them they can also have three rice. Marina carries the items to the counter and instructs me to add the points to know how many remain.

As a family, I know they have 2,100 points, as does Fabrice, who watches my additions the way an overzealous boss may scrutinize the actions of an underling, hoping for one small error, just one, so he may lash out at the novice and extend his authority over him.

Three hundred points remain. Claire returns to the shelves while Marina tells Fabrice in a mixture of French and English that when they come next week, we will have a gift, a petite cadeau, for the baby, who has remarkably remained quiet during all the commotion. Yet for reasons unclear, no sense of excitement or happiness crosses Fabrice's face. Instead, Marina's words seem to irk him. He wipes his hands over his face and then crosses his arms, a defensive move, as if preparing himself for another onslaught, another threat to be warded off, another obstacle to overcome. I do not understand how Fabrice has taken Marina's words; perhaps, he has only understood the words "semaine prochaine," next week, and has interpreted the phrase to mean he must wait again for something he could get today. Maybe the frustration he feels over our limited choices and the "one per person" rule has made him view any of our utterances with suspicion.

Fabrice's mistrust soon evolves into contempt. He spews a litany of fast French sentences I cannot follow, but his disdain for Marina's present, or at least what he has understood by her gesture, surprises both Marina and me. His anger towards her gift would be wonderfully confusing, such a break from the normal order of things, if only his resentment were not metastasizing before our eyes. It is building, becoming rage and something wholly uncontainable.

Marina tries to curb its rise, advising Fabrice to calm down because nothing she has said warrants such a reaction. The opposite is the case. She explains again what she said—Fabrice, your baby will receive a present next week—but no words can placate him, until Jean, a community volunteer from the DRC, intervenes. Jean has watched the entire episode unfold in silence; he speaks French and English and does not waste words. No fat around the edges. He is calm personified. His words relax. When he speaks to Fabrice in his soothing baritone, relief pours over me because I sense the Cameroonian's carapace soften a bit; his arms become uncrossed, and his demeanour cools. Where Marina and I have failed, Jean is succeeding. I am not sure how his explanation differs from ours, since he relays all the relevant information we have, but whatever the reason, Jean's words finally convince Fabrice to drop the gun, so to speak. We all smile at the turn of the events, and Fabrice confirms what Jean has told him: "You will have a present for my child next Friday." Marina and I both nod. "Okay," Fabrice says.

Simon

Cyprus is unique in that it allows asylum seekers to work while they wait for authorities to determine their case. After leaving the camp, they must wait one month and then apply for their labour card, allowing them to legally access the labour market and granting them some financial support after six months. Of course, some do not bother with such formalities and choose to work under the table and rely on whatever day jobs are on offer. You can see labourers mingling around downtown Nicosia, waiting for anyone to stop by with an offer. Many asylum seekers realize Cypriot adjudicators will never grant them refugee status, but because the status determination process can take years, they nonetheless see their time in Cyprus as a time to earn money and send some of it back home. Yet the Cypriot government is not as generous with its labour market access as it first seems. Asylum seekers only have access to certain sectors, specifically the ones citizens have no interest in doing. On its website, UNHCHR provides a helpful handout detailing those specific sectors, which include the following: agricultural and fisheries, processing, waste management, trade, service provision, food industry, as well as hospitality.

One of the services we offer at the centre is help with CV writing. Interested members must complete a questionnaire about their skills, past work history, education, and spoken languages. Members then book an appointment to work with a volunteer to fit their employment history into a Word CV template. Once the member is satisfied with their CV, we print five copies for them and email them the Word file.

When a member arrives with their completed form, we work together with them to craft an attractive CV for prospective employers. A young man from Cameroon, Simon, sits across from me as I review his completed document. Under skills, he has written "expert" in the entire Microsoft package—Word, Excel, PowerPoint. Although such expertise would normally be something job hunters would want to highlight, I know no Cypriot employer will find it impressive or relevant. For education, he has a degree in mathematics from a university in Douala; under job history, he has listed his various teaching jobs, including the head of the mathematics department at one secondary school. His last teaching job ended in 2019, and no other jobs are mentioned. I want to ask him what made him leave his profession and country behind to become underemployed in Cyprus because underemployed is what he will become. But I do not ask because my job is not to probe into the members' affairs but to provide some help. Beside me lies the document listing all the sectors asylum seekers may work within and all the professions they may occupy. I look at his job history and then the list. A heaviness descends, warming me beyond any level of comfort and increasing my internal temperature, for I feel the betrayal coming. "My friend," I say. "Have you any experience working in these areas?" my pen pointing to the list and its contents. Simon carefully reads the document, running his finger underneath each sentence and occupation. No sense of disappointment is obvious; I do not detect any flare of humiliation. Even if he does not say so, Simon must know what I am doing to him: I am deskilling him. I am asking this man to forget about his past studies—pretend they never happened—and ignore the years of teaching experience he has. I am asking him to erase part of himself because … well, because … employers do not care.

Simon stops in the service provision sector and tells me he has experience working in hotels. He still does not ask me why I need this information when I ask him the name of the hotel, its location, the jobs he performed, and the years he worked there. He does not express his confusion about why I ask about this particular job when he has other, more relevant ones to his schooling and what, perhaps, he would like to do again in the future. A hotel in Douala employed him from 2014 to 2015 and paid him to clean and tidy rooms. Simon worked there just before he attended university, as a way, I assume, to earn money for the cost of tuition. At the time, he must have thought this job was temporary, a necessary step on his journey towards his dream. Cleaning rooms was not his destiny, only a means to an end. Then he went to university, earned his degree, and set out to find employment. And he did. Starting as a part-time math teacher, he advanced through the ranks, becoming a full-time teacher and head of the department.

Now, he is applying for hotel work again. He has travelled back in time.

Paul

We have rules at the centre about who we can offer services to and what kind. For some rules, we are flexible, such as changing a member's shopping day and offering printing and labour card services to nonmembers. But one rule is sacrosanct: We can only offer food services to those who have left the camp within one month of registering with us. When new people come to register, the volunteer working at the door must check their alien certificate book to find the date they were released from the camp. If, for example, the person is released on July 5, and they come to register on August 10, we cannot help them. The centre targets people released from the camp because they need the most assistance securing food and accessing important legal documents. This rule leads to difficult conversations between us and those ineligible for food. We try to explain the rationale for our rule, particularly how it is the same for everyone, but our words do little to replace the disappointment. The conversations become more difficult and tense when the applicant counters our rule with this argument: The date on their alien booklet is incorrect. And it may well be. The date on the alien certificate is not necessarily the one they left the camp; it indicates the date they registered for asylum. For many reasons, the person may have had to stay in the camp longer than the date suggests, or the person may have left the camp but went directly to a hospital for necessary treatment and could not visit the centre until later. In this case, we ask for documents verifying either claim. Documents and documents. Asylum seekers are walking filing cabinets. I am amazed by the number of documents that spill from a person's bag whenever I ask for their alien registration booklet. Pages and pages. Copies upon copies. The top left corner of many are ripped and torn almost to the point of destruction because of how many times the document has been stapled and then restapled.

At the registration table, Paul, from Nigeria, sits with dozens of documents sprayed in front of him. There is no unity or organization to them. They are scattered. Yet they tell a story Paul desperately wants us to believe. According to his yellow alien certificate booklet, the most important document for our purposes, Paul left the camp in May, and since it is already the middle of August, we cannot register him unless he can prove he left the camp at a later date. "I am not lying," Paul keeps saying. I assure him I do not doubt the truth of his account, but I will need proof of it. He searches through the papers lying on the table, looking for anything that throws the validity of the yellow paper into question. He speaks fast, and I have difficulty understanding. There was a fire, I think, which required his hospitalization. Paul rolls up his sleeves, and purple and black welts stain both his biceps; he has endured pain there. Among his papers are records discussing the fire and his admittance to the hospital. Before or after the accident, he was transferred to a camp in Larnaca, transferred again, and then maybe again.

I tell Paul I need the date he was discharged from the hospital. Papers sail across the table. He desperately seeks the date that will grant him access to the food. I watch him scramble with an acute sense of shame building within me. I can still see his wounds peeking out from underneath his shirt sleeves. If it were up to me, I swear, if it were up to me, these lines I keep repeating to myself, watching Paul frantically search, looking, looking, looking for anything that might satisfy our rules. "Our rules are the same for everyone," I keep saying to Paul, even though he has stopped listening. "We believe you," I keep saying, even though we do not because if we did believe him, we would not subject him to such scrutiny. Document after document Paul flashes before my eyes has a June date, several weeks too late for registration. "I am sorry," I keep saying. "Do you have any date from July," I ask again and again. "Any record from a little later?" "Anything from July?" I know he does not, but I still ask, cruelly, maintaining a flicker of hope within Paul. If it were up to me, I keep saying. I swear to God if it were up to me... but I never finish the thought because, thankfully, it is not up to me. "Paul," I say. "I am sorry." He will not listen to me. He keeps looking and hoping.

Muhammad and Farahnaz

Muhammad and Farahnaz are a couple from Afghanistan. They and their two children fled Afghanistan after the Taliban's return to power in August 2021. They have found themselves in Cyprus as refugees; more specifically, they have found themselves in Cyprus as unemployed refugees. Muhammad has come to the centre today for help with his resume; Farahnaz is out looking for work, and the children are home alone.

Muhammad has pulled out his CV template. Under work history, he has written he has no work experience in Afghanistan, a frequent occurrence among members, for, I suppose, they assume what they had done in their previous home will hold no relevance for them here in Cyprus—they are partially correct. Nevertheless, we always tell members to include jobs they did in their country of birth, even though we will emphasize waiting tables over teaching children on their CVs. This I tell Muhammad. He looks at me and softly says, "I worked in the Ministry of Finance for seventeen years until the Taliban came." "Okay," I say, shocked by the revelation, "put that."

Muhammed looks frustrated. Fatigue has settled upon his body, making him look older than his forty-one years. He is only three years older than me, but my god, how much more experience, that of heartbreak and devastation, he must carry in his small frame. He appears to me as a ruined house, a forgotten home that had devolved from neglect, transforming from something sturdy and beautiful to a broken-down shanty. The anger rises inside of me—my acute emotional response to the injustice experienced by Muhammad and Farahnaz, the betrayals and catastrophes that pushed them from living a purposeful life in Kabul to seeking resume writing help from volunteers in Nicosia—this anger I must muffle for the moment because it is not mine to have and feel. It is Muhammad and Frahnaz's. I am a citizen of the West. I pay taxes to a government that has systemically and irrevocably failed the people of Afghanistan. We have betrayed them. We promised them democracy and peace, and we delivered the Taliban. The Taliban might have pushed them from their country, but the roots of their displacement were born decades ago through outside meddling and were nurtured through intervention after intervention, through mind-boggling corruption and incompetence, until all the Taliban had to do was knock on the door for the entire structure to fall and for the walls around Muhammad, Farahnaz, and their children to come crashing down.

Under skills, Muhammad has written the following: "I can drive very well. I can copy and print papers. I know about computers." From what I have learned about asylum seekers finding employment in Cyprus, I know what Muhammad has written here is less than useless. The Cypriot government recently declared asylum seekers could not obtain a driver's licence on the island, which blocks all newcomers from employment in the ballooning food delivery system. Muhammad's computer skills are also irrelevant, as is his experience working for the Ministry of Finance. He will not be working in an office. But I do not stop him from telling me about the work he did at the ministry, the documents he digitized and the database he helped create, and I do not ask him to remove these experiences from his CV. Displacement may destroy ways of life, but it can never destroy memory. And memory, regardless of how fleeting, ambiguous, and tenuous, can anchor someone in the here and now. It can convince some to stay. They are a record of a life lived. I cannot ask Muhammad to abandon his memories. Too cruel.

But I do need more. Muhammad looks confused when I ask him about the jobs he did before the Ministry of Finance employed him in 2004. Did he have any small jobs, anything part-time? Had he found employment in between bombings and gunfire? The Taliban were in power then, before the Americans came, and I wonder whether my questions may uncork more unpleasant sentiments from the past. I tread carefully and try to ask questions with easy, one-word answers. He tells me he did some cleaning, a revelation I latch on to because as an asylum seeker in Cyprus, having expertise in cleaning products will help him find employment far more than government experience. I ask him if he worked for a cleaning company in Kabul, and he looks askance, almost bewildered. He has become frustrated, I think, with all my questions about his employment before his career. Of what relevance could his cleaning history be if he has worked for the Ministry of Finance? No, there was no company; he only cleaned for family and people in his network. Maybe he only meant he cleaned his place. Regardless of what he cleaned, and for whom, I transform Muhammad into a self-employed cleaner with over two years of experience. For the skills he acquired during his tenure as one of Kabul's finest cleaners, I write he thoroughly and efficiently cleaned the homes of his clients, and as a self-employed worker, he showed resourcefulness and adaptability in securing a loyal client base.

I show Muhammad the page detailing the sectors asylum seekers can work within. As he runs his fingers over the words, trying to make sense of them, I glance at Farahnaz's template, which we will work on after Muhammad's CV. It is also almost blank, except for experiences working briefly at a restaurant in Nicosia and as a kindergarten teacher in Kabul. She and Muhammad, with their children, had built a life for themselves in Kabul, something they could look upon and feel a smattering of pride. I do not wish to romanticize their life before. I know not of its day-to-day rhythms. But I do know how quickly it was taken from them.

It's almost a year to the day the Taliban took Kabul. I replay the awful scenes of desperate men and women running after the last aircraft departing the city, some even clinging to metal parts, anything they could grab, as the plane ascended to the sky and took its hundreds upon hundreds upon hundreds of refugees, huddled in the hull, a belly full of desperation, towards the sky and away from danger. I remember watching those men lose their grip, the wind and speed proving too much, and fall to their deaths in Afghanistan.

I have finished Muhammad's CV. In addition to his seventeen years working for the government, I have added his experiences cleaning homes and driving. I ask Muhammad to review his CV and check for mistakes on my part, misspellings or inaccuracies. He seems satisfied, even though I know he has not understood all I have written. After I print his CV and hand him his copies, he stops me from starting to work on his wife's CV. He must return home. The children have already been alone too long, and he cannot risk another moment's separation, for who knows what could happen. Muhammad knows better than most how the world can suddenly stop spinning: A fire can be lit at any moment.

A few weeks later, Muhammad returns to the centre in a bad way. I overhear the conversation he has with Haley. He and his wife cannot find jobs. They cannot afford to eat. They cannot pay for their children's medical bills. He wants to return to Afghanistan. Haley's voice relates her shock to his request. "But Afghanistan is so dangerous," she says, and Haley doesn't even know what I do: Muhammad is a former government worker, someone the Taliban would be interested in meeting, since despite their assurances to the contrary, they have sought revenge against those they deem traitors to the cause. Haley's cautions, however, do little to sway Muhammad, as he reminds her Cyprus, too, is dangerous for him and his family, despite their being recognized refugees and despite Cyprus having a duty, enshrined in international law, to provide them sanctuary. But sanctuary means little without the tools to provide a life for yourself and your family. I have seen Muhammad's exhaustion firsthand—that burnout stemming from daily humiliations, from having doors slammed in his face, from having to beg for special favours. Muhammad's experience is a testament to the absolute failure of the international protection regime: He would rather return to Taliban-ruled Afghanistan than suffer the indignities of living as a refugee in Cyprus. And what of Farahnaz, his wife? And his children? What opportunities await them in Kabul? Has she agreed with Muhammad's plan? Has the situation for her become so untenable that she would rather return to Afghanistan and live with the consequences of that decision?

Muhammad wants to know about the government's return program and how much money they provide to people to leave. I think about the insidious nature of voluntary return programs and wonder how voluntary they are. Instead of investing that money into programs and services for newcomers, the government would rather use those funds to entice them to go away. We will pay you to go away. We will make life for you in Cyprus as difficult as possible. We will not provide you with accommodation, training, or resources. But do not worry. If you find the challenges too daunting, your situation too humiliating, you will always have an exit strategy: We will pay you to go away.

Haley walks towards me, on her way to ask Marina for guidance about Muhammad's request. I stop her as she passes. "Does he really want to return to Afghanistan," I ask, and Haley confirms what I overheard: No job, no money, no hope. I cannot fathom how his quality of life in Cyprus has deteriorated to the point he has asked for our help in his self-deportation. I am speaking to Haley, but I am only venting. He is a refugee. He should not have to pay for medical treatment. There must exist mechanisms that help refugees navigate the bureaucracy so they know to which rights they are entitled. Haley stops me. He has already been to Caritas six times." But, but, but…" I stammer. "Surely, it cannot be so bad that he would want to return to Afghanistan. He just needs someone who can clearly articulate to him what resources he has available to him. He is a refugee." I am rambling again. "He is a refugee. He should not have to pay. He should not have to. He just needs reassurance, something practical, a glimmer of hope—evidence he should stick it out."

Haley goes to find Marina.

The Children

My apartment looks down on a playground. Every evening, I can hear the laughter of children as they bounce up and down on trampolines and propel their little bodies higher on the swings. Mirth overwhelms them and pushes them from activity to activity. Little balls of excitement, these children are. When I sneak a peak of the goings-on, I cannot help but smile at all the commotion. Tiny bodies in motion. Arms and legs flexing power. Voices laced with excitement. Their specific words die in the commotion, in each's effort to do everything all at once, as if each tiny person realizes, deep inside the caves of their mind, that childhood is fleeting and ephemeral, just a brief second of fearlessness before conformity and perfectionism and a desire to become invisible replace that courage.

From time to time, children appear at the market alongside their parents. They help carry bags, select items, and try to stay out of the way. The more precocious among them will grab a croissant or a bag of potato chips only to have a parent snatch away the item and return it to the shelf. Sometimes, though, the parent will acquiesce to the child's request. We give them a little ice cream when we have extra in the fridge.

My first morning in the shop, an Afghan family enters: a mother and her three children, two girls and a boy. They all look the same age, and the girls are almost identical, save for a slight variation in hair length. They might be triplets. I don't know. The market and all of its items excite the children. The boy grabs a piece of chocolate while the girls focus on the cookies. They must not be used to such abundance, all this choice. The mother manages to apprehend the little robbers and confiscate the goods, much to the thieves' protest. She, though, does weaken at the sound of her little ones' protests, eventually capitulating to their demands: Each can choose one item to buy.

I want to focus on this interaction, but my eyes remain locked on those of the children. An infection coats their eye sockets, cellulitis maybe. The skin has turned red, and the resulting irritation causes the children to swipe and scratch at their eyes every few minutes. The condition, however, does not lessen their enthusiasm for the market and its treasures, bouncing as they do from goodie to goodie, much to the chagrin of their mother, who must focus on what the family needs in terms of nutrition and subsentence. Their eyes, though, bother me. I am unaccustomed to children looking like they do—sick. It's an alien presence, a sensation I do not often associate with children. Revulsion. The sickness in their eyes repulses me. Children should not look like they do. Their bodies are too young, too innocent, to be subjected to the ravages of disease. Illness belongs to adults. Let adults carry the burden of diseases. Children should not have their bodies invaded by bacterial forces, as the fight is unfair. The opponents are not evenly matched, but life, and all the killers it breeds, has no regard for justice.

I do not run from the children and their eyes. I take the little pieces of chocolate from the children's equally little hands. I wave back when they shyly wave at me. I help them and their mother put their goods inside a plastic bag. Not for one moment do I reveal how they make me feel. Ashamed. My smile hides the shame well.

Weeks later, I am sitting on the patio of a Greek restaurant waiting for my takeaway. The patio sits on Ledras Street, the main thoroughfare of Nicosia, and from my chair, next to the air conditioning, I watch tourist families lick ice cream cones and drink bottled water, doing everything they can do to stay cool and protected from Cyprus's unrelenting August sun. People drinking Keo and eating fat pita sandwiches surround me. There is little desire to do anything except sit, drink, and eat. In this heat, excessive movement is not recommended. Just sit. Stay still. Have something to drink.

But then a blur and another. Something small shooting across Ledras and then disappearing into the children's playground, the one my apartment looks down upon. Quick on their feet. Nimble. Not the cumbersome steps of an adult, whose hulking presence can never be hidden. No. The swift steps of a child. A child at play. Their breeziness bespeaks a terrain in which the barriers of the adults' world have not been planted. No potholes or fences terrorize the land. Only space. Meadows. Fields. Sun. Blue sky. There is no rule except to play and play well. And then another flash, a boy, easily weaving his way around the slouching pedestrians, heavy with heat, and then vanishing into the land of trampolines and swing sets. He has gone to join the game of the other two, whose importance only the three are privy: the secret world of children.

The three have returned to the street and huddle together at the playground's edge, deep in conversation. I recognize them, but from where? Straight brown hair falls down both girls' backs; they could be twins. And, yes, that's it. It's the Afghan children who visited the centre a month ago, whose eyes had left such an indelible impression on me. Their sickness had made me flinch. But here they are now, roaming freely on the streets of Nicosia— at play. The cellulitis has retreated; their little bodies have vanquished the foe. Each's eyes sparkle with wonder and vitality. They are planning and plotting. Secrets pass between them. Codes and passwords. The three then burst across Ledras again, circumventing and manoeuvring around dreamy tourists, and enter a passageway beside the restaurant, whose staircase must lead to their residence. This stretch of street belongs to them. Between their home and their playground. A mere twenty steps, but perhaps a whole new beautiful world for children who had just been pulled from a shark's mouth. Here, there are no sharks but only the slow path towards hope, a long passageway to a future still hidden by weeds and dead leaves. I see shears, though, in their tiny hands. A rake, too.

One girl has found something shiny on the ground and inspects it. A two-euro coin. Emboldened by her discovery, she proudly holds it high in the sky for all to see. Something remarkable then happens: She marches right into the restaurant to the waiter lazily waiting for patrons to come and order from his menu. The girl barely reaches the man's waist, yet her diminutive size causes no consternation. She holds the coin high, demanding the man's attention. What lessons has this child already learned? Entry without such shiny objects is strictly prohibited; she must already know this on some level and has already become accustomed to money and the attention and respect it can buy. But now she has something shiny, and she wants respect. Her action does produce a chuckle in the waiter, who looks down at the little girl with a degree of bemusement, yet he makes no motion for her to enter the paradise of his restaurant, where great food is prepared, whose smell must waft into her apartment and keep her wondering what she must do to get some of that deliciousness herself. But now she holds the key to this magical world, and like all who have come before her, she wants what is hers. But the man only stands there, and the wave the little girl waits for does not arrive. Soon, the man's smile dissipates, replaced by a closed lip expressive of annoyance, and he points for the girl to return from where she came, just to his right, her apartment entrance. Vanish, his body screams. But the little girl will not be bullied into disappearance; she will not go until she has in her hands what the shiny object must deliver. She waits and holds the coin as high as her arms can reach. Nothing rocks her attention. Not the waiter's increasing frustration. Not the other patrons who pass her into the restaurant. Not the feelings of humiliation that would befall anyone else in her situation. After a few more minutes, though, because her arm has become tired or she has grown exhausted at waiting for this waiter to do what the coin commands, she takes the matter into her own hands and marches. Holding the coin up high, she strides past the waiter and into the restaurant, on the hunt for the manager or anyone who understands the value of what she holds.

The White Woman

During my time volunteering, over 95 per cent of my fellow volunteers have been white and Western, and over 95 per cent of the displaced persons I have encountered have been nonwhite and non-Western. This reality births unhealthy assumptions about who can be a refugee and who is in a position to help them. The humanitarian world is very white. A snowstorm. A crisis burns uncontrollably, and we come with our squalls and ice to neutralize it. Never mind that our governments, as well as the histories (and privileges) we inherited, played a not insignificant role in starting the fire in the first place. And if the helpers are perpetually from one place and the helpees from another, this state of affairs becomes naturalized. Nothing is shocking about it, just like no one is shocked when winter gives way to spring and then spring to summer. This is what is supposed to happen. No further inquiries are necessary.

The white woman takes me by surprise. She just appears outside the market, in the hallway. Without warning, she is just there. A middle-aged and large woman, I need a moment to register her presence, to make sense of it, because on the surface, based on everything I have seen and heard, she should not be here among the others, the ones whose presence does make sense to me. Her words are in a language I do not immediately recognize, and when my English sentences prove beyond her comprehension—"How can I help you" "Is there something I can do for you"—her body tightens and her mouth surrenders not one but several whimpers. She is upset. "No English," she says. The market and its food keep grabbing her attention. A great force pulls her to the shelves and its goods, the carbohydrates and calories. Tears accumulate in her eyes and threaten to overflow. The store beckons. I anticipate her attempt and subtly move my body, just some centimetres, not even a metre, to block her entrance. My denial registers within her body, not the first, I am sure, but an idea then seems to strike her, as her fingers and hands search her person before retrieving a card and handing it to me. The card's presence in my hand enlivens her spirits, for she believes, rightly, that as a gatekeeper, someone who distinguishes between the deserving and undeserving and distributes food based on that decision, I require proof, documents or cards or papers, before I can make my decision, before I can rule on her case—before I can adjudicate. She wrongly, however, believes her document will suffice and does not realize that before she even opened her mouth or before she even entered the premises, I had already denied her request. Her card is a Bulgarian EU identity card and how it glitters in the light. A diamond. A ruby. Sapphire. For many of the members, the plastic she hands me represents the ultimate goal of their journey—European citizenship. Yet here she is, begging for something she cannot have. That very card precludes her from shopping and forbids her from entering the shop. She is entitled to zero points. She is entitled to nothing but "I am so sorry, but we cannot help you." I wonder what the other members think of her presence. Do they feel any compassion for her? Does she represent only another human being needing help? Or does she represent a squandered opportunity? If one is white and cannot succeed in this world, do they only have themselves to blame?

I stare at her card longer than I need to, buying time, trying to think about how to extricate myself from this unpleasant situation. I find Marina, explain the situation, and ask whether we can do anything for her. But I already know what she will say: There is nothing we can do. This is what Marina tells the woman, but her words keep falling against the woman's incomprehension. Marina abandons this approach and asks me if we have anything small to give her, something that may appease her and send her on her way. There is the bowl of free peaches we have set out for members, and I suggest filling a plastic bag for the woman. Marina consents and motions for the woman to sit and wait. The peaches' fuzz massages my fingertips as I inspect each one for bruises and other sore spots, selecting only the best for the woman who waits. Ten or so now fill the plastic bag, which I tie. Peaches in hand, I approach the woman humbly because I have a request. In exchange for the peaches, I want her to go away. That's all. Just go away. Her look is of a broken thing. Of course, not broken. No. She still breathes; thus, she still acts and chooses. Her bloodshot eyes evidence tears. Yes, tears have fallen. And some still do, I notice, as I hand her the bag of peaches. The more I study her eyes, careful my glance does not linger too long, the more I want to know, from afar, of course, maybe as some kind of special interest project, about what caused her to depart her native Bulgaria for the divided island of Cyprus and about what led her to beg for food at a charity servicing only asylum seekers. Her body yields no answers except struggle. Although she accepts our peaches and cup of water with gratitude and thanks, nothing about her acceptance suggests our gesture is anything but a short break on an otherwise arduous journey.

Samuel

Every Tuesday and Thursday, Samuel, an asylum seeker from Sierra Leone, works in the centre, helping members apply for their labour cards online. Since Samuel has lived in Nicosia for over two years and has much experience navigating the country's labyrinthine bureaucracy, the NGO has hired him for his expertise. He contracted polio as a youth in Sierra Leone but uses his experience as a disabled person to help other disabled asylum seekers in Cyprus, founding an organization that advocates for their rights and which sometimes meets at the centre. On a break one afternoon, he asks me about the education system in Canada, particularly about higher education, and whether the government offers any support for students, and I tell him about loans, grants, and scholarships. The information brightens his mood. He says how important it is for people to have the opportunity to study even if they cannot afford it. He however has not let me finish, since I was going to add, and now must do so, that most government assistance is reserved for Canadian citizens and residents only and that universities often charge exorbitant fees for international students. Such information suffocates the spark in Samuel's eye, killing any far-flung ideas that might have momentarily seized him.

Samuel wants to attend university to study computer science, to eventually assist other disabled people, but the Cypriot government offers no financial support for asylum seekers. He cannot afford the fees on his own. Two years in Cyprus, and he still waits for his first asylum interview, his status as an asylum seeker relegating him to the worst jobs available on the island. "There is no work," he says. He works for the centre twice a week and is grateful for the opportunity, but it is not enough. I sense he is tired of picking up other people's trash, cleaning other people's things, and building other people's dreams. He wants to focus on his. "I am not getting any younger," he tells me, a note of desperation tainting his voice. Pushing thirty, he may sense his productive years, when one focuses on a dream and works to make it a reality, are almost behind him. A university degree is another three or four years. He must find work and establish a career, which will take more years. He does the math and does not like the results. How much longer will he have to wait for his life to begin? Will it ever? Robbery is the long-term effect of displacement.

The barricades across the island of Cyprus will remain for the foreseeable future. Just a few steps from my apartment are barrels and wreckage and other debris used to separate one side from the other, and just down the street, a soldier is standing at a look-out position watching me whenever I pass, camera slung over my shoulder, to make sure I do not snap a photo in his area, a sensitive zone in which photography is prohibited. I have been caught taking photographs in such areas before, but I only had to play the dumb tourist card to silence the soldier's shouts. Yet whispers have begun to spread about a thawing of tensions, about an end to partition, and the return of a land in which no wire splits its side, where the displaced may return to the cities they were forced to flee fifty years ago. In the north, ghost towns sit on beautiful beaches. Their buildings and stores are quiet and vacant. Kitchens and bedrooms have all the trappings of life—cutlery and beds—but no people to use them, not since they ran to the south all those years ago. If the wall comes down, if the peoples of Cyprus can coexist again, what might those cities look like? Will the ghosts of 1974 metamorphose into real people once again? Will those forgotten beds once again provide rest and comfort? What is a return if not a kind of resurrection? Displacement's end is very much like a rising. And for those now asking Cyprus for sanctuary and safety, will they, too, rise?

I receive a message from Samuel a few weeks after leaving Cyprus: He has been accepted to the University of Nicosia and has started a GoFundMe campaign to pay for his tuition. On his fundraising page, he talks about how at the age of five, during the civil war in Sierra Leone, he suffered an accident, which eventually led to him contracting polio, rendering him disabled. He talks about receiving little support from his family and society at large, his homelessness, and eventually his arrival in Cyprus. He talks about wanting to complete his undergraduate degree in computer science to eventually design learning programs that better cohere to the needs of disabled children. He talks about how even after all he has suffered both in Sierra Leone and Cyprus, he never abandoned his dreams. A few months later, I receive another message from Samuel: It is his University of Nicosia identification card with his name and face. It is up to Cyprus whether they choose to squander the gifts Samuel and others like him are ready to give.

6
Subotica

September and October 2022

Northern Serbia resembles the ugly tip of an even uglier triangle. The country is not a perfect triangle by any metric, but look hard enough and the familiar contours do appear. Plump at its southern parts, the republic gets increasingly skinnier the more north it extends. Its three northern neighbours—Croatia, Hungary, and Romania—apply pressure from the east, north, and west, squishing and squeezing Serbia's northern extremities. As a result, travellers heading up the E-75 from Novi Sad, and not wanting to stay in Serbia, can exit east, towards Sombor, and enter Croatia, exit west, towards Kikinda, and enter Romania, or proceed north, through Horgos, and into Hungary. Thus, Serbia provides a plethora of options for onward travel, plenty of options for the hardier and more experienced travellers, but not so adventurous that they would ever cross a frontier without proper documentation, without some marker explaining to anyone requesting to look that they belong somewhere else, to another body or regime, and they want nothing else but to journey onwards and only for a fraction of time, maybe a week or two, and they demand nothing else except the right to enter and then to exit. They need nothing else but the permission afforded to them by the little booklet they hand to anyone who asks. Words are rarely required with the proper documentation. For those without, the borderlands are a place of violence. Among abandoned buildings, vacated farms, and well-hidden forests, these men, women, and children wait for a chance to cross into Croatia, Hungary, or Romania. Every day, hundreds of people try to cross, and most fail. Officials beat them back. I volunteered with an organization providing humanitarian aid to people in these borderlands. Here are a few of their stories.

The Man Going to Italy

The bus from Belgrade to Subotica is full—a mixture of locals and foreigners. Each has their destination and reason for travel. I am on the window seat and watch cars pass us on the AI. The windshield wipers work hard in the rain. The countryside is flat, remarkably so, but verdant. Farmland for as far as the eye can see. Green and green and green. The earth here possesses a remarkable vitality, rich enough to feed the belly of Serbia and beyond. Sitting next to me is a man I would guess does not call Serbia home. He speaks Arabic and travels with three other men. They are close in age and possess a closeness born only from proximity, from having one another's backs no matter the circumstances. A camaraderie exists between them. They are accountable to one another. When the bus stops, they all go out for a quick cigarette and return together. Serbia is not the first country they have travelled through, and it will not be their last.

The man beside me sends a WhatsApp message on his smartphone, which is Italian, and the man expresses his love for whoever is on the receiving end: Ti amo. He then switches back to Facebook and scrolls through dozens of stories written in Arabic. The phone has seen little love; cracks appear at the screen's outer edges and slowly snake their way to the centre. And they will grow, I think, until the screen and the information it displays finally go dark. Now and then, the man will turn to his fellow travellers and speak, and they will return words in kind as if confirming the thing the man had asked.

The seats are less than roomy, especially not for taller and bigger men like me and him. Once, purely by accident, he nudged my arm with his elbow while maneuvering himself in his seat, and he raised his hand in apology for a slight that, in my mind, did not warrant acknowledgment, but maybe experience has taught him that even the slightest accident could be misconstrued, especially by people like me.

We enter Subotica, and I glance down at the map on my phone to determine the distance between the bus stop and my apartment, which is not far, as well as the distance between my apartment and the volunteer house, also not far. The map shows that within the vicinity of my apartment, I have supermarkets, internet service providers, bars and restaurants, pharmacies, and ATMs. I am calculating the distance, about a ten-to-fifteen-minute walk, when there's a tap on my shoulder, and I turn to see the man staring at me. "Subotica," he says, pointing downwards, and I nod. My affirmation seems to settle whatever tremour propelled him to ask a stranger about what town they were approaching. I would never ask directions from a stranger unless my life were at stake, only if my phone were broken in the middle of a snowstorm, and I were helplessly lost in the squalls.

His request does provoke warm feelings inside me. I like he thinks I know something he does not, or I appear so confident in my manner and behaviour he assumes I must know exactly where we are. I like I blend in. I like I can disappear into a sea of faces without drawing attention to myself. Attention is catnip for anxiety. I avoid the spotlight as much as possible. For him, though, my travelling companion, it makes perfect sense to assume I, a white man, know exactly where I am going. Why wouldn't I? Nothing in his experience would ever dissuade him from thinking a man like me would never not know where he was going. What follows can only assure his original hypothesis, for once the bus stops and the passengers depart, I grab my bags and head for my new apartment in my new city, while he and his companions, I notice as I walk past them, engage in a lively debate with a taxi driver about the price of their next journey.

The organization I volunteer with provides showers, food, hygiene items, charging stations, and sometimes clothing to people on the move in Northern Serbia. In the back of our van is a giant water tank we fill every morning. We have a battery-powered water pump, a water heater, two shower heads, a bunch of tubing, two shower tents, and two palettes. With these tools, we can provide mobile showers. Before each distribution, we triple-check we have everything for the day. With everything packed, the team meets outside the warehouse to discuss the day's distribution, go over the site, and highlight any issues we may encounter. We talk logistics and contingency plans. We double-check everyone has their passports in case we meet the police. We ask questions and answer them. Once everyone is on the same page, we set off. Today, we are visiting the site known as River.

Much rain has fallen over the last few days in Northern Serbia. Puddles cover roads and sidewalks; everything is wet. For those paths not blessed enough to be covered in asphalt or concrete, the water has transformed them into muddy lanes, making them unsurpassable by vehicles, unless they happen to be four-wheel drive. We do not have such a car. One such road leads to a squat frequented by people on the move. It sits deep in a forest on the banks of the Tisza River, which not far from the site, just up the river, becomes the border between Serbia and Hungary. So on any given day, between one and two hundred men, women, and children will sleep under the cover of branches and blankets, waiting for the smugglers to organize the boats that will ferry them across Tisza and into the Schengen Zone.

The closest community to the site is the hamlet of Srpski Krstur, literally "Serbian Cross." Krstur has three streets, a stadium, a church, and a few convenience stores. Each street terminates in the farmland leading to the river, but the most southern one, Svetog Save—named after Serbia's national hero Saint Sava—does not completely die at the fields; instead, it metamorphoses into a dirt road that circumvents the cornfields and heads into the forest. Our team normally takes this road on drier days when the road does not resemble a mud bath. Normally, we would drive into the forest, park the van a stone's throw from the camp, and set up the showers, charging tables, and the food distribution. Today, though, as soon as Sava's pavement ends, a large mud pond greets us, as well as a few other vans parked around its outer edges. The vans belong to MSF, and the doctors recommend in the strongest terms we do not try and drive the van over this road to the site, for they did and almost did not make it out. Once the dirt and clay get wet, the substance becomes almost like ice, making it impossible for normal tires to gain any traction, leading to endless spinning. The second car in our team, comprised of volunteer doctors and nurses, decide they will make a go of it and try to get at least halfway to the camp, which means they can transport some of our supplies. We decide to forego the showers and charging and only to distribute the food and NFI we have.

Lindsey, a fellow volunteer, hops into the van and starts handing down the crates full of food packages, each one a brown bag containing three hundred grams of onions and five hundred grams of potatoes, as well as the crates containing the small plastic bags of sugar and salt. There are also the cardboard boxes full of eggs— 180 a box—the duffle bags full of women's and children's clothing, and the razors and soap. We stuff the brown bags into backpacks and cram as much as we can into the car. For the remaining supplies, we must carry the kilometre or so to the squat site. Christina, a volunteer, jumps into the car, super excited to drive it through the trenches. A confessed adrenaline junkie, she asks Heidi, another volunteer, to follow on foot alongside the car and to point any possible potholes or craters to avoid. And off they go: Christina at the wheel, plowing through the mud, and Heidi running just ahead, on the lookout for any hidden hazards. The rest of the team sets out with packs on our backs or boxes of eggs in our arms. The ground is slick, slippery, and we take each step with extra caution, for we do not want to lose any eggs to the ground. Now and then, young men will pass us carrying plastic bags full of food and water, bought at a local convenience store, whose proximity to the squat site must do wonders for its business. These men are much more confident on their feet than we, since their journeys have taken them through far more intimidating terrain than this. Lindsey notices a man carrying more than he can handle, and she offers to take one of his hands, which he agrees to.

The scenery is picturesque. Farmland meets forest in an eye-pleasing way. Clouds float across the sky, threatening rain, but the sun always triumphantly resurfaces. Today, it's never hidden for long. This scene reminds me of Southern Ontario: the lush farmland, rolling hills and never-ending forests. My family and I would walk our dog through such geography almost daily. We never associated forests with violence.

I could be walking anywhere in Southern Ontario now, except I would not see these men passing me with their bags on their backs and wearing the flimsiness of shoes. I would not see the man with the limp, who responded "Not so good" when we asked him how his day was going. I would not see the man with a bandage around his thumb or the man wearing a flipped-up cap whose behaviour suggested his intoxication. There is nothing serene about the forest we march towards.

Christina can drive the car no further. The earth has too many scars; long and deep wounds cut into the ground, the remnants of previous vehicles' journeying, and the rain has rendered them no longer as helpful lanes but as slippery valves, whose mud and sludge could send a tire into a maddening spin. So, Christina parks, and we hike the remaining distance with bags on our backs. The forest comes. There are trees, fallen branches, and mosquitoes. But as much as the confines strike me as familiar, a particular atmosphere exists that I have never associated with a forest. There is no peace here.

We set up the table and unpack the food bags. Melissa, the shift lead, goes with two other volunteers deeper into the forest, along the pathway, and to the squat to do outreach, basically informing the people living there what we have to give. We have strict rules about entering people's living areas; we only do so with permission and only when there's a chance people may not know about our organization. And because here in the forest, what with the river and Hungary only a stone's throw away, the turnover is typically fast, and since we park our van (on dry days) a short distance from the site, some people may not know about us. Otherwise, we do not enter people's places of residence. It's a matter of respect. While Melissa is gone, Lindsey and I distribute the food and hygiene items to the people passing. After a few minutes, a mother comes with her daughter, asking about clothes for her little one, and Lindsey invites them behind the table to the red duffle bag full of children's clothing. There in the forest, underneath a canopy of green leaves, a mother and daughter debate which shirt looks best. Lindsey and the mother take turns holding a shirt against the girl's body to see how it would fit and wrap itself around the young body's frame. Some are too large, and some are too small; it takes a few tries, but soon, the girl has in her possession a shirt she and her mother adore. And both Lindsey and I say how nice we think the shirt looks, and upon hearing my voice, the girl turns and looks at me, neither with a smile nor a frown, but only the understanding that no matter how lovely the shirt may look, nothing about this encounter in the forest is nice.

More and more people emerge from the forest and queue for food, razors, and soap. Some ask for things we do not have, like jackets and shoes, whereas others just take food, nod thanks, and disappear back into the woods. I notice a guy's eyes on me; he is studying my features. I ignore him; no good can come from exchanging words with him. I have nothing beyond what lies in crates before me, nothing but the most basic of nutrition and the most rudimentary of hygiene items. But he persists and waves in my direction, and I can no longer pretend he is not there, wanting something from me. But what? He speaks to me in Italian, but when my blank expression meets his words, he tries to express his meaning through body language. He points at himself and then at me and keeps saying, "Belgrade. Belgrade. Belgrade." He then mimes sitting down and standing up, again and again, but even my fake laughter and superficial smile cannot disguise my ignorance to his meaning, and he sees it. He speaks more in Italian, and judging by the rise and fall of the sentence and his intonation, he is asking me a question, one that I cannot answer because its content eludes me, so I can only say to the man that I am sorry, but I do not understand.

My anxiety grows because I cannot satisfy his desire for me to remember him and cannot cool the frustration growing within him. My eyes return to the brown bags and blue razors, the comfort of inanimate objects, and my hands continue to pass out the items to those men and women who queue. My body language is clear: I am done with this interaction. I am done with this game of charades, of my failing to guess what he means. I don't know the name of the movie or the actor. Please take your food, soap, and razor and go. But he persists and starts yelling to those within earshot, asking whether anyone speaks Italian. Christina turns from her conversation and replies in the affirmative, and the man's eyes light up, and he explains to her who I am to him, and as soon as he does, it hits me: I know who this man is. We rode the bus together from Belgrade; he sat next to me. He told someone he loved them. He asked me whether we had arrived in Subotica. Shame and embarrassment replace my anxiety. How could I have forgotten him so quickly? How could his features not have jarred my memory? I watch him explaining the situation to Christina, and I marvel at how different our journeys from the bus station have been. I walked to my apartment, checked in, and enjoyed the comforts of a large apartment in the city centre; he and his companions took a taxi to the forest and have since waited for smugglers to arrange their transport across the river.

"He took the bus with you from Belgrade," Christina says, and I pretend to only acknowledge my memory of him then, not the fifteen seconds early. I act so surprised and apologize profusely for failing to recognize him. He only gives me a fist bump and then takes his food back into the forest.

Mahdi

Mahdi is a volunteer from Tunisia, and his presence in the organization intrigues me because in my experience, non-Western volunteers are a rare breed. We are usually white, and we are usually well-to-do. Mahdi, though, had to get a visa to travel to Serbia, all that work just to volunteer in Subotica for a month. He's a hard worker, even if he takes one-too-many smoke breaks. When he weighs the potatoes and onions, his concentration is impressive; he stares at the scale with great intensity, as if willing the correct numbers to appear. Dumping cups of salt into plastic bags is another of his jobs. Hundreds of them. I call him "salt man," which he enjoys, and he calls me "sugar man," since I am doing the same with sugar. "How many?" "How many?" he periodically shouts at me, wanting to know how many sugar bags I have completed, and I am always ahead, not because I am faster but because, as I said, too many cigarette breaks. Mahdi is charming and makes us laugh. He chats with a volunteer photographer about different kinds of editing software and the advantages of each relative to the subscription costs. He has an interest in photography and videography. It's not the first time he has been to Serbia, either. A few years earlier, he visited different borderland sites, chatted with people, and took photos. His Arabic language skills will prove useful in the field and save us the time and effort of resorting to translation apps to make ourselves understood. I am curious about the interactions he will have with the other Tunisians he will meet in the field, those who have come to Serbia not to volunteer but to leave it as soon as possible.

The day before Mahdi went missing, he told the other volunteers he was going to meet a friend and help him find a hotel in Subotica. Later that night, he sent a message to volunteer saying, "I am in trouble." After that concerning message, we lost all contact with him. Most of his clothes were still in his room as were his expensive laptop and camera. He intended on coming back. What happened to him? What kind of trouble found him? The next day, the coordinators reported him missing at the local police station and gave the officers a description of what he was wearing, as well as a timeline of his movements. The NGO's director contacted the legal team for advice and even planned to visit the Tunisian embassy in Belgrade to report one of their citizens missing. Later that night, though, towards midnight, Mahdi Facebook messaged a volunteer and explained what had happened: He had decided to go on game and was now waiting at the River site to cross into Hungary. His intention had always been to go on game but had wanted to volunteer first, maybe to do a little reconnaissance work before actually attempting, but the smuggler with whom he was in contact told him the window of opportunity at River was quickly closing and in two or three weeks, it might be shut, so Mahdi paid the man two thousand euros and took his spot at the River squat.

The fact we might have worried about his disappearance did not seem to register with him, and the news we had reported him missing with the police greatly alarmed him, since he did not want the police looking for him. We told him if his crossing proved unsuccessful, we would welcome him back to the volunteer house but only for forty-eight hours—to collect his belongings and plan his onward journey. If he happened to be successful, we would mail his belongings to his new European address.

Unfortunately for Mahdi, the window at River had closed. The next day, the Serbian police conducted a widespread eviction at there, and Mahdi was one of the many people rounded up. After the eviction, the Serbian minister for the interior did a press briefing at River in which he talked about taking more action against such "scum." While he spoke, the police were transporting Mahdi and the others to Dimitrovgrad camp, hundreds of kilometres away, on the Bulgarian border. A closed camp, authorities did not permit people to leave and took their passports to be processed. Whether or not Mahdi would be released or pushed back into Bulgaria was impossible to know.

We learned all of this from Mahdi himself, as he used a friend's phone to relay information to us from the camp. In the meantime, the volunteer coordinators had contacted his family in Tunisia, who were distraught over the news, especially since it had been Madhi's parents who had pressured him to go on game. His sister implored us to do everything in our power to get Mahdi out of camp and get him home. He didn't want him to go, his sister said. She wanted answers, some information, anything, about the whereabouts of her brother, about what was happening to him.

But we just don't know. We don't know.

Vitaminka

Vitaminka is the largest squat. We pack for 420 people, but we always run out of food. The site sits on farmland near the Hungarian border and consists of three abandoned houses, each housing people from a particular country and region. Despite each person on the move having the same goal, tensions and animosities do exist between the nationalities, particularly concerning which group may ultimately have the best shot of getting asylum, and violence does sometimes occur, which is why they remain separated as much as possible. Food distribution rarely goes smoothly, as four to five hundred people slam into the table, shoving and pushing their way to the front. Forming an orderly line is a near impossible task, so we often have to rely on the help of smugglers to manage the crowd, even though they may have their own favourites among the queuers. The situation is wholly undignified as people jostle for position over a bag of potatoes, onions, eggs, and salt and sugar. As for the distributors, we just try to handout the food as efficiently and as fairly as possible. We barely have time to look the receiver in the eyes, as someone is always waiting.

After the food disappears, things tend to mellow. People are generally friendly and chat with us about this and that, particularly music. They teach us dance moves. They want pictures with us. They want our social media information, which we do not give out. They want to know where we come from. Showers are popular. There is a steady stream of people. One man tells me he hasn't showered in a week; I imagine the same is true for most people here. Another man has his foot bandaged and carefully wraps a bag over it for fear of it becoming wet.

Later, a Moroccan tells me about how he almost made it to Vienna. He and his fellow travellers crossed the Hungarian border by foot, took a taxi to Budapest, and then boarded a train to Vienna. Twenty kilometres from the Austrian border, Hungarian police entered the train, spotted the foreign-looking travellers, and asked for their identification. When the travellers could not provide any identification except their Serbian camp one, the officers removed them from the train and promptly returned them to Serbia. The Moroccan tells me all he wants is a good life. He just wants to work.

Dozens of tents are pitched in the vicinity of several abandoned buildings near the Horgos border. Here, hundreds of mostly Moroccans and Tunisians wait for the most opportune time to try and cross. Most have already been pushed back; most will try again. We meet Adil, a Moroccan who has been on the move since 2016, first in the UAE and now on Europe's borderlands. He hails from Essasouria, a touristy town on the Atlantic with some of the best surfing on the continent. Adil still speaks nostalgically about his country and how he misses his family and cannot really think about Morocco without becoming emotional. He is homesick for familiar things like the food. But he will not go back. He will never give up on his dreams. No matter the violence he suffers at the hands of border police, no matter the violations and humiliations, he will never go back. He will never give up. He will survive. He will try again and again. He says these words in an almost romantic, dreamlike manner as if the violence he has suffered no longer touches him. He still walks with a limp from when he broke his foot falling from the fence separating Serbia and Hungary. But there is something utterly detached in the way he speaks; perhaps, he has learned to compartmentalize the pain, tuck it away somewhere, until a time he can properly come to terms with it, when he is living safely in Germany or France or the UK. When I ask him whether he has a final destination in mind, he just shrugs his shoulders and says "anywhere."

Hamza

We arrive at the Border site, and Hamza, one of the main smugglers, wants to talk. Hamza is from Algeria and has worked at the site for almost seven months. He has a chatty, charismatic personality and charms listeners with his vast knowledge of the smuggling network. He knows how to get things with his words and how to manoeuvre situations to his advantage. What he lacks in height, he makes up for in compactness. He is a bulldog—and has a few teeth missing. The others respect him; they all know his name. Everyone listens to him. AirPods jut from his ears; a Marlboro Red never strays far from his mouth. A black bag is strung around his shoulder. He carries a blue lighter.

He gathers the volunteers around him as if a boss prepared to delegate the day's tasks to his workers. The site has split into two, he tells us, in French. Half of the people have already moved to a site closer to the border, a few kilometres away; the rest will follow shortly, even though we have already heard from a few people they have no desire to move closer to the border, since they fear aggravating the police, whose presence they are already wary of. We have heard stories of how at night, Serbian police stop people on the move for a shakedown, demanding money in exchange for their looking the other way. We are hesitant about moving locations, since we do not know the situation at the other site and do not like to make drastic changes to the plan while out on distribution. The other site too has a reputation for increased tension, as not two months ago, a van full of right-wing vigilantes stopped in front of the squat and fired bullets into the air. We tell Hamza we would consider changing sites in the following weeks if needed, but for today, we must stay here. The Algerian does his best to hide his disappointment, still acting cheerful and ingratiating, but he does let slip a few passive-aggressive remarks about the nature of our work and how if we wanted to help the people, we would go to where the people are. We tell him we want to help the people, but we can only do it here for today. After much and back forth, it is agreed we will set up distribution here, and Hamza will ask the people who have already left to return to the site to collect their food, have a shower, and see the doctors.

The distribution proceeds calmly as more and more people arrive from the other site. Another man from Algeria, an Amazigh, assists us in distributing the food packs. He is trying to reunite with family members in France. As for why he left Algeria, he will only say the relationship between the Amazigh and the Algerian state is not good. In front of the table, we have set the bulletin board with information about the work we do documenting pushbacks. Written in several different languages, the documents on the board explain if a person has experienced a pushback, they can make an anonymous report with us if they wish. The board always generates a lot of attention and discussion among viewers. Some want to talk to us; others are more apprehensive. We do not pressure anyone to share their stories, but we are ready to listen if they are ready to share. In my experience taking testimonies, I have sensed the people experience a measure of catharsis in relating what happened to them. They get to unburden themselves. Even though their telling will not heal their police-inflicted injuries any quicker or return the money and items stolen from them, they do get to know their story will not die with them and that maybe their telling will lead to some change and some accountability for those who have hurt them. As it stands, the borderlands around Northern Serbia are a lawless place, an area where border police and the military that supporting them may carry out their violence with impunity. They may hit, kick, threaten, and steal with no consequences. They act with more criminality than the men and women who cross borders irregularly and the people who help them.

Hamza has many stories, and he has seen everything. He left Algeria in 2016 and spent six years in Greece, three of which were in prison. He does not say what for, just that he had problems. He opens his phone and shows me on MAPS.ME the route his clients take from Horgos to Budapest; it is a series of red dots, each corresponding to a location with specific information, about whether the place is suitable to sleep or what other amenities are nearby. The journey involves a two-day hike through Hungarian forests (the "jungle" as Hamza calls it), hidden from view and away from the public's prying eyes. A nondescript Hungarian town meets them at the end as well as its train station and train to Budapest. The logistics of smuggling networks have always fascinated me. At other locations, a taxi awaits people at the other side of the fence and whisks them through Hungary as quickly as possible. They need not worry about train stations, as making it to Budapest does not guarantee success. Of course, an awaiting taxi is no guarantee of success here. Car accidents involving people on the move are common in Hungary. Speed is in the name of the game, which often results in crashes, injuries, and even death.

Hamza gestures to a family of five sitting just outside one of the abandoned buildings. Imagine walking through the forest for two days with such little ones, he says, and I cannot. He says he prioritizes families, doing everything possible to increase their chances of a successful journey. Hamza has tried five times to cross into Hungary; after the last time, he decided to stay put and work instead. From his experiences of being pushed back, he has seen a lot of bad things. I ask him how the police steal from people on the move, and his face brightens in anticipation of enlightening an ignorant audience. He is a conscientious teacher who takes great pride in imparting knowledge to his students. The police force people to sit on their knees with their hands wrapped behind their heads. They must always keep their eyes on the ground. The police then walk behind the line of kneeling men and women and take whatever they fancy from their bags and pockets. One group who had been pushed back the other day had fifteen hundred euros stolen. The police like iPhones, which they will help themselves to; less expensive phones, they smash. Men have had water dumped over their heads; women have been beaten. Yet the only time Hamza approaches a point of rage in remembering what he has seen and experienced is when he recounts an episode with a Czech border officer. "Fuck the Quran," this man told Hamza. And when he repeats what the man says, he does it clandestinely and asks me to come close, as if he were telling me a secret and does not want anyone to hear the words from his mouth. "You do not say this," he says. "You do not." I am struck at how much the officer's words have cut Hamza, more so, apparently, than the physical beatings he suffered. "You are a Christian," Hamza says (I do not correct him), "and I am a Muslim, and we must respect each other's beliefs." He looks at me hard, with a penetrating glance that unnerves me, until I agree with him, and I do. A smile then replaces his anger, and he reminds me he watches and listens to the happenings around the border, and if I ever have any questions, all I have to do is ask.

A man on a bicycle stops in front of the van. He is not a local looking for trouble, but he does know this spot intimately, perhaps better than the hundreds of other men resting in the sun and waiting for night to fall. He was here ten years ago looking for a way into Europe. And maybe, for him, not much has changed. I imagine these same buildings still stood, and these same farmlands still grew. I imagine he, too, sat among others hoping for a new life in Europe, the promised land. He had fled from Iran and the Ayatollah, and his journey had taken him through Serbia, Horgos, and Hungary. But here he is again, ten years later, on a bicycle. He has found refuge in Germany and has residency, meaning he can live a full life in the open without fear of detention and deportation. Yet his words for his fellow travellers are not of perseverance or hope. He does not tell them to hold onto their dreams. He does not tell them their long journey is almost at an end, and if they can hold on for a moment or two longer, if they can withstand the cold, dirt, and beatings for a day or two more, all of their dreams will present themselves. The man says none of this. Instead, he tells whoever will listen to return to their countries. Europe does not want you, he says. Europe does not care about your problems. Even if you do make it, even if you reach your destination and get status, it's not worth the years Europe will take from you. It's not worth how Europe will make you feel, he says. They will isolate you. They will make you feel you do not belong and never will. I wish I had never left Iran, he says. The man is returning to Iran on a bicycle, retracing the journey he took a decade ago but in the opposite direction. He will probably face consequences from the Iranian government, but he does not care. He wants to be in Iran while the country teeters on the brink of revolution, led by defiant schoolgirls and young women who have had enough of being told what to wear.

I do not know how much his words affect those fighting to get into Europe, but I have often wondered how much people on the move know about the reception awaiting them at Europe's borders when they set out. And for those with no asylum claim, a life living in the shadows awaits them. An undocumented life. No legal protections. No social services. No healthcare. Are they prepared to hide from the police daily? Are they prepared to withstand the hateful, antimigrant rhetoric spewing from the mouths of right-wing politicians who have never had to risk anything in their lives?

During the border violence reports, we also ask respondents to look through the binder we provide of different police officers and the uniforms they wear and see if they can identify the type of officers and vehicles involved in their pushback. There are photos of the Hungarian border police military and their counterparts from Croatia and Romania, police vehicles, and the different European flags officers might have sewn on their sleeves. I always enjoy watching respondents flick through the binder, looking for the type of officer who assaulted them. Excitement takes them, as does an expectation of justice, as if they were in a police station flipping through mugshots of their attacker. They become animated and debate among their friends about who it was that hit them, stole from them, and humiliated them. They get to talk; they get to retell what happened without fear of retaliation or further abuse. More often than not, they select Hungarian police and military, the latter having a particularly fearful reputation;

however, they also note Hungarian officers are also joined by those from Germany, Austria, and Czechia, making the violence perpetrated at the border and the resulting gross undermining of international law, a pan-European affair. Although they know any hope for justice is illusory at this point, our presence provides them with its semblance, only the crumbs of justice, but if more and more people share their story with us, a reckoning may still come.

I have known about police violence at the Hungarian-Serbian border for some time, yet the stories I record from respondents still shock me with the cruelty and malice they contain. One stands out, though. A Moroccan man with bandages along his hand sits in front of me. I have laid out a carpet for us to sit on, away from the commotion and attention of the Vitaminka site. He is a big man, well into his thirties, which makes him older than most other travellers. As he stretches out on the carpet, delicately moving his body, with only one good hand, I see a heavy force weighs on him, something ugly and gargantuan. He speaks some English, certainly enough to articulate his experience at the border. But his sentences arrive in trembles; each word produces a little earthquake within him. This big, strong man strikes me as a child who must recount to a parent something scary they saw, an event or figure so terrifying that their words struggle to form. But recount he does. Two nights ago, around one in the morning, he and four other Moroccans departed the Vitaminka squat for Hungary. While the man was climbing the border fence, he severely cut his hand on the barbed wire. Not long after, on the other side, Hungarian police intercepted the group and told them to sit on the ground. The man asked the police for some water, but the officers ignored him. He told the police how much pain he was in, but they just told him to keep sitting on the ground, preferably in silence. Thirty minutes later, a few more officers arrived; the Moroccan showed his bleeding hand to a woman officer, who laughed at him. She encouraged him to sever the injured hand from his arm if it bothered him so much. The Moroccan pleaded with the officers. "I am a human being," he said. The officers only laughed and smoked.

The Moroccan understands the officers have a job to do, even though he wishes they would just let the people pass. They have no desire to stay in Hungary. I hear this question all the time from people on the move. They want to know why Hungary will not let them pass. In the silence between his words, the big man examines the bandages on his hand and grimaces ever so slightly. Pain has him in its grips, but more than his physical injuries, the mental anguish of what he experienced, I feel, weighs more heavily on him. These are cuts that will not heal as quickly as his physical harm. "If they won't let us pass," he says, "why cannot they return us to Serbia in peace." This is the true meaning, I think, of the expression "going on game." It is a game played between people on the move and the police. The former tries to cross, and the latter tries to prevent them. Where there is some disagreement is the number of times the game can be played. People on the move believe the game continues until they win; the police, though, want to make it so that their competitors will think twice about playing again. Hence, the violence. The baton beatings to the ribs and ankles. The kicks to the stomach and chest. The pepper spray and dogs. The threats. If you ever come back again, we will break you. If you ever come back again, we will kill you. Hence, the taking of money and phones. You cannot move if you cannot afford the way, and you cannot move if you do not know the way. If police just returned them intact, without inflicting harm, the men and women would have no incentive to reflect on whether their continued effort to cross would be worth the consequences.

The Moroccan does not want to understand the logic behind the police violence because, although some officers may honestly enjoy torturing people who do not look like them, which puts their victims outside their realm of morality, the cumulative effect of their actions is to stoke fear among those who wait and plot in the borderlands. Europe's fear of the other has granted a license to these officers to instill fear in the other. I believe the Moroccan when he says he hates Hungarians now, whereas before he left his home, he didn't know anything about the country or its people. Fair enough. But the violence the police did to him goes beyond the woman who laughed at him. It is condoned and legitimized by the silence emanating from Brussels and Strasbourg.

The Monster of Majdan

Majdan is a village in northwestern Serbia. It seems a place time has forgotten. Horses and buggies often meander along the road's shoulder, seemingly in no great hurry to get anywhere, and inconvenience the trailing cars with their slow speed. The inhabitants are primarily farmers, and the surrounding topography is table-flat and green. Fields stretch for miles in every direction, giving the impression one may wander for hours without having to circumvent any great obstacle or worry about getting lost. One may just go. Looks, however, can deceive, and what makes Majdan unique is not its endless space but rather its location sandwiched between two borders: Only a few kilometres to the east lies Romania, and only a few kilometres to the north sits Hungary. Majdan's proximity to these two borders makes it an attractive setting-off point for people on the move seeking entry into Hungary or seeking entry into Romania to later cross into Hungary. Thus, among the few abandoned buildings dotting the otherwise picturesque landscape, hundreds of people seek shelter from the elements and wait for an opportune time to cross.

Today, a helicopter hovers in the distance, floating just over the farmland, which, we learn, is the Romanian border, and then disappears behind a group of trees. The pilot is hunting for people on the move. Romanian border police have quickly established themselves as acting as brutally as their Hungarian counterparts. People here talk about one Romanian officer in particular who takes great pleasure in beating the displaced people he comes across. He is big and walks with a dog. The doctors we sometimes work with talk about the injuries they treat that have resulted from police brutality; it's such an often occurrence that at the end of each shift, the doctors tally how many cases of police brutality they have treated. I remember asking a man at Vitaminka whether he and his friends tried to cross into Hungary daily. He scoffed at my ignorance and said they maybe try every four or five days for the simple reason they have to let the injuries they sustained from the police heal first. The men today in Majdan all have stories about pushbacks; some have tried ten, fifteen, or even twenty times to get through Hungary. Many do make it through the jungle to Szeged or even to Budapest; the problem then becomes getting out of Hungary. Many are caught on the train ride from Budapest to Vienna or Bratislava. What does routinely getting so close to the destination only to be flicked away like some bug do to a person's psyche? How does one summon enough strength and perseverance to withstand the psychological and physical trauma of a pushback and to try again? For many, the answer is simple: They cannot go home.

It's an unseasonably mild late-October day, although fall is still in the air. The leaves clinging to their branches have all changed colour; the days are getting shorter, and the nights cooler. Winter is undoubtedly coming. The squat is relatively quiet; only about forty people, mostly Syrians, are currently staying. A border patrol car slowly drives by the squat but does not pull in; the vehicle's appearance puts everyone on edge as they watch it pass, thankful the cops inside only give them a passing glance. It's an odd feeling when the arrival of police produces not reassurance but anxiety among people. Anxiousness sets in. They are more like the mafia than law enforcers, entities that must be paid to go away. Their presence affects everyone and handcuffs them in silence. At Vitaminka, a person on the move was telling me about his pushback experience when an unmarked car arrived, a police officer stepped out, and the squat went quiet. The man with whom I spoke immediately stopped talking and would not say another word until the officer left and would not be seen leafing through a binder filled with pictures of officers. At Horgos border, two men would not continue their story of being tortured by Hungarian police until the cop car driving slowly passing had disappeared from view.

At Majdan, once the police car has vanished, the men want to play music. One of the doctors retrieves her speaker from the car, and within minutes, music blasts from it. The music's beats and rhythms infect the men, possessing them with a spirit and energy that seem at odds with the squat and its trash and smoke. The music makes them remember. I have always found music to be one of the most effective modes of time travel. If I hear a song I love, the music immediately transports me back into time to all the different moments it infused my life with feeling, not only joy but also melancholy. I am there, and I relive it. I see myself, and I experience what he does, again and again. A song remembered is a potent thing, and the way Majdan's music has affected the men around me, causing them to lock hands and dance, I sense the sounds have transformed each back to Aleppo, Damascus, or Homs. They go around in a circle, and every few seconds, they bend their knees and then raise their left foot in a coordinated, choreographed fashion. It's a dance they all know, and they make the movements look deceptively simple. Laughter comes from them, and the smiles arrive easily. Here in the northeastern corner of Serbia, men dance and have their hair cut while helicopters fly overhead and police cars drive by. And the music makes them forget as easily as it makes them remember. For a moment, the squat vanishes.

People on the move often talk about the fear they have of police officers' dogs. But in the forests ahead, a monster lurks more vicious than any dog. Dogs have teeth, claws, speed, and agility. If mistreated, they can grow vicious and ferocious. But there is no malice. Dogs do not attack for pleasure. They are either defending themselves or have been instructed to attack—to bear their fangs. Many of the houses on the outskirts of Subotica have dogs roaming around their fenced-in yards, and when I happen to pass, some do lunge at me through the spaces between the steel rails. They intimidate me, to a degree, especially the Rottweilers, but I am unsure about whether if there were no fence separating us whether they would sink their teeth in my fleshy legs or whether they would just let me pass when they realize I pose no threat to the family and property they protect. Their hostility to my presence has been taught; they have a job to do, nothing more. And those who do attack do so not from enjoyment but from loyalty to their owner. I do not believe dogs are born bad.

As for the monster prowling the borderland fields, those picturesque and pastoral acreages separating Serbia from Romania, I cannot say. Monster is a useless term when applied to humans and their unsavoury deeds. We call bad people monsters because we want to separate them from us. We feel uncomfortable calling them kin because if kinfolk could do such a thing like beat a helpless man and steal all his possessions, then who's to say you or I couldn't become one. After all, the monster the men of Majdan speak of does not have hoofs or a pointed tail. He has no claws or no fangs. He is a man—this the men agree. He has two legs, two arms, etcetera. He is balding, though, and wears an earring. I have heard of no monster like that. Romanian authorities have also tasked him with a very un-monster-like job: patrolling the border zone between Romania and Serbia and hunting for anyone who does not have the requisite permission to pass. Yet this man, who wears all black and a balaclava to match, does not merely direct travelling folk back to their squat. He is not like the kind stranger of the park who sees an overexcited toddler wander away from their parents and then directs them back to safety with a little push and shove. The officer is far more interested in their presence. Of course, he does want them there. They have illegally snuck into his country. Such disrespectful behaviour will not stand. No self-respecting Romanian will stand for it. Etcetera. Etcetera. But this officer does not want them to go just yet. Stay a little, he implies, when he asks each person he meets to sit on their knees or lie on their bellies. Don't go just yet. Because, well because, and this is where the people start to tremble when they talk about meeting the man in the forests and farms, away from other people and other eyes, because he wants something from them. The man in black without a doubt wants their money, as over the last two months, he has stolen close to four thousand euros from the Majdan men, but there is something far more existential he wants to impart to them. It's they do not matter. Yes, something like this. They are figurines, toys, in which the man in black can do whatever he pleases. They are inanimate objects, and with objects, people can become rather imaginative in their cruelty. There are no consequences.

I suspect the Romanian officer loses little sleep over what he does to the Majdan men. The fact he told a sixteen-year-old to drop to his knees, close his eyes, and then put a pistol to his head in a kind of mock execution would not cause him to lose a second of sleep, I would hazard to guess, because why would it? Do monsters view themselves as monsters? I doubt it. Perhaps they understand on some level they have broken the rules of polite society, but whether their actions would stop them from enjoying time with their children or having a drink with their friends, I think not. I bet the Romanian officer beat the Majdan men with batons and then went home without a single trouble on his mind. I bet when he threw the men's clothing, phones, and other belongings into a pile and set it on fire, he could still go about his daily activities without the slightest inkling of guilt or self-doubt. And I bet when he told the men to prostrate themselves on the ground and then proceeded to urinate close to their heads, he still found nothing troublesome about his actions, for, and this is the rub, there is nothing consequential about pissing on your toys.

A Shower in the Forest

It's my first time inside the actual campsite at River. We are carrying the remaining food packs into the site, for not many people came to distribution, which we attributed to their reluctance to venture far from the camp. Tents of various sizes and shapes dot the landscape, looking like overgrown mushrooms. They add some needed colour to the area. There's some activity. Men cook over fires, and children run about. Yet most people, it seems, still rest within their shelters. We see the two teenage girls, sisters from Tunisia, who a few minutes earlier were searching through our blue beauty bag and examining each of the skin creams we brought. The girls, along with their brother and parents, have been here for three weeks. They smile at our presence and direct us further into the camp, after we motion, asking with our hands, whether we may go further, careful as we are to have permission to take more steps. Our food packs draw their attention, as their fingers delicately open the brown bags and note the bread and eggs. From an elevated structure, like an old bunk house, a woman peers from the door and directs a man down below to grab a couple of bags from us. Another woman, with her head peeking out from her tent, takes a bag before quickly zipping back up the entrance. Others are not so interested. We approach a group of men sitting around their tents and diligently watching their phones. We throw them our pitch, explaining we are handing out some bread and eggs, and they are free to take some, but our words provoke no response among them, registering not a single movement. Our voices meet an impenetrable wall. Their eyes stay locked on their phones; nothing they do acknowledges our presence.

Behind the men is their foe, the Tisa River, and since the ground is slightly elevated, we have an expansive view of it through the branches and leaves. About one hundred metres separate the banks, and today, the water seems calm and easily swimmable; that is, of course, if you know how to swim, have a pair of dry clothes waiting on the other side, and have a way to transport your belongings without them becoming soaked. The other side looks strikingly similar to this one: trees and trees. It is still Serbia, the last of it, the remaining few acres. A few hundred metres upriver, maybe a kilometre or two, the opposite side transforms, almost magically, into Hungary. It is that shore the boats carrying the people would paddle towards if any remained.

Back at the distro site, a family of five prepares their youngest boy for a shower. The father joins his son inside the shower tent and undresses him to his undies; meanwhile, the mother lays out a fresh set of clothing atop the black crate resting behind the shower and tries to block the showerer's sister and brother from getting a peek at the goings-on inside the tent. Once the father has successfully prepared the boy for showering, he takes the showerhead in his big hand and asks me for water. In deft movements, the father manages to lather the boy in soap and water without getting himself soaked and then takes the brown rag he brought and starts to rub the boy down, cleaning him from the dirt and grime that have accumulated on his skin over the past days. The boy does not make a peep, keeps his eyes focused on the ground, and lets his father work. Soapy water collects under the palette and runs towards the van and then underneath, pooling underneath the wheels, and I wonder how much effort it will take to dislodge those tires from their new home in the mud. The mother has a hard time keeping the other two children from spying on their brother, as both are drawn to the happenings inside the tent. She yanks them by the arm when they get too close, desiring as she does for their sibling to have a little privacy, if such a thing were possible here in the forest, but as soon she gets them to act respectable and then turns her back, they race back to the shower to get another eyeful of their brother getting soaked. The boy did not have to act with such curiosity because once the father tells me to stop the water, he quickly dresses the showered son in the new, clean clothes, releases him back into freedom, and then grabs the brother and tosses him into the shower, repeating the same process with him.

A parent washing their child is an intimate rite of passage. Before the child knows how to wash themselves, which parts need the most attention and care, and before they understand how cleanliness can prevent the march of disease, the parent must instruct them. Normally such lessons should transpire in the privacy of the family washroom, with doors that close. Here, no such privacy exists, and I am careful not to intrude upon this parent-child ritual and give them the space they need to finish their work. But the reality of existing on the move shatters any notion of privacy. Everything is communal; everything is shared. All bodily functions become public; there is nowhere to hide the body's workings, nowhere to run from the eyes.

Not long after the father has finished cleaning and dressing his sons, I spot two police officers marching along the path towards us. "Police," I shout, and everyone becomes alert, their bodies primed and ready for any possible attack. Rabbits and foxes. Some people dart and disappear into the woods, not wanting anything thing to do with the cops and perhaps thinking they are only the first of more to come, perhaps another eviction, perhaps another beating, perhaps another excursion to a camp. Instead, they take refuge among the trees and brush. Others, the families in particular, stay huddled around the charging station while one man, who is next to take a shower, continues to shave his face with an electrical razor. The police walk in a manner befitting their authority. Their steps crush the ground beneath them. Both are young, in their twenties, and have shaved heads. I wonder if they took part in the eviction. I wonder if they helped beat the shit out of Mahdi.

"Dobar dan," we all greet the officers, and they return the greeting. All volunteers rest against the van and have our passports ready to be checked. The crowd around the charging station do their best to ignore the cops' presence. Lisa, the shift leader, explains our presence here, what we are doing and who we are. She retrieves our legal documents and hands them over; the younger of the two, who has a pronounced baby face, rifles through them, and their contents, whatever they say, seems to satisfy him. He asks whether we speak Serbian, which I interpret as a concession his English is not good enough to engage us in conversation. But he soon corrects my assumption, after we all shake our heads, by asking us whether we called the police to this spot. The news surprises us, and we dissuade him of the notion. No one here called the police. No one here would dream of calling the police, certainly not people on the move. I am suspicious of his claim and watch the young cop grab his cell phone and call someone with likely more authority than he possesses. The other cop, meanwhile, engages us in harmless small talk, as he asks us whether we know how many people are currently staying in the camp. We say we haven't the slightest idea, since we do not visit the camp, only set up our distribution on its cusp. This is, of course, a lie. We have a decent idea of how many people are staying in the camp, but we will not do their job for them. We will not facilitate in any way the forced removal of these people from the forest.

The officers soon lose interest in us and walk over to the people at the charging station. They want to know whether they are staying at the camp deeper in the forest. Each gives the most perfunctory of nods, only the bare minimum of recognition, just the slightest of affirmation. I am amazed by the indifference these men, women, and, yes, some children display towards these badge holders. Yes, they listen; yes, they answer. But a cool nonchalance infects their actions; it's as if they refuse to acknowledge the power the police project; it's as if they say even though I must listen to you, I do not need to afford you any more than the slimmest amount of my attention. Some continue to watch their phones. Some continue to chat among themselves. Their reaction starkly contrasts with ours, as we moved fast to accommodate the police officers' presence. Here are our documents. Yes, here they are. Yet when the officers ask the people whether they have their documents, they reply "no," without any further elaboration. And when the officers press the issue and ask why they do not have their documents, highlighting for their audience that we, the volunteers, standing at a distance, do have our documents and that everyone should, must have documents, the people remain silent and do not engage further with the officers' questions. They might have destroyed their documents, as some people on the move are wont to do, so to make it as difficult as possible for authorities to identify them, thus, hopefully, slowing their deportation. Or they might have their documents tucked safely inside their tents. Wherever their location, the people at the charging station do not disclose to the police their whereabouts, nor do they provide any more information about what exactly they are doing in the forest or what their plans may be. Is it based on advice from the smugglers that the people act so cavalier towards these men with guns? Do they specifically tell them not to reveal any information to the police? Whatever the reason for their indifference to the police, the officers soon lose interest in the group and begin to return in the direction from where they came, but before they go, the younger officer turns to us, smiles, and says, "That's that."

Minutes later, some of the people return from their hiding spots, and the conversations among the people resume. The police's interjection does not lessen the conviviality among the group. Laughter soon returns. The man goes back to trimming his beard, holding the shaver in one hand and the mirror in the other. Precision cuts. He knows how he wants to look, and he will make it so. In any other circumstance, I would admire the man's skills with the razor and his steadfast desire to look his best even in the most degrading of places. But his is the last shower before we can pack up, and as much as I explain to him we need to leave soon, he just waves me away, indicating he understands what I am saying but will not allow my impatience to disrupt the flow of his routine. When he is finally satisfied with the way he looks, when he likes the face in the mirror smiling back at him, he races over to the shower, undresses, and jumps in.

Taxis

On the outskirts of Sombor stands a restaurant that no longer serves food but instead works as a waiting station for people organizing their smuggling route and waiting for their smugglers to give them the green light. Inside there are rooms with beds and running water. The conditions are less than sanitary, but they are better than a factory or train tracks. Here, the more moneyed displaced stay. The more money displaced people have to spend, the greater their chances of a successful crossing. Money talks. Just like any facet of life. People forget it is never the most destitute who leave; without money, there is little hope for asylum or safety.

People here prepare for their journey, their odyssey, into the EU. Taxis come and go with an impressive frequency. Men and women stuff clothing into their backpacks. Smugglers chat with drivers and tell them to wait a minute or two as they organize the waiting men and women and decide who will go in which car. Doors are constantly slammed. Cigarettes are perpetually smoked. And names are continuously yelled. It's a revolving door of movement. A beehive. It buzzes. There is an air of apprehension tinged with excitement. People follow smugglers' instructions to a tee. Little argument. Little debate. With Europe so close, it's best to do as one is told. The worry is real. I see it on their faces. Taxi drivers, though, look calm and collected, quietly milling about as they wait for their next passengers. The reality they are aiding and abetting a smuggling operation does not seem to bother them, as it is more than likely smugglers have paid off the less scrupulous police officers to look the other way. A smuggler walks about with a speaker hung around his neck, blasting out Eminem.

From here, taxis will take people to a spot along the border, where they will climb the fence, and then get into the waiting taxi, which will whisk them through Hungary into Austria. We hear stories while we distribute water from the tank, the only service we provide at the restaurant. As they fill their containers, they tell us stories. A group of Syrian minors tell us of trying to cross the Evros River from Türkiye to Greece. Ten Greek officers wearing balaclavas intercepted the group and proceeded to whip, beat, and kick them. During the attack, one Syrian was pushed into the river and drowned. Another man tells us a friend of his successfully made it to Hungary only to die in a car accident.

As dusk descends, a family—two parents and a boy and a girl—emerges from the house. By the entrance, they stand and wait. The boy wears a blue toque, and the girl, a yellow one. They both have a slight cough and look so small next to their parents. Night soon comes, and its unrelenting blackness is broken only by headlights and cigarettes. And the stars. It's a clear night, and they have come out in full force. Impressive and dazzling. We, the volunteers, look for constellations, and the North Americans among us learn that in Germany, the big dipper is known as the wagon, which the constellation looks nothing like. Maybe a wheelbarrow. But a wagon? Preposterous.

The children do not make a sound. They stay huddled close to their parents, awaiting their instructions. I have often wondered how children process displacement and how their developing minds interpret what is happening to them. They may only trust in their parents' wisdom and hope they find a place that does not require them to sneak through the night like a ghost. Children do protest and often will not silence themselves even after much threatening from their parents. Little ones make their opinions known. Any perceived slight will be heard about, which makes them less than ideal travel companions. Noise is the enemy of clandestine movement. A child's cry will attract border police. They will come charging. Parents, then, in their desperation, will do everything in their power to keep the children quiet during the journey, which may include giving them something to make them sleep.

These children, though, look ready for the journey ahead. They are as stoic as statues. Nothing seems to rattle them. They project a maturity beyond their age, and as for the upcoming journey, one undoubtedly fraught with peril, their demeanour screams "Bring it on." Or maybe the terror of their surroundings has rendered them speechless. But what does a parent tell a child in this situation? How do you make them understand?

When their taxi arrives, the children and mother climb into the backseat. The father talks with the smuggler, undoubtedly receiving last-minute instructions about what will happen next. Inside the taxi, the driver waits. The overhead light illuminates him and the girl in the backseat, who has leaned forwards to get a better view of what transpires outside, what her father is up to. The driver is past middle age; his hair has greyed, and he wears glasses. He cleans his steering wheel with a wipe and then lights a cigarette. He does not acknowledge the passengers sitting behind him, only watching the conversation happening outside his window, which the car's lights have illuminated. He strikes me as the impatient type, someone who enjoys the structure schedules provide. Yet if this waiting annoys him, his behaviour does not suggest it. He waits as do the mother and children sitting behind him. In the taxi's limited light, I see only the driver and the girl, both sitting patiently, surrendering only the slightest of movements. In the girl's portrait, I see the tenacity of the will to move. She represents an effort for betterment. A desire for a future. I do not wish to romanticize the journeys people take for a better life, for they are both degrading and dangerous, but there is something heroic about setting out upon the open road with only the belongings they can carry. In any other case, a Western audience would applaud their initiative and self-determination. But for every girl that makes it, an untold number do not. Some are never found.

The father climbs into the front seat. Not a word passes between him and the driver, as nothing needs to be said. Both understand the roles they play and the tasks they must perform. There is nothing complicated about this business relationship, and that is all it is. A transaction. The engine starts. And without further display, the car drives away and disappears into the night.

Budapest

On October 23, 1956, a large group of students, soon followed by other Budapest residents, took to the streets with a petition demanding their leaders address the nation's ills, including the end of forced collectivization, the release of political prisoners, and the closing of internment camps. In short, they rebelled against Hungary's subordination to the Soviet Union, against those policies emanating from Moscow. During the revolution's first week, the rebels had much success. Imre Nagy became premier and agreed to establish a multiparty system. He then declared Hungary's neutrality in the growing Cold War and asked the UN for help, but the Western powers were in no mood to confront the Soviet Union, so they stood idly by when Soviet forces invaded Hungary on November 4 and did nothing when Nagy was executed for treason two years later. Fearing the chaos resulting from both the revolution and its eventual crushing, 170,000 Hungarians fled over the border into Austria, likely taking the same journey the Afghan, Iranian, Syrian, Algerian, and Tunisian men, women, and children would take sixty-five years later. At the border, the Hungarians were not met with batons but with humanitarian aid. NGOs offered shelter and food for the arriving refugees, and some even worked to offer resettlement to these Hungarians. Tens of thousands went to Canada, the US, Australia, and New Zealand.

Hungary wants to remember this dark chapters of its history, the time it was subjugated to both Nazi and Communist brutality. The House of Terror serves this purpose. The square building sitting at Andrássy Avenue 60 was first used by the Nazi Party to detain, torture, and kill suspected enemies and then was used by the Soviets in the postwar period for the same purpose. The museum strives to protect the memories of those who lost their lives within the building's walls.

Towards the end of the House of Terror exhibition, visitors are greeted with the "Victimizers Room." Whereas the rest of the museum works hard to remember those who perished under the Nazi and Communist regimes, this room identifies the perpetrators of the violence, those men and women who greased the steel arteries of the great violent machine and made sure everything hummed along smoothly. The room is neatly situated just after the prison cells, through which visitors can walk and try to imagine the dissidents entrapped there, waiting either for their torture to extract false confessions or their execution for said confessions. Visitors first see the crimes and then the perpetrators. A blood-red paint covers the room, and the lighting makes the red pop. A small sign defines "victimizer" for visitors, lest there be any confusion over terms and designations. According to the museum, a victimizer is anyone "who contributed to the creation and maintenance of the totalitarian systems [Nazi and Communist] during times of foreign dominance as well as actively supported them or occupied positions of authority in the executive branch in either of those systems." These people either committed the crimes themselves or gave orders for them to be completed. They worked for organizations that routinely committed crimes against humanity as well as war crimes. The sign concludes with a sombre message: "Their lives before or after do not acquit them from their individual responsibilities." No information is provided about their lives before or after they inflicted suffering upon the victims of the Terror House, but however sweet and kind they were as children or whatever they did (or not) to atone for their behaviour after the fact does not sweep their sins under the carpet. There is no more hiding. After the secrets and lies of the past totalitarian regimes, there will be transparency and accountability. Victims will have their stories known and circulated. Perpetrators, too, will have their stories known and circulated.

The red room is full of the victimizers' pictures. The framed photos neatly hang in rows, and there are easily hundreds. Each contains a portrait photograph of the individual, their position, as well as their date of birth and death. Their positions ranged from administrators to ministers. Each person is smartly dressed in their respective uniforms; some even smile, or at least grin, for the photographer. These are not mug shots. These photos were taken while they were doing the work that would result in having them appear in the victimizer's room in a museum for all future generations to judge and scold. The smiles are eerie; they hide the interiorities of the photographed well. Viewers would be forgiven for acting surprised to hear any of these individuals could have beaten a person until a confession was extracted. These are professional people. They wear uniforms. They are dedicated, hard-working, and upstanding citizens. I'm sure most had families and children. Some probably went to church and socialized with friends on the weekend.

As I gaze at these men and women, these officers for whom the museum wants the world to know, I do not question how seemingly banal human beings—people who go to work and raise families—can commit monstrous acts. My time in Europe's borderlands has rendered that question moot. People do horrible things to other people, especially to those who exist outside any accountable legal framework, where perpetrators believe there will be no consequences for their actions. And I wonder whether fifty years from now—that is, if the atrocities committed against people on the move in Europe's borderlands are ever recognized for the crimes against humanity they are—whether a new museum will emerge in Budapest exploring the violence committed against displaced persons, and instead of photos of Nazis and communists, it will hang photos of smiling Hungarian border patrol officers.

Afterword
Ukraine

In the leadup to Russia's invasion of Ukraine, I was volunteering in Sarajevo. My fellow volunteers and I debated whether Putin and his army were prepared to bring war back to Europe. I knew about Putin's obsession with Ukraine, or rather his obsession with the inexistence of Ukraine as a country and people, but I did not truly believe he would launch a three-pronged attack against the democratic nation of forty-four million people not only because of the violence and death it would entail for Ukrainians but also because of the suffering it would unleash on the Russian people themselves. We debated whether Putin would use the eight-year-long war in the Donbas region of Eastern Ukraine as a pretext to invade the country. We debated NATO. Was Putin justified in his anger towards NATO expansion? Did eventual Ukrainian membership in the military alliance pose an existential threat to Russia? My position was since Ukraine is a sovereign nation, unbeholden to Russian interests and fully capable of deciding its future, Putin's opinion on Ukraine's bid to join NATO was largely irrelevant. I became frustrated with the anti-imperialist left whose lazy analysis equated NATO and Putin in terms of their violent desire to expand. Although I did not support NATO's bombing of Belgrade, which resulted in the deaths of civilians whose families have still received justice, the attack was done to stop Milosevic's ethnic cleansing of Kosovo. And for all of Putin's rhetoric concerning the Ukrainian government's genocide against the people of the Donbas and the need for intervention to protect them, no evidence has ever been mounted to justify these claims.

Moreover, Eastern European countries did not join NATO so they could more easily launch an attack against their former overseer but rather better protect themselves from being attacked.

Yet for all his bluster and posturing, I still believed Putin was only working to leverage his position in any negotiations with the West over the status of Ukraine vis-à-vis its NATO membership. So, when I awoke on the morning of February 24, 2022, to headlines that Russia had launched its invasion, an intense feeling of foreboding gripped me, since it was now obvious Putin no longer cared to negotiate Ukraine's status; for him, the country never existed. Volunteering with displaced people in Bosnia and Herzegovina, the site of Europe's last great conflict, while watching war return to the continent and the exodus of millions of Ukrainian refugees was both surreal and disheartening. The lessons of history had gone unlearned. Nationalism remains a disease for which we have no cure, and war remains a drug from which we cannot wean ourselves. We seem destined to walk in circles—heavily armed.

Yet the speed at which the world united around the Ukrainian cause has been inspiring and surprising. People worldwide have watched with awe and admiration as ordinary Ukrainians abandoned their jobs as teachers, lawyers, and engineers to take up arms against the invading force to defend their country. They have also watched with sadness as the violence has claimed innocent lives, separated families, and caused a million refugees to flee into Poland, Hungary, and Romania. In response, politicians and citizens alike have sprung into action. Governments around the world have announced widespread sanctions aimed at weakening the Russian economy and punishing Putin and his allies. Citizens have donated money to organizations working to support the refugees fleeing Ukraine. Volunteers have arrived at the border to welcome the refugees and provide much-needed food, shelter, and information. Ordinary families have agreed to house refugees until they can find their own accommodation. Remarkably, within a week of the invasion, the EU triggered its 2001 temporary protection directive, which provides immediate protection to displaced persons from non-EU countries. The directive is particularly useful when the EU confronts a large influx of people and processing asylum claims individually would prove impossible. In terms of rights, temporary protection provides the following: a residence permit for the duration of the protection period, opportunities for family reunification, as well as access to employment, accommodation, social welfare, medical treatment, and education for minors. Although the directive has existed for more than twenty years and Europe has had opportunities to use it before, the EU has never triggered it until now: Ukrainians arriving in the EU will receive temporary protection for at least three years. Even more remarkably, beyond the directive's triggering, was how little protest the directive's activation generated among the EU states hit hardest by the refugee flow. Hungary, Slovakia, and Poland have been known to act aggressively to stop asylum seekers from reaching their respective territories. Recently, the European Commission referred Hungary to the EU Court of Justice for failing to align their domestic laws concerning asylum to EU ones and for continually pushing asylum seekers back from their borders. In 2021, when Lukashenko opened Belarus's border to Poland to asylum seekers from the Middle East, Afghanistan, and elsewhere in retaliation for Western sanctions on his country, Polish authorities detained them in a forested area without access to medical treatment or any other support. Others were returned to Belarus even though they had requested international protection. Polish authorities refused to grant media, humanitarian organizations, and lawyers access to the restricted area. Numerous UN reports, though, still detailed the inhumane conditions experienced by asylum seekers in the area and noted the death of some along the Polish-Belarussian border due to exposure.

Thus, images of Poles and Hungarians welcoming displaced Ukrainians to their country have been perplexing, since it's unclear, at least on paper, what distinguishes a person fleeing the Taliban's takeover of Afghanistan from a person fleeing Putin's invasion of Ukraine. Indeed, none of the typical hysteria that tends to concern large flows of refugees—about security issues, burden sharing, or cultural differences—followed Ukrainians as they crossed into the EU. A sense of solidarity with Ukraine and its people spread across Europe and the world. As the media coverage of fleeing Ukrainians intensified, however, a discourse emerged that tried to distinguish not only the invasion of Ukraine from the wars ravaging other parts of the world but also the refugees fleeing Kyiv, Kharkiv, and Odesa from those fleeing Kabul, Damascus, or Juba: "They look like us." The war itself and the refugees it produced did not seem to shock Western journalists as much as the place and people under attack. Something about the attack on Ukraine seemed particularly egregious, an event more tragic than the wars and displacement happening elsewhere. CBS News senior foreign correspondent Charlie D'Agata said Ukraine is not a place "like Iraq or Afghanistan that has seen conflict raging for decades. This is a relatively civilized, relatively European [country]." Daniel Hannan wrote the following in the *Telegraph*: "They seem so like us. That is what makes it so shocking.

Ukraine is a European country. Its people watch Netflix and have Instagram accounts, vote in free elections and read uncensored newspapers. War is no longer something visited upon impoverished and remote populations." In this logic, solidarity with an oppressed people does not originate with a deep hatred of injustice but with similarity. The scale of a coordinated response to a catastrophe becomes predicated on how much the people affected look like you, how much they are your mirror, and not on a moral and ethical duty to help others in need. I do not recognize myself in you; thus, you are outside my conception of humanity.

In the summer of 2022, I volunteered at Szfa Dobra, a free shop for Ukrainian refugees living in Krakow. The clothes hanging from the hangers and racks were all donated by Polish people, underscoring the generosity, warmth, and empathy with which Polish citizens opened their arms (and sometimes even their homes) to these refugees. Boxes upon boxes of sorted clothing and accessories filled the store. The donors had forgotten the historical animosity existing between the two nations and instead pledged not to let the presence of millions of refugees undermine Europe's united front against Putin's invasion.

This free shop was the most dignified place I volunteered. The shop had many supporters and backers. Every morning, volunteers met at the back of the shop for orientation. Coordinators explained the rules of the free shop and the jobs the volunteers would do. There were two groups: Polish-speaking and English-speaking. The former included locals from Krakow who made time to volunteer around their daily work schedule, and the latter included foreigners who travelled to the city to volunteer.

Volunteers came from all over the world to support the Ukrainian community in Krakow: Singapore, Chile, and even Russia.

There were also many American volunteers, more so than at any other place I had volunteered, many of whom had used their two weeks of vacation to travel to Poland. These volunteers were also much older. At the other sites I worked, volunteers were usually in their twenties, fresh from graduating from university, and European or British. In Krakow, they were in their thirties, forties, fifties, and even older. They were professionals. They were retirees. It was heartening to see these eager and determined faces every morning, ready to sacrifice their time to make the situation of another a little better.

Volunteers chatted over coffee and sweets in the back room during breaks, away from the shop's hustle and bustle. They talked about their reasons for volunteering and how they couldn't sit at home while so many innocent people suffered. Putin's invasion compelled them to act. They had to do something. Everyone was engaged. They debated Putin's motivations, his end game, and what it would take for him to stand down. None were optimistic about the war ending soon, although all were encouraged by the West's resolve not to let Putin weaponize refugees. Such compassion existed among them.

Yet I could not help but compare the reception of Ukrainian refugees to that experienced by other groups arriving at Europe's borders, those men, women, and children from Afghanistan, Syria, Palestine, Iran, and elsewhere I met in Serbia, France, Bosnia and Herzegovina, Greece, and Cyprus. I could not help but compare the warmth Ukrainians received with the abuse suffered by those arriving from more distant places. In the store's warehouse section, where all the sorted boxes of clothing were kept, there were rooms filled with even more boxes. This place, a coordinator joked, was where misbehaving volunteers were sent to and never heard from again. The rooms were disquieting, shrouded as they were in darkness, with boxes stacked almost to the ceiling, some teetering precariously. Each of the hundreds of boxes contained winter clothing—jackets, ski pants, and other accessories—items of no use during summer. We had become a warehouse of discarded winter clothing; thousands of items sat unused and unworn. Even though the organization had explicitly stated they no longer needed winter clothing and all volunteers had been instructed not to accept any, they still arrived by the box full. They did nothing but accumulate dust.

Under Polish law, or the license outlining the operational parameters of the organization, none of the received donations can go to displaced persons outside Poland or Ukraine. Goods can be sent to Ukraine directly but not elsewhere, even if those organizations assist Ukrainian refugees, say, in Moldova or Romania. When I first arrived at the warehouse and saw those mountains of boxes full of winter clothing, my thoughts returned to my fall and winter in Belgrade, Calais, and Sarajevo and how we were always short on good quality winter clothing for people on the move, who often did not have the accommodation options available to Ukrainian refugees. These people either were on the move, travelling overland through unforgiving terrain, or sleeping rough. A good coat could mean the difference between appropriate bodily warmth and hypothermia. Looking at all those boxes, I thought about how the NGOs serving these people would love to take some of those items, even if it required storing them for a few months. The weather turns brutal early in Calais, Sarajevo, and Belgrade. But if a Krakow coordinator were to send clothing to any organization outside of Poland or Ukraine, they would jeopardize their entire organization. It's a classic case of separating displaced persons into deserving and non-deserving ones. The Polish state understands Ukrainians as deserving of assistance and compassion, yet if any of that help happened to find its way to other displaced persons who desperately need it, the same state would declare such action illegal.

As much as my experiences volunteering with displaced people around Europe have shocked me, I am grateful for them. They have revealed to me the extent to which European leaders will forego their commitment to human rights to manage and protect their borders better.

Externalization agreements with Libya, Tunisia, and Mauritania mean that Europe's borders become more mobile, moving south to empower local authorities to prevent asylum seekers from reaching Italy, Spain, or Greece. The brutality Europe's borders and its managers inflict on the world's outcasts reveals without ambiguity how human rights apply to only those people who can claim to belong to England, France, and Germany, only to people with the right paperwork. Sophisticated surveillance technology. Pacts with authoritarian figures. Billions of dollars spent. All of this is to keep the undesirables out.

Instead of a place where the legal rights of asylum seekers are protected, Europe's border zones have become an extralegal space where state officials can deny these same rights with impunity. Despite the illegality of pushbacks, for example, the European

Commission has done little to punish states that continue to push back asylum seekers and refugees. To date, only Hungary has had an infringement procedure brought against it, which Budapest has largely ignored. Border-monitoring schemes have proven largely ineffective. Croatia, for example, recently implemented such a mechanism after months of discussion with the European Commission, which had insisted on the country finding a solution to the continuing reports of pushbacks from the country. Although this border-monitoring method aims to prevent pushbacks from happening, little evidence suggests the scheme will do that in practice.

The West, though, has welcomed Ukrainians. There is burden sharing. There is solidarity. Paths to opportunities and integration have been opened for the displaced. They will not be sent back. Yet as much as the West's response to Ukrainians has been inspiring, it has revealed a glaring double standard in terms of who is worthy of refuge. For every Ukrainian offered protection, another deserving person is languishing in a refugee camp or risking their life to cross borders irregularly. As Poland, Hungary, and the Baltic states offer sanctuary to those fleeing Putin's violence, those same leaders busy themselves building walls to prevent other asylum seekers from entering their territories. These leaders adopt a bevy of terms to separate Ukrainians from others. The former are worthy, whereas the latter are not. The former are legitimate refugees, whereas the latter are economic migrants. The former are deserving of protection, whereas the latter are asylum shopping. Yet in my experience supporting displaced people on the ground, the only difference separating them from Ukrainians is the country of their birth and, thus, the content of their culture and the colour of their skin. The people I met on the road would not subject themselves to such daily humiliation—the persistent and ubiquitous threat of violence from both cop and criminal—if the homes they fled were not worse than these degradations. They would not risk drowning in the English Channel or being beaten to death in Hungary if home offered anything other than a threat. The West has grown comfortable in thinking war and displacement are unfortunate things that happen to other people in other parts of the world—never to us. Russia's invasion of Ukraine has put to bed such a notion. But instead of recognizing war is always an unnatural state of affairs and is never inherent to a particular world region, Western leaders have concluded this anomaly has made Ukrainians even more deserving. Ukraine is the exception that proves the rule: War only happens outside the West. Yet war respects no border, and displacement knows not just one culture. The West, too, will know displacement again. Its citizens will experience displacement again. What, then, should they expect from others? How would they like to be welcomed?

References and Further Reading

Introduction

For refugee statistics, please see UNHCR. "Global Trends Report 2023." *The UN Refugee Agency*, UNHCR, 2023, https://www.unhcr.org/sites/default/files/2024-06/global-trends-report-2023.pdf.

For EU deterrence policies, please see Wallis, Emma. "New EU Migration Policies Expected to Get Even Tougher in 2025." *InfoMigrants*, 3 Dec. 2024, https://www.infomigrants.net/en/post/61516/new-eu-migration-policies-expected-to-get-even-tougher-in-2025.

Chapter One

For NATO's campaign in Serbia, please see the following sources: "Interim Agreement for Peace and Self-Government in Kosovo (Rambouillet Accords)," *Peacemaker*, 2019, https://peacemaker.un.org/kosovo-rambouilletagreement99; Zivanovic, Maja, and Serbeze Haxhiaj, "78 Days of Fear: Remembering NATO's Bombing of Yugoslavia," *Balkan Insight*, March 22, 2019, https://balkaninsight.com/2019/03/22/78-days-of-fear-remembering-natos-bombing-of-yugoslavia; Amnesty International, "Serbia: Impunity for NATO—Ten Years after Operation Allied Force." *Amnesty International*, 23 Apr. 2009, www.amnesty.org/en/latest/press-release/2009/04/serbia-impunity-nato-e28093-ten-years-after-operation-allied-force-20090423/. Schapiro, Mark, "Serbia's Lost Generation," *Mother Jones*, 1999, www.motherjones.com/politics/1999/09/serbias-lost-generation/.

Chapter Two

For the statue and its interpretation, please see the following sources: "The Story behind the Sculpture." *Parisian Fields*, Nov. 11, 2011, https://parisianfields.com/2011/11/27/the-story-behind-the-sculpture/. "The Burghers of Calais," *The Met*, https://www.metmuseum.org/art/collection/search/207812. "The Burghers of Calais," *Rodin Museum*, https://rodinmuseum.org/collection/object/103361; "Monument to the Burghers of Calais," *Musée Rodin*, https://www.musee-rodin.fr/en/musee/collections/oeuvres/monument-burghers-calais-0;

Offenstadt, Nicolas. "History Refuses to Look Kindly upon the Good Burghers of Calais," *The Guardian*, 15 Aug. 2002, https://www.theguardian.com/education/2002/aug/15/highereducation.news.

For more information about how the French police treat migrants in Calais, please see Human Rights Watch, *Enforced Misery: The Degrading Treatment of Migrant Children and Adults in Northern France,* 7 October 2021, https://www.hrw.org/report/2021/10/07/enforced-misery/degrading-treatment-migrant-children-and-adults-northern-france.

Concerning the migrant drownings, in a subsequent investigation, French authorities revealed that when the migrants saw that their dingy was taking on water, they phoned the French Coastguard for help. Instead of sending help, the coastguard let them drift into British waters. No help came from either side. A 2023 UK investigation showed that British coastguards thought the migrants were exaggerating the danger they were in: Pascual, Julia "Investigation of 2021 Drowning of 27 migrants in Channel Shows Rescue Services Ignored Calls for Help," *Le Monde,* Nov. 14, 2022, https://www.lemonde.fr/en/france/article/2022/11/14/investigation-into-2021-death-of-27-migrants-in-the-channel-shows-rescue-services-ignored-calls-for-help_6004228_7.html; van Brunnersum, Sou-Jie. "UK Investigation into 2021 Channel Tragedy Reveals Coastguard Assumed Migrant Calls for Help Were 'Exaggeration.'" *InfoMigrants,* 9 Nov. 2023, https://www.infomigrants.net/en/post/53135/uk-investigation-into-2021-

channel-tragedy-reveals-coastguard-assumed-migrant-calls-for-help-were-exaggeration.

For third-safe country critiques, see Hathaway, James C. "Why Refugee Law Still Matters." *Melbourne Journal of International Law*, vol. 8, no. 1, 2007, pp. 89-103.

For an overview of the UK government's now-abandoned plan to send asylum seekers to Rwanda for processing, see Bullen, Poppy, and Naomi Bartram. "Rwanda Plan Explained: Why the UK Government Shouldn't Be Sending Refugees Anywhere." *International Rescue Committee*, 13 June 2022, updated 19 July 2024. https://www.rescue.org/uk/article/rwanda-plan-explained-why-uk-government-should-rethink-scheme.

Chapter Three

For the Death March, see "The Death March." *Remembering Srebrenica*, 2021, www.srebrenica.org.uk/learn/the-death-march.

For an overview of the Bosnian refugee numbers, see "Report of the United Nations High Commissioner for Refugees, 1992." *United Nations General Assembly*, Official Records, Forty-seventh Session, Supplement No. 12 (A/47/12), 28 Aug. 1992, https://www.unhcr.org/publications/report-united-nations-high-commissioner-refugees-1992.

For an overview of the Dayton Accords, see Hegglin, Oliver. "The Dayton Accords 28 Years Later: The Security Landscape in Bosnia-Herzegovina." *Human Security Centre*, 11 Dec. 2023, http://www.hscentre.org/europe/dayton-accords-28-years-later-security-landscape-bosnia-herzegovina/

For pushbacks in Croatia, see "M.H. and Others v. Croatia." *European Court of Human Rights*, Applications nos. 15670/18 and 43115/18, 2021, hudoc.echr.coe.int/fre#{%22itemid%22:[%22002-13480%22]}; Şimşek, Ayhan. "EU Governments Behind Illegal Pushbacks of Refugees at Borders: Report." *Anadolu Agency*, 7 Oct. 2021.

https://www.aa.com.tr/en/europe/eu-governments-behind-illegal-pushbacks-of-refugees-at-borders-report/2385533.

For the Sharifi case, see "Sharifi and Others v. Italy and Greece." European Court of Human Rights, Application no. 16643/09, 2014, www.asylumlawdatabase.eu/en/content/ecthr-sharifi-and-others-v-italy-and-greece-no-1664309-article-2-3-13-article-4-protocol-4.

Chapter Four

For an overview of the 2016 EU–Türkiye deal, see Terry, Kyilah. "The EU-Turkey Deal, Five Years On: A Frayed and Controversial but Enduring Blueprint." *Migration Policy Institute*, 8 Apr. 2021, https://www.migrationpolicy.org/article/eu-turkey-deal-five-years-on.

For Greek pushbacks, see "Greece: Investigate Pushbacks, Collective Expulsions." *Human Rights Watch*, 16 July 2020, https://www.hrw.org/news/2020/07/16/greece-investigate-pushbacks-collective-expulsions.

For Erdoğan's border opening, see Smith, Helen and Mattha Busby, "Erdoğan Says Border Will Stay Open as Greece Tries to Repel Influx," *Guardian*, March 2020. https://www.theguardian.com/world/2020/feb/29/erdogan-says-border-will-stay-open-as-greece-tries-to-repel-influx.

For the European's court ruling on Greek pushbacks, see Mellersh, Natasha. "ECtHR Finds Greece's Border 'Pushbacks' Illegal in Landmark Ruling." *InfoMigrants*, 8 Jan. 2025. https://www.infomigrants.net/en/post/62120/ecthr-finds-greeces-border-pushbacks-illegal-in-landmark-ruling.

For an overview of the CCAC camp, see "One Year Since Greece Opened New 'Prison-Like' Refugee Camps, NGOs Call for a More Humane Approach." Refugees International, 20 Sept. 2022, https://www.refugeesinternational.org/statements-and-news/one-year-since-greece-opened-new-prison-like-refugee-camps-ngos-call-for-a-more-humane-approach/.

For the Turkish-Greek transfer, see Hirschon, Renée. "'Unmixing Peoples' in the Aegean Region." *Crossing the Aegean: An Appraisal of the 1923 Compulsory Population Exchange between Greece and Turkey*, edited by Renée Hirschon, Berghahn Books, 2003, pp. 3-12; Iğsız, Aslı. *Humanism in Ruin: Entangled Legacies of the Greek-Turkish Population Exchange*. Stanford University Press, 2018.

Chapter Five

For an overview of the refugee situation in Cyprus, see "2022 Update AIDA Country Report: Cyprus." *European Council on Refugees and Exiles*, 14 Apr. 2023, https://claude.ai/chat/8d136cb4-1356-4456-80a2-0c4d08e1cb22.

For a history of the Cypriot conflict, see Skitt, Laura. "How Cyprus' Green Line Earned Its Name More than 60 Years Ago." *Forces Network*, 4 Mar. 2024.

Chapter Six

For an overview of the 1956 Hungarian Revolution, see "1956: Hungarian Revolution." H*oover Institution Library & Archives*, Stanford University, 2023, https://www.hoover.org/library-archives/histories/1956-hungarian-revolution.

Afterword

For Ukraine and the temporary protection directive, see Luyten, Katrien. "Temporary Protection Directive." *European Parliamentary Research Service*, July 2024, https://www.europarl.europa.eu/RegData/etudes/BRIE/2024/762373/EPRS_BRI(2024)762373_EN.pdf.

For the European Commission and Hungary, see "EU: Hungarian Council Presidency Takes Aim at Refugees and Asylum-Seekers." *Statewatch*, 3 Oct. 2024, https://www.statewatch.org/news/2024/october/eu-hungarian-council-presidency-takes-aim-at-refugees-and-asylum-seekers/.

For Belarus, see "ACAPS Briefing Note: Belarus/Poland: Migration Crisis on the Belarus-Poland Border (2 December 2021)." *ReliefWeb*, 2 Dec. 2021, https://reliefweb.int/report/belarus/acaps-briefing-note-belaruspoland-migration-crisis-belarus-poland-border-2-december.

For coverage of the Ukrainian crisis, see Bayoumi, Moustafa. "They Are 'Civilised' and Look Like Us: The Racist Coverage of Ukraine." *The Guardian*, 2 Mar. 2022, www.theguardian.com/commentisfree/2022/mar/02/civilised-european-look-like-us-racist-coverage-ukraine.